REVIVING THE BALANCE

The Authority of The Qur'an and The Status of The Sunnah

THE INTERNATIONAL INSTITUTE OF ISLAMIC THOUGHT
P.O. BOX 669, HERNDON, VA 20172, USA
www.iiit.org

LONDON OFFICE
P.O. BOX 126, RICHMOND, SURREY, TW9 2UD, UK
www.iiituk.com

ISBN 978-1-56564-690-2 *limp*
ISBN 978-1-56564-691-9 *cased*

REVIVING THE BALANCE

The Authority of the *Qur'an* and the Status of the *Sunnah*

•

Taha Jabir Alalwani

Translated by
Nancy Roberts

THE INTERNATIONAL INSTITUTE OF ISLAMIC THOUGHT
LONDON • WASHINGTON

Contents

Foreword

TAHA JABIR ALALWANI'S *Reviving the Balance: The Authority of the Qur'an and the Status of the Sunnah* studies the position of the Sunnah in Islam and its fundamental relationship to the Qur'an.

The work carefully examines the sensitive issue of the development of the oral and written traditions, the problems scholars faced despite painstaking work verifying the authenticity of reports as well as the character of narrators etc., and the ever growing complexity of a body of narratives, with a labyrinthine shroud of scholastic views, that were making the simplicity and clarity of the Prophet's (ṢAAS)* life, words, and actions, a burgeoning maze of information. Taking the without doubt praiseworthy intention and effort to emulate the Prophet into account, the author nevertheless makes the case that once the Sunnah had been collected, the Muslim community began to neglect the Qur'an in favor of narrations of what the Prophet had done and said on the pretext that such narratives "contained" the Qur'an, and it is with the aim of restoring the relationship between the two that this work has been written. The author stresses that the Qur'an should be given precedence with the Prophetic Sunnah tied inextricably to the Qur'an in a way that allows for no contradiction between the two.

The IIIT has undertaken in recent years to produce abridged versions of its key publications, and this translation is taken from the abridged Arabic edition, *Ishkāliyyah al-Taʿāmul Maʿa al-Sunnah al-Nabawiyyah*.

We live in an age in which time is at a premium in virtually all spheres of life, including those of writing and production. Copious intellectual, cultural and informational output continues unabated as

*ṢAAS – *Ṣalla Allāhu ʿAlayhi wa Sallam*: May the peace and blessings of Allah be upon him; said whenever the name of Prophet Muhammad is mentioned or whenever he is referred to as the Prophet of Allah.

part of efforts to keep pace with changes in the public and private spheres alike, while publishing houses and websites vie to provide people with the latest, and most up-to-date information in the easiest, most effective manner. The knowledge economy that now dominates the world requires a process of 'creative adaptation' of information as one of the building blocks of the world community at large, hence the IIIT's series of abridged works. The aim is to help readers benefit from available information as easily, effectively, and efficiently as possible and to further develop their critical faculties so they become better able to contribute to the development of humanity..

The abridged texts have been written in a clear, easy to read style, and while the essential contents of the original works have been preserved, readers will note that, in the interests of space, the abridged editions contain far fewer endnotes than do the original works. The only notes retained are those needed for clarification or the proper establishment of an idea, since the principle aim of this endeavor is to facilitate rapid absorption of the content being conveyed. Readers who wish to go more deeply into the topics of concern or to find full documentation of quotes may refer to the original works, which contain all necessary citations.

The work is being published to widen discourse, and to clarify the relationship between the Sunnah and the Qur'an. No doubt the subject is a delicate one, but it is hoped that for the most part both general and specialist readers alike will benefit from the perspective offered and the overall issues examined.

Where dates are cited according to the Islamic calendar (hijrah) they are labelled AH. Otherwise they follow the Gregorian calendar and labelled CE where necessary. Arabic words are italicized except for those which have entered common usage. Diacritical marks have been added only to those Arabic names not considered modern. English translations taken from Arabic references are those of the translator.

Since its establishment in 1981, the IIIT has served as a major center to facilitate serious scholarly efforts. Towards this end it has, over the decades, conducted numerous programs of research, seminars and conferences as well as publishing scholarly works specialising in the social sciences and areas of theology, which to date number more than four hundred titles in English and Arabic, many of which have been translated into other major languages.

We would like to thank the author, translator, as well as editorial and production team at the IIIT London Office, and all those who were directly or indirectly involved in the completion of this book. May God reward them for all their efforts.

JANUARY, 2017

Introduction

THE PURPOSE of this book is to clarify the relationship between the Sunnah* – the sayings and actions of the Prophet – and the Qur'an. This relationship, which has been described in disparate ways and from a variety of perspectives based on changing historical circumstances, has given rise to varied forms of knowledge and expertise. This knowledge and experience have, in turn, left their mark on the sciences through which we examine the Sunnah. Earlier and later[1] hadith scholars adopted differing viewpoints and attitudes, while the stances taken by Islamic schools of thought – both juristic and philosophical – on specific types of Sunnah narratives reflected the concrete life conditions of the scholars in question. Similarly, differences over whether to categorize a given narrator as trustworthy or untrustworthy reflected disparate juristic, theological or philosophical principles that might lead some to reject this or that narrator while approving another, to accept this or that hadith while rejecting or reinterpreting those that contradict it, to accept or reject the criteria for criticizing the content of hadith narratives, and so on.

The question of how to approach the Sunnah had not yet arisen during the time of the Prophet, who instructed his followers to emulate him as he adhered to the Qur'an. It was he who showed them how to apply the Qur'an, translating its teachings into concrete behavior and using it as their guide in life. In order to ensure that the Sunnah fulfilled the practical role for which it was intended, the Prophet made a point not to allow the Qur'anic text to be confused with any other. Similarly, he discouraged the Muslim community from preoccupying itself with any text other than the Qur'an, even if divine authority was claimed for it. God has rendered the Qur'an so complete that it contains the entire

*For the various senses in which the word *sunnah* is being used in this translation, see the entry for "Sunnah" in the Glossary of Terms.

Islamic religion. It is the Qur'an that provides the explication of everything, while the Prophet's example provides a comprehensive demonstration of how to apply everything taught in the Qur'an.

The Messenger of God was determined not to allow believers' minds and hearts to be occupied by anything that might set itself up as a rival to the Qur'an, or to let their attention be diverted by things far less worthy. Consequently, he warned the Muslim community against writing down, or concerning themselves with, anything but the Qur'an alone.

However, once the Sunnah had been collected, the Muslim community did, in fact, neglect the Qur'an in favor of narrations of what the Prophet had done and said on the pretext that such narratives "contained" the Qur'an. They then abandoned the Sunnah narratives in favor of Islamic jurisprudence on the pretext that Islamic juristic texts tacitly included both the Qur'an and the Sunnah.

In sum, I hope this book will provide answers to the troublesome questions that so frequently arouse controversy or disagreement among those who concern themselves with the study of the Prophetic Sunnah and Islamic tradition.

I

Prophethood and the Prophet's Duties

[FIRST] The Prophet as Messenger and Human Being

THE FINAL message of God to humankind encompasses the experiences of all previous prophets combined. It provides an overview of the history of the divine messengers with their peoples, some of whom accepted their message, and others of whom rejected it. The Qur'an presents us with many of these encounters and deals with the differences, both overarching and minute, between prophethood and divinity lest the new community of faith repeat the errors of former nations who had lost the ability to distinguish between prophethood and apostleship on one hand, and lordship and divinity on the other, as well as between human free will and divine ordainment. The Qur'an emphasizes the humanity of the Apostle and the need to obey whatever commands he brought from God. The Apostle thus warned people against revering him excessively. He said such things as, "I am a mere human being, who forgets just as you do," "I was born of a woman who eats jerked meat," and, "Do not turn my grave into the site of yearly religious rites or celebrations (*lā tattakhidhū qabrī ʿīd*). At the same time, the Prophet's followers were forbidden, for example, to raise their voices over his (cf. *Sūrah al-Ḥujurāt*, 49:2).

At one point the Muslim community was in a state of such discord that its members ran the gamut of extremes in their approach to the Prophet. Among the Bedouin Arabs there were those who thought of him as nothing but a tribal chief. Hence, they had no hesitations about calling him by name without preceding it with the title "Prophet" and following it with the prayer, *Ṣallā Allāhu ʿAlayhi wa Sallam*, "may God's blessings and peace be upon him," while others in the community went so far as to ascribe to him attributes of lordship and divinity.

The Concept of "Prophet"

The Arabic words for prophet (*nabī*) and prophethood (*nubuwah*) are derived from the triliteral root *n-b-'*, meaning to be elevated, high or raised. Hence, the *nabī*, or prophet, might be likened to an elevated rock escarpment which serves as a landmark or guide for travelers. The *nabī* is also one who has informed (*anba'a*) others about God, the Arabic noun *naba'* referring to a piece of news or information about an individual of high standing. Al-Iṣfahānī wrote that the word "*nubuwah* refers to a site raised above the surrounding area." Grammatically speaking, the noun *nabī* might be found in the form of the active participle *munbi'*, referring to someone who brings tidings about God, or a passive participle *munba' minhu*, referring to someone from whom the tidings have gone out. However, the term *nabī*, with a doubled *ī* sound at the end, is the most commonly used.

Among Jews and Christians, the prophet is an inspired individual who informs others about the realm of the unseen. In ancient Hebrew the word for prophet was used to refer to someone who spoke of legal matters. Among Muslims, the term *nabī* refers to someone to whom God has given a revelation; if this individual is commanded to communicate the revelation to others, he is referred to as a *rasūl*, that is, an apostle or messenger. Hence, every apostle or messenger is also a prophet; every *rasūl* is also a *nabī*. *Sūrah al-Aʿrāf* speaks of those "who believe in Our messages, those who shall follow the [last] Apostle, the unlettered Prophet whom they shall find described in the Torah that is with them, and [later on] in the Gospel" (7:156-157). We read in *Sūrah Āl ʿImrān*: "And Muhammad is only an apostle (*rasūl*); all the [other] apostles (*ruṣūl*) have passed away before him" (3:144). In *Sūrah al-Anʿām*, by contrast, the word *ruṣūl* refers both to angels and human beings: "And We send [Our] message-bearers only as heralds of glad tidings and as warners..." (6:48).

The Concept of "Apostle"

The Arabic word for apostle – *rasūl* – is derived from the verb *arsala*, meaning to send. The verb *arsala* is used in a negative context in *Sūrah Maryam*, where it is used to refer to God's "letting loose" satanic forces against those who willfully disbelieve: "Are you not aware that We have let loose (*arsalnā*) all [manner of] satanic forces upon those who deny the truth... (19:83)?" The difference between God's sending (*irsāl*) of His prophets and His letting loose (also *irsāl*) of satanic forces against His enemies is that in the first case, He is sending His prophets to warn others of judgment to come. The singular of apostle, *rasūl*, is found in *Sūrah al-Tawbah* – "Indeed, there has come unto you [O mankind] an Apostle (*rasūl*) from among yourselves (9:128)" – and *Sūrah al-Shuʿarā'*, where the singular form, *rasūl*, is used to refer both to Moses and Aaron together (26:16). The plural form, *ruṣūl*, is used to refer sometimes to angels, and sometimes to prophets: "[Whereupon the angels] said: 'O Lot! Behold, we are messengers (*ruṣūl*) from your Sustainer!'" (*Sūrah Hūd*, 11:81). In *Āl ʿImrān* we read: "And Muhammad is only an apostle (*rasūl*); all the [other] apostles (*ruṣūl*) have passed away before him" (3:144). In *Sūrah al-Anʿām*, by contrast, the word *ruṣūl* refers to both angels and human beings: "And We send [Our] message-bearers (*ruṣūl*) only as heralds of good tidings and as warners" (6:48). The word *arsala* may, moreover, refer to the sending of something desirable, such as life-giving rain (*Sūrah Nūḥ*, 71:11), or to something undesirable, such as divine chastisement (*Sūrah al-Dhāriyāt*, 51:33).

The Difference Between Prophethood and Apostlehood

The Qur'an draws a distinction between prophet and apostle, or messenger. Both the prophet and the apostle have received a message revealed by God. However, the message that has been revealed to an apostle (*rasūl*) is legislative in nature, whereas the revelation given to the prophet (*nabī*) contains no new legislation. Rather, the prophet is subordinate to and follows the legislation brought by the apostle who preceded him. Both prophet and apostle are held accountable before God for communicating the revelations they have been given and for inviting their people to follow the messages they have brought. The function or duty of the apostle is to recite the message he has received and to communicate to others whatever God has revealed to him by way of legal commands. As we read in *Sūrah al-Nūr*:

> Say: "Pay heed unto God, and pay heed unto the Apostle." And if you turn away [from the Apostle, know that] he will have to answer only for whatever he has been charged with, and you, for what you have been charged with; but if you pay heed unto him, you will be on the right way. Withal, the Apostle is not bound to do more than clearly deliver the message [entrusted to him]. (24:54)

As for the function of the prophet, or *nabī*, it is to teach and lead others by calling upon them to follow the message brought by the apostle who came before him. Prophethood entails a pedagogical mission; hence, a prophet is, as we have seen, subordinate to the apostle who preceded him. This meaning is illustrated in the story of Moses and Aaron. Speaking of Moses, God says, "We granted unto him his brother Aaron, to be a prophet [by his side]..." (*Sūrah Maryam*, 19:53). Hence, Aaron was a prophet; at the same time, however, God sent him with Moses to Pharaoh as Moses' source of support; as such, he supported an apostle as well. The difference between the two brothers was that Moses had been given a divinely inspired message, whereas Aaron had not. Rather, he was in the service of the message revealed to Moses. Similarly, the other prophets sent to the children of Israel were subordinate to the message that had been revealed to Moses rather than being bearers of new legislation from God. They were given commands and instructions in response to which they were to guide others on the basis of Moses's message. The only exception to this was Jesus, to whom himself was revealed a message from God. As such, he was an apostle, and was granted divine protection from being harmed by others.

In this connection, the Qur'an draws another distinction between the prophet and the apostle based on the notion of what is termed in Arabic *ʿiṣmah*, which might be rendered "divine protection." Prophets are not granted such protection. Rather, like all other human beings, some of them have been killed. Nor are they granted divine protection from human failings and foibles such as error, forgetfulness, and falling into disobedience. The prophet, being a knower of God, fortifies himself against lying and other acts of disobedience by the power of his human will. In other words, it is a self-protection that all people are called upon to engage in. As God commands believers, "And hold fast (*waʿtaṣimū*), all together, unto the bond with God" (*Āl ʿImrān*, 3:103). The Arabic word used in the command to "hold fast," that is, *iʿtaṣimū*, is derived from the verb *ʿaṣama*, which means to preserve, guard, defend, or render immune. Hence, believers are being exhorted to guard themselves against the forces of disunity by clinging to God's "rope."

As for the *ʿiṣmah*, or the protection afforded an apostle, it is marked by two aspects. The first is protection from being killed, the purpose being to enable the apostle to complete his mission. The second aspect of the *ʿiṣmah* enjoyed by an apostle is protection against error when proclaiming the words of the revealed message. The revelation is thus preserved both in the memory of the apostle and in the manner in which it is uttered so that there will be no error in the process of transmitting it to others. When an apostle finishes transmitting to others the message with which he has been entrusted, his role as apostle comes to an end and his role as prophet begins. Given the fact that the apostle is the first person to have received the message newly revealed and, therefore, the first one to be held accountable for responding to it, his role as prophet is to act on the revealed message, teach it to others, and call on them to accept and apply it themselves.

Prophethood did nothing to negate the prophet's humanity. Rather, it accorded him the role of scholar and teacher. Nor, when a prophet became an apostle, did this negate his humanity or his task as a prophet. Rather, maintaining his full humanity and his Prophetic role, he took on the role of apostle as well, saying at God's command, "I am but a mortal man like all of you" (*Sūrah al-Kahf*, 18:110). Moreover, since prophethood confers the status of teacher, and since prophets are the most illustrious of scholars, then prophets are the most qualified of all to engage in interpretation (ijtihad) of the divine message. The prophet engages in ijtihad when teaching, inferring rulings and gleaning information from the divinely given message, and inviting others to embrace and practice it. If, on the other hand, he is [also] an apostle, he uses the message that has been revealed to him. Hence, given these three distinctions between a prophet and an apostle with respect to the message given, the kind of protection afforded, and the practice of ijtihad, it is generally agreed that an apostle is a prophet to whom divine legislation has been revealed, and that a prophet is subordinate to an apostle, hence the principle that "every apostle is a prophet, but not every prophet is an apostle."

One does not become a prophet through some acquired experience or accomplishments. Rather, one becomes a prophet by being chosen by God for this role. It is a role that involves one in acquiring and imparting knowledge, leadership, and calling others to embrace the divine message. Whatever suffering an ordinary human being might endure, may be endured by a prophet as well, and whatever immunity to imperfection and sin a prophet enjoys, he enjoys by dint of his own will and effort. As a scholar, moreover, the prophet is entitled to engage in ijtihad.

As for the apostle, his status is that of someone who has been commissioned to deliver God's message to people; he has been commanded to do nothing but recite and deliver the message. He has no right to offer his own interpretations of the message's content as delivered. The apostle enjoys divine protection from losing or forgetting any of the message; he is given the ability to utter the message perfectly, and is protected from being killed in order that he might complete his mission.

Based on the foregoing, we may conclude that the status of prophethood is linked to the person of the prophet himself. Hence, the station of prophethood comes to an end upon the death of the prophet as happened in the case of the prophet Aaron, whereas the station of apostleship is linked not to the person of the apostle, but, rather, to the message he has been given. Hence, if an apostle should die, this has no effect on the message he has brought; this is illustrated in the fact that after Moses' death, the Torah that had been revealed to him lived on. Prophethood is tied to time and place, while apostleship is universal and ongoing after the death of the individual who fulfilled this role. Given this distinction, it may be said that Muhammad's prophetic mission was to the Arabs, while his apostolic mission is for all people everywhere. As God declares, "Say [O Muhammad]: 'O mankind! Verily, I am an apostle of God to all of you'" (*Sūrah al-Aʿrāf*, 7:158). And in fact, the message brought by the Prophet Muhammad as embodied in the Qur'an continues to spread among people all over the world. Contrast this with the hadiths, or narratives of the Prophet's words and actions, many of which have been, and continue to be, the subject of heated discussion and disagreement among Muslims. When the process of revealing the religion of Islam, which had begun in the days of Noah and continued through Abraham, Moses and Jesus, reached completion with the Prophet Muhammad, may God's blessings and peace be upon them all, this meant of necessity that there would be no more need for prophets. Instead, the completed, final message has continued to be conveyed from one generation to the next via scholars, each of whom fulfills the role of prophet in his or her generation. Given the knowledge and means at their disposal, such scholars teach people, call them to truth and justice, and derive relevant rulings from the divinely revealed message in order to provide remedies and solutions to newly arising issues and problems in the life of society.

All speech addressed to a prophet, whether explicitly or implicitly, is pedagogical and instructional in nature, its purpose being to guide people to a better way and to the best possible solutions given their current circumstances. It is not, however, new legislation. When we encounter discourse that begins with the imperative, "Say...," we need to examine the content that follows. If it contains legal rulings such as those we find, for example, in *Sūrah al-Baqarah*, 2:222, which deals with marital relations when the wife is menstruating, then the person addressed with the imperative "Say" is the Messenger of God in his role as apostle. If, however, the text is simply instructional, such as, "Say: 'He is the One God....'" (*Sūrah al-Ikhlāṣ*, 112:1), then he is being addressed in his role as prophet. If the discourse contains the word "apostle" (*rasūl*) explicitly and the text is related to legal rulings or obedience to God, then the discourse is addressed to the Messenger of God in his role as apostle, whereas if it has to do with instructions or repetition following an act of obedience to God, then it is directed to him in his role as prophet.

Prior to being chosen by God, no one knows that he will become a prophet or an apostle. He has no foreknowledge of this event, nor would such a person seek out such a calling. Rather, "[In His Almightiness,] God chooses message-bearers from among the angels as well as from among men. But, behold, God [alone] is All-Hearing, All-Seeing [whereas their knowledge is limited]" (*Sūrah al-Ḥajj*, 22:75; see *Sūrah al-Anʿām*, 6:124). It is essential that we understand the concepts of prophethood and apostlehood as they are set forth in the Qur'an itself, and not as some present them based on their own whims and fancies.

[SECOND]
Prophets in the Qur'an

The Qur'an clears the prophets who came to the children of Israel of the false accusations that have been leveled against them, and stresses their full humanity:

> For [even] before your time, [O Muhammad,] We never sent [as Our apostles] any but [mortal] men, whom We inspired – hence, [tell the deniers of the truth,] "If you do not know this, ask the followers of earlier revelation" and neither did We endow them with bodies that could dispense with food, nor were they immortal. (*Sūrah al-Anbiyā'*, 21:7-8)

The Qur'an sets forth the broad outlines of how to view and respond to the prophets, whose stories as told in the Qur'an provide systematic foundations for defining the contours of the human societies with which the prophets dealt in a variety of time periods. The Prophet is quoted in *Ṣaḥīḥ al-Bukhārī* as having described the "prophetic structure" of societies in the words:

> The relationship between me and the prophets who preceded me might be likened to a man who built a house. The house was well-made and beautiful except for the fact that it was missing a brick in one corner. People walked around the house and marveled, saying, "Why was this brick left out?" I am that brick. I am the seal of the prophets.

Both the Qur'an and the Sunnah affirm the infallibility (*ʿiṣmah*) of the prophets in the sense that no true prophet would be capable of committing a major sin. After all, in order for them to fulfill the purpose for which they were sent, the prophets must be worthy examples to emulate. They must be above any action that would call their integrity or their message into question, and be fortified against the possibility of disobeying God by violating the revelation given to them.

The Relationship Between the Prophet Muhammad and the Prophets Who Preceded Him

The Qur'an sums up the relationship between the Prophet Muhammad and the prophets who preceded them in the words, "Verily [O you who believe in Me,] this community of yours is one single community, since I am the Sustainer of you all: worship, then, Me [alone]" (*Sūrah al-Anbiyā'*, 21:92). God's prophets make up "a single community" with respect to their messages, the source from which these messages have come, their call for adherence to God-given ideals and self-purification, and their call to lay the foundations of human civilization on Earth. The Qur'an sets forth the points of commonality and difference among the prophets and messengers; similarly, it shows the constants and variables in the messages they brought. Specifically, the Qur'an stresses four important dimensions: (1) doctrine, (2) human values and morals, (3) divinely revealed law, and (4) human interactions in society. As for detailed and newly formulated laws, these differ from one society to the next based on variables of time and place.

The Acts of Worship Engaged in by the Prophet Before he Received His Divine Calling

Were the acts of worship engaged in by the Prophet before and after he received his divine calling based on the laws and traditions adhered to by those who had received revelation before his time? Scholars of the fundamentals of Islamic jurisprudence may be divided into three categories based on their answer to this question. One group of scholars denies that the Prophet worshipped in accordance with the rites of those who had come before him. A second group affirms that he did worship in accordance with former practices. And a third group expresses no opinion on the matter.

The difficulty here results from a faulty understanding of the Qur'anic context. Those belonging to the second group cite *Sūrah al-Anʿām*, where God commands the Prophet to "follow the guidance" of those "whom God has guided" (6:90). They also cite *Sūrah al-Naḥl*, where God says, "We have inspired you, [O Muhammad, with this message:] 'Follow the creed of Abraham, who turned away from all that is false, and was not of those who ascribe divinity to aught beside God'" (16:123), as well as other Qur'anic passages which affirm the oneness of the sources in the monotheistic tradition with respect to faith in God alone, worship, values and morals. Through this affirmation of oneness, such scholars have argued that if Jews and Christians truly believe in the divine revelation that preceded Islam, then they are obliged to accept the guidance and light brought in the Qur'an, since they are essentially the same guidance and light that were brought by previous revelations. As for divinely inspired legislation, it will differ from one prophet to the next, but has been crowned at last by the message of compassion and alleviation brought by the Prophet Muhammad. As we read in *Sūrah al-Aʿrāf* (7:158):

> Say, [O Muhammad]: "O mankind! Verily, I am an apostle of God to all of you, [sent by Him] unto Whom the dominion over the heavens and the earth belongs! There is no deity save Him; He [alone] grants life and deals death!" Believe, then, in God and His Apostle – the unlettered Prophet who believes in God and His words – and follow him, so that you might find guidance!

Hence, we may say that the divine message revealed to all apostles and prophets is founded upon specific pillars, which are: the oneness of God, the full humanity of the prophets and the truth of their messages, and the command given to all prophets to follow the message revealed to them.

[THIRD]
The Tasks Assigned to the Prophets

God has assigned His prophets and apostles tasks and responsibilities which they must carry out precisely as given. The Qur'an was revealed in order to clarify what these tasks are. It cites the examples of bygone religious communities whose perceptions of who their prophets were had become distorted, and warns against falling into the same errors into which they once fell. The Qur'an stresses the full humanity, and sinlessness, of all God's messengers with a clarification of the meaning of the miracles they performed. It emphasizes the finite nature of the prophets' human capacities, reminding its readers that whatever signs these messengers and prophets performed were the doing of God alone, Who has no partner, and Who granted them these miracles in order to confirm the truth of their messages:

> Say thou, [O Prophet:] "I am but a mortal like you. It has been revealed to me that your God is the One God: go, then, straight towards Him and seek His forgiveness!" And woe unto those who ascribe divinity to aught beside Him. (*Sūrah Fuṣṣilat*, 41:6)

The revelations given to earlier prophets took the form of commands to adhere to the rulings that had been revealed to them. They were to exhort their peoples and show them how to practice the revealed teachings, thus applying what might be termed "the jurisprudence of piety." Their lived examples were not an end in themselves, but were, rather, an extension of the revelations they had been given. Hence, as the Torah relates concerning Moses, Aaron and all other prophets sent to the children of Israel, these individuals would inform the people of what was being revealed to them. Then they would exhort them to act on it and warn them against violating it.

[FOURTH]
The Tasks Assigned to the Seal of the Prophets

Task Number 1: Tilāwah (recitation, or "following" the revealed message)

God commanded his Prophet to recite or convey the Qur'an. Thus, we are told in *Sūrah Āl ʿImrān* that "Indeed, God bestowed a favor upon the believers when he raised up in their midst an apostle from among themselves, to convey His messages unto them (*yatlū ʿalayhim āyātihi*), and to cause them to grow in purity, and to impart unto them the divine writ as well as wisdom..." (3:164). Another meaning of the Arabic word *yatlū*, often rendered as "recite" or "chant," is to follow or imitate. God says, "Consider the sun and its radiant brightness, and the moon as it reflects the sun!" (*Sūrah al-Shams*, 91:1-2). A more literal translation of the phrase rendered "reflects the sun" (*wa al-qamari idhā talāhā*) would be "as it [the moon] follows it [the sun]." The moon derives light from the sun, and in this sense it is the sun's "follower" or "successor."

God asks rhetorically, "And what of him who stands upon a clear sign from his Lord, and a witness from Him recites it...?" (*yatlūhu*) (*Sūrah Hūd*, 11:17, A.J. Arberry). In this context, the verb *yatlū* might also be understood to mean "acts on the basis thereof." Hence, the recitation – *tilāwah* – of God's revelations may mean not only to recite them, but to follow them in the sense of acting on the commands, prohibitions, and exhortations they contain. Its meaning also includes the notion of conveying from on high, as when God states, "This message do We convey (*natlūhu*) unto you" (*Sūrah Āl ʿImrān*, 3:58).

Task Number 2: Tablīgh (announcement, declaration)

The verb *balagha*, from which the intensified verb *ballagha* (verbal noun, *tablīgh*) is derived, means to reach one's final or intended destination, whether in a geographical, temporal, or metaphorical sense.

We read in *Sūrah al-Nūr*: "Withal, the Apostle is not bound to do more than clearly deliver the message (*al-balāgh al-mubīn*)" (24:54). The Qur'anic phrase *al-balāgh al-mubīn* intimates that when apostles deliver God's message, they deliver it in its totality and enable people to comprehend it fully in the sense of applying it properly, setting it up as the model they emulate, instructing others in it, and seeking self-purification.

Task Number 3: Bayān (explication)

The purpose for explicating the Qur'an is to prevent or, at least, to reduce disagreements among people over how to understand the Qur'an's message. God says to the Apostle, "And upon you [too] have We bestowed from on high this reminder, so that you might make clear (*li tubayyina*) unto mankind all that has ever been thus bestowed upon them..." (*Sūrah al-Naḥl*, 16:44). The process of making the revelation clear takes place through words, actions, and the act of approving this or that idea or action. God declares:

> O people of the Book! Now there has come unto you Our Apostle, making clear (*yubayyinu*) unto you much of what you have been concealing [from yourselves] of the Book, and pardoning much. Now there has come unto you from God a light, and a clear divine writ. (*Sūrah al-Mā'idah*, 5:15)

The act of clarifying or making clear might address different levels of meaning. On a more general level, it might address concepts such as lordship, divinity, and the divine attributes. On a more specific level it might address itself to issues of belief, doctrine, law and rites of worship, all of which are areas in which people need clarification. Another area where clarification is called for has to do with what we mean when we say that the Qur'an determines what is true in earlier revelations, or that it confirms the truth of whatever still remains of them (cf. *Sūrah al-Mā'idah*, 5:48), bearing in mind that through his lived example, the Prophet provided a practical model for how to preserve the best and truest of what the earlier revelations contain.

Consequently, God has untiringly preserved His final revelation for His exalted name alone. In *Sūrah al-Qiyāmah* God says to the Prophet:

> Move not your tongue in haste, [repeating the words of the revelation:] for, behold, it is for Us to gather it [in your heart,] and to cause it to be read [as it ought to be read]. Thus, when We recite it, follow you its wording [with all your mind]: and then, behold, it will be for Us to make its meaning clear (*bayānuhu*). (75:16-19)

In another verse God declares, "Behold, it is We Ourselves who have bestowed from on high, step by step, this reminder, and, behold, it is We who shall truly guard it [from all corruption]" (*Sūrah al-Ḥijr*, 15:9). Hence, just as God gave no one but Himself a part in sending down the revelation from high, neither does He give anyone else a part in preserving the revelation, reciting it to His final Prophet, explaining the meanings of its unequivocal verses, "gathering" it in the Prophet's heart and causing him to recite it in such a way that he is in no danger of forgetting any of it, then clarifying it in such a way that it, in turn, can serve to clarify everything else. In this way, the various authoritative references for human beings have been united in the Qur'an, which is the final revelation given to the Seal of the Prophets in a sacred land. Therefore, the Qur'an's authority to validate or invalidate other scriptures is absolute. Similarly, the Qur'an stands in judgment over the guidance brought in the Sunnah of the Prophet. This means that the Qur'an removes all the distortion and falsification to which the heritage brought by previous prophets had been subjected. It also corrects uninformed interpretations by the ignorant and self-deluded, thereby presenting the message anew in a true, purified form.

Task Number 4: Nuṣḥ (proffering sound advice)

The Qur'an relates that the Prophet Hūd once said, "O my people! There is no weak-mindedness in me, but I am an apostle from the Sustainer of all the worlds. I am delivering unto you (*uballighukum*) my Sustainer's messages and advising you truly and well" (*Sūrah al-Aʿrāf*, 7:67-68). The phrase rendered here as "advising you truly and well" might also be rendered, "and I am to you a faithful advisor" (*wa anā lakum nāṣiḥun amīn*). The task of providing trustworthy advice (*al-nuṣḥ*) follows that of delivering the message (*al-tablīgh*), since the advice proffered is based on the message that has been delivered. The Qur'anic concept of *nuṣḥ* encompasses a number of actions, one of which is to recommend behavior which, if the person being advised engages in it, will benefit him or her. It is understood here, of course, that the person offering the advice wants nothing but the best for the person he or she is advising.

Task Number 5: Taʿlīmuhum al-kitāba wa al-ḥikmah (teaching them the Book and wisdom)

We read in *Sūrah al-Jumʿah*: "He it is who has sent unto the unlettered people an apostle from among themselves, to convey unto them (*yatlū ʿalayhim*) His messages, and to cause them to grow in purity, and to impart unto them (*wa yuʿallimuhum*) the divine writ (*al-kitāb*) as well as wisdom (*wa al-ḥikmah*) – whereas before that they were indeed, most obviously, lost in error" (62:2).

"Wisdom" (*al-ḥikmah*) is a broad concept that encompasses everything from the laws of the cosmos to human knowledge and discoveries. Once we learn of such things, we become able to combine a reading of the divine writ – written revelation – and wisdom as it manifests itself all around us. The Prophet taught his Companions how to benefit from the wisdom and knowledge God has deposited in the world so that they could learn to live in harmony with the creation rather than combating it or disregarding it in ignorance.

Task Number 6: Tazkiyat nufūs al-nāsi waʿuqūlihim (purifying people's hearts and minds)

In the verse quoted above we read about the Prophet's task of causing people "to grow in purity" (*yuzakkīhim*) (62:2).

Task Number 7: Ittibāʿ (teaching them to follow)

The verb *ittabaʿa* (verbal noun, *ittibāʿ*) means to follow someone or to walk in his or her footsteps. God declares that "those who follow My guidance (*man tabiʿa hudāy*ā) need have no fear, and neither shall they grieve" (*Sūrah al-Baqarah*, 2:38). The act of following spoken of here is similar to that of imitating when it relates to another person. However, unlike imitation, the following spoken of here is based on understanding and evidence. Hence, when one follows a godly individual, one does so based on the soundness of this person's behavior and arguments. *Sūrah al-Baqarah* (2:120) and other Qur'anic passages highlight the difference between following based on understanding and knowledge, and following based on mere whim. They analyze the outcomes of these disparate ways of following so as to make it easier for us to make the right choices. Sound "following" is based on reliable guidance and knowledge, not on conjecture and caprice. As God says on the lips of the Prophet Abraham, "O my father! Behold, there has indeed come to me [a ray] of knowledge such as has never yet come unto you. Follow me, then; I shall guide you onto a perfect way" (*Sūrah Maryam*, 19:43). God commanded His apostle to follow the revelation that had been sent down to him, saying, "Follow you what has been revealed unto you by your Sustainer" (*Sūrah al-Anʿām,* 6:106). Similarly, He commanded those who had believed in the Apostle to follow him: "Say

[O Prophet]: 'If you love God, follow me, [and] God will love you and forgive you your sins; for God is Much-Forgiving, a dispenser of grace'" (*Sūrah Āl ʿImrān*, 3:31).

Task Number 8: Taʿlīmuhum al-iqtidā' bihi (teaching others to imitate him)

God commanded the Prophet to imitate (*iqtadih*) those who had been guided before him (*Sūrah al-Anʿām*, 6:90). The act of imitation in this context consists of following a leader's way of dealing with proofs and evidence, be this leader a prophet, a proponent of virtue, or whatever else.

Task Number 9: Taʿlīmuhum al-ihtidā' bi al-hadī (teaching others to be guided by truth)

The process of being guided, or finding guidance, has to do with what we seek or aspire to and the choices we make in relation to earthly or spiritual matters. God "has set up for you the stars so that you might be guided by them in the midst of the deep darkness of land and sea" (*Sūrah al-Anʿām*, 6:97). And, speaking to the Prophet, God said:

> Say [O Prophet]: "O mankind! The truth from your Sustainer has now come unto you. Whoever, therefore, chooses to follow the right path, follows it but for his own good; and whoever chooses to go astray, goes but astray to his own hurt. And I am not responsible for your conduct." (*Sūrah Yūnus*, 10:108)

God's guidance of human beings is of four types. The first is the type of guidance given to every morally accountable human being by way of reason and necessary knowledge and information. As Moses stated to Pharaoh, "Our Sustainer is He who gives unto every thing [that exists] its true nature and form and thereupon guides it [towards its fulfillment]" (*Sūrah Ṭāhā*, 20:50). The second is the type of guidance God gives to people by calling them through one of His prophets. God said to the Prophet:

> And indeed, [O Muhammad,] We did vouchsafe revelation unto Moses [as well]: so be not in doubt of [your] having met with the same [truth in the

> revelation vouchsafed to you). And [just as] We caused that [earlier revelation] to be a guidance for the children of Israel and [as] We raised among them leaders who, so long as they bore themselves with patience and had sure faith in Our messages, guided [their people] in accordance with Our behest – [so, too, shall it be with the divine writ revealed unto you, O Muhammad]. (*Sūrah al-Sajdah*, 32:23-24)

The third is the type of guidance that is provided in the form of divinely-given success. As we read in *Sūrah Muḥammad*, "It is such as these whose hearts God has sealed because they [always] followed but their own lusts, just as for those who are [willing to be] guided, He increases their [ability to follow His] guidance and causes them to grow in God-consciousness" (47:16-17). As for the fourth, it consists in guidance to Paradise in the hereafter. This is the type of guidance referred to in God's words, "Indeed, from on high have We bestowed messages clearly showing the truth; but God guides onto a straight way [only] him that wills [to be guided]" (*Sūrah al-Nūr*, 24:46).

These four types of guidance are founded upon one another. Without the first, the second will not take place. Conversely, if the fourth takes place, this means that the preceding three types have also taken place.

No one can guide anyone else by means of anything but supplication and invitation, and by setting forth the paths that lead to truth. God told the Prophet:

> And thus, too, [O Muhammad,] have We revealed unto you a life-giving message [coming] at Our behest. [Ere this message came unto you,] you did not know what revelation is, nor what faith [implies]: but [now] We have caused this [message] to be a light, whereby We guide whom We will of Our servants, and, verily, [on the strength thereof] you, too, shall guide [men] onto the straight way." (*Sūrah al-Shūrā*, 42:52)

In a reference to the other types of guidance, God tells the Prophet, "Verily, you canst not guide aright everyone whom you love: but it is God who guides him that wills [to be guided]; and He is fully aware of all who would let themselves be guided" (*Sūrah al-Qaṣaṣ*, 28:56).

The types of guidance God withholds from wrong-doers and deniers of the truth are the third type mentioned above, that is, the divinely given success that is granted only to those who have sought out true guidance, and the fourth type, which consists in entry into Paradise in the life to come. As we read in *Sūrah Āl ʿImrān*, "How would God bestow His guidance upon people who have resolved to deny the truth after having attained to faith, and having borne witness that this Apostle is true, and [after] all evidence of the truth has come unto them? For, God does not guide such evildoing folk" (3:86).

Some types of guidance are beyond any human being's power to provide, including even the Prophet himself. These are: the provision of reason, divinely given success, and entry into Paradise. As God told the Prophet, "It is not for you to make people follow the right path, since it is God [alone] Who guides whom He wills" (*Sūrah al-Baqarah*, 2:272). In *Sūrah al-Isrā'* we are told that "he whom God guides, he alone has found the right way; whereas for those whom He lets go astray you can never find anyone to protect them from Him" (17:97), which means that those who seek out guidance will be granted success by God and brought to Paradise. We read in *Sūrah al-Insān*: "Verily, We have shown him the way: [and it rests with him to prove himself] either grateful or ungrateful" (76:3), and in *Sūrah al-Balad*, "Have We not given him two eyes, and a tongue, and a pair of lips, and shown him the two highways [of good and evil]?" (90:10), where "the two highways" refer to what can be ascertained about good and evil through reason and the law. Speaking of people's ability to deceive themselves through their willful choices, God warns:

> ...As it was He Who brought you into being in the first instance, so also [unto Him] you will return: some [of you] He will have graced with His guidance, whereas, for some a straying from the right path will have become unavoidable: for, behold, they will have taken [their own] evil impulses for their masters in preference to God, thinking all the while that they have found the right path! (*Sūrah al-Aʿrāf*, 7:29-30)

As for God's saying, "No calamity can ever befall [man] unless it be by God's leave: hence, whoever believes in God guides his [own] heart [towards this truth]; and God has full knowledge of everything" (*Sūrah al-Taghābun*, 64:11), it is a reference to the God-given success that a person is capable of seeking. (On the subject of guidance, see also *Sūrah al-Anʿām*, 6:87, and *Sūrah al-Nisā'*, 4:68).

Task Number 10: Taʿlīmuhum al-ta'assī bihi (teaching them to emulate him as their model)

The Arabic word rendered "model" or "exemplar" (*uswah*) is found in only three places: "Verily, in the Apostle of God you have a good example (*uswatun ḥasanah*) for everyone who looks forward (with hope and awe] to God and the Last Day, and remembers God unceasingly" (*Sūrah al-Aḥzāb*, 33:21), "Indeed, you have had a good example (*uswatun ḥasanah*) in Abraham and those who followed him..." (*Sūrah al-Mumtaḥanah*, 60:4), and, "In them, indeed, you have a good example (*uswatun ḥasanah*) for everyone who looks forward [with hope and awe] to God and the Last Day" (*Sūrah al-Mumtaḥanah*, 60:6).

One of the ways in which to emulate the model found in the Prophet is to abide by the teachings of the Qur'an itself. Once, when asked about the Prophet's character, ʿĀ'ishah replied, "Do you not read the Qur'an? His character was embodied in the Qur'an."

Emulation of someone whom we take as our example requires that we view this person's words and actions as all growing out of particular causes and occasions, and as being linked to rulings or precepts of some kind. This person's words and deeds must not be examined piecemeal, but in their entirety, as an overall phenomenon ordered by universal laws and principles that can be studied and analyzed so that, having placed the model's statements and actions within a larger framework, we can search for the purposes and aims behind all that this individual said and did.

Task Number 11: Al-Haymanah (the exercise of finality and supremacy)

The process or act of *haymanah* is spoken of in *Sūrah al-Mā'idah*, where God says to the Prophet, "And unto you have We vouchsafed this divine writ, setting forth the truth, confirming the truth of whatever there still remains of earlier revelations and determining what is true therein" (5:48). The phrase "determining what is true therein" is a rendering of the Arabic phrase *muhayminan ʿalayhi*, which means to watch or guard over, to oversee, and hence to exercise supremacy or ascendancy over someone or something. This is the role the Qur'an is described as exercising in relation to the scriptures that preceded it: determining what truth they still contain and confirming that truth. Being the final revelation, the Qur'an becomes the unified source of religious authority or governance for human beings. As such, it removes whatever distortions, falsehoods, and misinterpretations had been introduced into, or imposed on, the message brought by previous prophets as passed down from one generation to the next, and presents this message in its pristine form.

[FIFTH]
The *Āyah* (Miracle or Sign) in Previous Messages and in the Final Message

It was necessary in the divine wisdom for the prophets to be specially chosen, since it was they who would bring God's messages of guidance and light to humankind. As God declared to the Prophet, "And, truly, We sent forth apostles before you, and We appointed for them wives and offspring" (*Sūrah al-Raʿd*, 13:38). Although the prophets are human beings from the physical standpoint, they are, from the spiritual standpoint, part of the realm of divine command prepared to receive divine inspiration and spiritual power for which they have been singled out. Concerning Jesus, God states, "And We vouchsafed unto Jesus, the son of Mary, all evidence of the truth, and strengthened him with holy inspiration" (*Sūrah al-Baqarah*, 2:253) and, addressing Muhammad, "trustworthy divine inspiration has alighted with it from on high upon your heart, so that you may be among those who preach in the clear Arabic tongue" (*Sūrah al-Shuʿarā'*, 26:193-195). They were enabled to receive inspiration through the mediation of angels, while the human bond they shared with those around them equipped them to deliver to others what had been revealed to them. As God explains in *Sūrah al-Anʿām* regarding the Prophet's opponents:

> They are saying, too, "Why has not an angel (visibly] been sent down unto him?" But had We sent down an angel, all would indeed have been decided, and they would have been allowed no further respite [for repentance]. And

> [even] if We had appointed an angel as Our message-bearer, We would certainly have made him [appear as] a man... (6:8-9)

The Qur'an talks about how, in all ages, people have asked the prophet in their midst for a "sign," or *āyah*. When this request grew out of a sincere desire to find the truth, it was met with a positive response, whereas, when it was made with other motives, the prophet concerned would refuse to engage in this sort of "bargaining" with the Almighty.

A miracle, or sign, serves as a declaration by God that His servant has spoken the truth. However, it does not cause the messenger to cease being a mere human being. Nor does it abrogate the laws of nature or aim to paralyze human reason or force it into abject submission.

1. *The Qur'anic Distinction Between a Miracle (Muʿjizah) and a Sign (Āyah)*

It has become commonplace to use the phrase "the *miracles* of the prophets" in place of the more Qur'anic concept of "the *signs* of the prophets." The question then arises: What outcomes have resulted from this confusion? One might say that even though both "miracles" and "signs" were originally seen as evidence of, or a witness to, the veracity of the person through whom God had brought about the event in question, the confusion between the concepts of "sign" and "miracle" has entrenched an attitude of stubbornness and defiance among those prone to resist the truth. The difference between the two is actually quite significant. The stuff of "the miraculous" tends to stir up resistance and defiance among those who witness it. As for the "sign," it includes the element of miraculousness, but presents the miraculous event as a kind of evidence, the function of a "sign" being to prepare those who witness it to listen more attentively, and to be more receptive to the message and the message-bearer.

2. *The Term "Miracle" (Muʿjizah): Its Definition, and its Qur'anic Usage*

The Arabic term *ʿajz* conveys the sense of failure, weakness, or inability to do something; as such, it connotes the opposite of ability or strength. As Cain cried out, "Oh, woe is me! Am I then too weak (*ʿajaztu*) to do what this raven did...?" (*Sūrah al-Mā'idah*, 5:31). Elsewhere God states, "Verily, that [reckoning] which you are promised is bound to come, and you cannot elude it (*wa mā antum bi muʿjizīn*)" (*Sūrah al-Anʿām*, 6:134). In other words, they are unable either to slow the coming of the divine judgment for themselves, or to prevent others from following the prophets. In *Sūrah Saba'* we find another derivative of the root *ʿ-j-z*, as God speaks of "those who strive against Our messages, seeking to defeat their purpose (*muʿajizīn*)" (34:5) in the mistaken belief that there is no resurrection, reward or punishment in the life to come. The same root appears in the Prophet's warning to deniers of the truth that "you cannot elude Him on earth (*wa mā antum bi muʿjizīna fi al-arḍ*)" (*Sūrah al-Shūrā*, 42:31).

As will be clear, the Qur'anic usage of terms derived from the triliteral root *ʿ-j-z* has nothing to do with the signs, or *āyāt* brought by the prophets in support of their messages. In fact, there is nothing to indicate that the words *muʿjizah* and *āyah* are synonymous. Hence, there is a need to reclarify Qur'anic concepts, such as sign, or *āyah*, and to distinguish them from non-Qur'anic ones, such as that of miracle, or *muʿjizah*. There is a constellation of complementary Qur'anic concepts, the use of any one of which will evoke associations with other, complementary, terms and concepts. However, if some extraneous, non-Qur'anic concept is interpolated among them, they lose their coherence and mutual complementarity, which in turn distorts them and robs them of their meaning.

Al-Qāḍī ibn al-Bāqillānī has mentioned four conditions that must be met in order for something to be termed miraculous (*muʿjiz*). These four conditions are: (1) that God alone would be capable of it; (2) that it is so out of the ordinary that it may be said to violate a law of nature; (3) that no one but a prophet would be able to manifest the likes of it; and (4) that it take place at the hands of an apostle who is challenging the people to whom he has been sent, and with the claim that it is a sign of the truth of his message.

3. *The Meaning of the Term Āyah*

The word *āyah* has been defined as a sign or signal. It may also refer to a unit or verse of the Qur'an. According to Abū Bakr, "The reason a verse of the Qur'an is referred to as an *āyah* is that it serves as a sign that a unit of speech has ended, and that another unit of speech is beginning." It has also been suggested that the reason each verse of the Qur'an is referred to as an *āyah* is that, as a set of words from the Qur'an, it reveals God's signs and wonders. Further, the word *āyah* can refer to a lesson or moral, as when God says, "Indeed, in [the story of] Joseph and his brothers there are messages for all who search [after truth]" (*Sūrah Yūsuf*, 12:7).

4. *The Concept of Āyah in the Sayings of the Apostle*

It has been narrated on the authority of Abū Hurayrah that the Messenger of God said, "Every prophet has been given signs (*āyāt*) on the basis of which people have placed their trust in him. What I have been given is a revelation with which God has inspired me. Hence, I hope on the Day of Resurrection to be the one with the greatest number of followers." Note that he did not use the term "miracle" (*muʿjizah*); rather, he used the Qur'anic concept of "sign," or *āyah*.

5. *The Concept of Āyah in the Qur'an*

Al-Iṣfahānī defined *āyah* as a clear, visible sign. The term *āyah* has also been used to refer to a tall building, as when Hūd says, "Will you, in your wanton folly, build [idolatrous] altars (*āyatan*) on every height and make for yourselves mighty castles...?" (*Sūrah al-Shuʿarā'*, 26: 128-129). The word *āyah* is derived from the verbal noun *al-ta'ayyī*, which is the act of settling and establishing oneself on something. The verb *ta'ayya* has also been defined more or less synonymously with the verb *arfaqa*, meaning to be useful to, or serve, or with the verb *awiya*, meaning to provide lodging for shelter for.

6. *The Meanings Associated With the Words Āyah and Āyāt in the Qur'an*

It will be necessary here to draw a distinction between an *āyah* in the sense of a structural unit of the Qur'an, and an *āyah* in its more purely logical sense. Used in the first sense, every clause in the Qur'an that conveys a ruling or a self-contained meaning would be an *āyah*, whether the linguistic unit in question constitutes an entire surah, or chapter, of the Qur'an, or just one part or division of a surah. Alternatively, every clause separated from another by a verbal marker might be referred to as an *āyah*, on which basis we calculate the number of verses (*āyāt*), in a surah. The following are three senses of the word *āyah*:

a) "Signs," or *āyāt* in the sense of the ongoing patterns and laws observant in the cosmos. This sense of the word is found in the passage that reads:

> And among His wonders is this: He creates you out of dust, and then, lo! you become human beings ranging far and wide! And among His wonders is this: He creates for you mates out of your own kind, so that you might incline towards them, and He engenders love and tenderness between you: in this, behold, there are messages indeed for people who think! And among his wonders is the creation of the heavens and the earth, and the diversity of your tongues and colors: for in this, behold, there are messages indeed for all who are possessed of [innate] knowledge! And among His wonders is your sleep, at night or in daytime, as well as your [ability to go about in] quest of some of His bounties: in this, behold, there are messages indeed for people who [are willing to] listen! And among His wonders is this: He displays before you the lightning, giving rise to [both] fear and hope, and sends down water from the skies, giving life thereby to the earth after it had been lifeless: in this, behold, there are messages indeed for people who use their reason! And among His wonders is this: the skies and the earth stand firm at His behest. (*Sūrah al-Rūm*, 30:20-25)

b) Social "signs" such as those we find in the stories of the prophets. This sense of the word may be seen in the following passage:

> As God declares, "And indeed, [in times long past] We sent forth Noah unto his people, and he dwelt among them a thousand years bar fifty; and then the floods overwhelmed them while they were still lost in evildoing: but We saved him, together with all who were in the ark, which We then set up as a symbol (*āyah*) [of Our grace] for all people [to remember]. (*Sūrah al-ʿAnkabūt*, 29:14-15)

c) The verses of the Qur'an. This sense of the word is found in *Sūrah al-Naml*, which reads, "These are messages (*āyāt*) of the Qur'an – a divine writ clear in itself and clearly showing the truth" (27:1).

7. *The Āyāt, or "Signs" of the Prophets*

In the Qur'an the word *āyah* appears sometimes in the singular, and at other times in the plural, *āyāt*. In *Sūrah al-Mu'minūn* it is used in the singular: "And [as We exalted Moses, so, too,] We made the son of Mary and his mother a symbol (or "sign") [of Our grace]" (23:50). The singular form, rather than the dual, is used because each of these two individuals – Jesus and his mother Mary – contributed to a single, greater "sign" through their relationship to each other. Speaking of Moses, God says, "And indeed, We gave unto Moses nine clear messages (*āyāt*)" (*Sūrah al-Isrā'*, 17:101). In *Sūrah al-Aʿrāf*, the Prophet Sāliḥ speaks to the people of Thamūd, saying:

> O my people! Worship God alone: you have no deity other than Him. Clear evidence of the truth has now come unto you from your Sustainer. This she-camel belonging to God shall be a token (*āyah*) for you: so leave her alone to pasture on God's earth, and do her no harm, lest grievous chastisement befall you. (7:73)

This "token" was sent to present the people with such a clear sign that they would have no excuses before God should they fail to respond to it with faith and obedience. Again, we read in *Sūrah al-Anʿām*, "Yet whenever any of their Sustainer's messages (*āyatun min āyāti rabbihim*) comes unto them, they [who are bent on denying the truth] turn their backs upon it" (6:4), and in *Sūrah Yūnus*: "Say: 'Consider whatever there is in the heavens and on earth!' But of what avail could all the messages (*al-āyāt*) and all the warnings be to people who will not believe?" (10:101).

8. *Signs Intended to Inspire Fear or to Present a Challenge*

God declared:

> And nothing has prevented Us from sending [this message, like the earlier ones,] with miraculous signs [in its wake], save [Our knowledge] that the people of olden times [only too often] gave the lie to them: thus, We provided for [the tribe of] Thamud the she-camel as a light-giving portent, and they sinned against it. And never did We send those signs for any other purpose than to convey a warning. (*Sūrah al-Isrā'*, 17:59)

The "signs" referred to here are those which were sent to bygone nations in order to arouse holy fear in those who witnessed them. As for the generation of people among whom the Prophet was born, God affirmed that He would not overtake them with chastisement. Rather, in dealing with these people, God limited Himself to evidence rather than inflicting on them the punishment that they had so foolishly sought to hasten (*Sūrah al-ʿAnkabūt*, 29:54).

9. *Distinguishing Features of the "Sign" of the Final Message*

The final message to humankind as it pertains to miracles (*al-muʿjizāt*) and signs (*al-āyāt*) differs from previous revealed messages in style, form and content. God caused Muhammad's prophethood and message to be founded on knowledge and reason. By the Prophet's day, human beings had been prepared to comprehend the Creator's final discourse addressed to them. As such, they began realizing their capacity to draw the proper connections between the signs of the cosmos (the observed patterns and laws of nature) and the written "signs" found in the Qur'an in such a way that they were led to believe in the reality of the Unseen Source of all. God addresses the people of the Prophet's day, saying, "Would you, perchance, ask of the Apostle who has been sent unto you what was asked aforetime of Moses? But whoever chooses to deny the [evidence of the] truth, instead of believing in it, has already strayed from the right path" (*Sūrah al-Baqarah*, 2:108). God's intention for us is to further develop tools for investigation, reflection, contemplation on the expanses of the universe and its laws, and strengthening the bond between ourselves and the One who has placed the Earth and its resources at our disposal. The cosmos and its laws are miraculous signs (*āyātun muʿjizāt*) that have been manifested to human beings in order for them to contemplate their meanings on both the material and spiritual planes and, having done this, put them to use in the service of the Earth and all its inhabitants.

The sign granted to Muhammad, the last of God's prophets, was the Qur'an. In giving this sign, God left humanity with the responsibility to discover, investigate, and reflect on the realities of the universe in successive ages. As we read in *Sūrah al-Dhāriyāt*, "on Earth there are signs (*āyātun*) [of God's existence, visible] to all who are endowed with inner certainty, just as [there are signsthereof] within your own selves. Can you not, then, see?" (51: 20-22). Here we have an exhortation to combine a reading of written revelation in the form of the Qur'an, and the natural revelation manifested in the universe around us.

This exhortation is found in numerous passages of the Qur'an, since it is through this "double reading" of revelation that we are empowered to fulfill our God-given responsibility as vicegerents and stewards on Earth. It is through this same double reading of revelation that we develop tools with which to reason, reflect, investigate, understand, explain, interpret, reinterpret, and put our knowledge to creative uses.

All these functions require autonomous, effective, sound reasoning abilities. The message of the Qur'an directs us to the realm of the unseen not to paralyze reason, but rather, to put our reason to work, and to help us see that the realm of the unseen is subject to the same Majestic Creator to Whom the visible world is subject and that the relationship between these two realms is precisely ordered and controlled. Hence, there is no reason for us to fear Nature, or to flee from the unknown. Rather, we are called upon to study and understand it with assistance from the "signs" of the revealed Book. As for the universe, is it not intended to dazzle or frighten us into a submission born of ignorance. Rather, it is a realm for the constructive action that lies at the heart of true stewardship.

If we confuse Qur'anic concepts with notions that are extraneous to the Qur'anic frame of reference, we endanger our ability to understand the Qur'an properly. The reason for this is that notions derived from non-Qur'anic sources or frames of reference will be laden with presuppositions or premises that differ from, and may well conflict with, the Qur'anic perspective. Hence, the interpolation of such notions into our constellation of Qur'anic concepts, which derive directly from God, will obscure and distort the Qur'anic conceptual framework. And this, in fact, is what has happened in relation to the concepts of sign (*āyah*) and miracle (*muʿjizah*), the former of which is Qur'anic, and the latter of which is not. When scholastic theologians and Muslim philosophers replaced the phrase "the signs of the prophets" (*āyāt al-anbiyā'*) with the phrase "the miracles of the prophets" (*muʿjizāt al-anbiyā'*), this worked at cross purposes with the divine intent behind the concept of *āyah*, or sign, which fosters an association between manifestations of the Divine in the physical universe and its manifestations in the written revelation. Given the proper understanding of the concept of *āyah*, or sign, the finality of the Prophethood and message of Muhammad is reflected in people's ability to connect the concrete signs of God's existence and attributes in the natural world with the linguistic signs of the Divine in the Qur'an, with or without the direct presence of a prophet.

As time went on, a confusion arose between the sign that had been given to the Prophet – the Qur'an – and the miracles that had been wrought at the hands of earlier prophets such as Moses, Jesus and others. The miracles of former prophets, particularly Moses and Jesus, were observable events in the material world that were appropriate to the eras in which their associated divine messages were revealed. In many such situations, those whose hearts were hardened to God's message demanded miracles. Following the miracles' occurrence however they persisted in their unbelief and were destroyed by God, which served as a warning to others. As God states in *Sūrah al-Isrā'*, "And nothing has prevented Us from sending [this message, like the earlier ones,] with miraculous signs [in its wake], save [Our knowledge] that the people of olden times [only too often] gave the lie to them" (17:59).

Unlike earlier messages from God, the Qur'an served as an announcement of both warning and good tidings. Moreover, it was conveyed in a way that did nothing to paralyze or hinder human intellectual powers. The miraculous signs given to Moses in the time of Pharaoh, which were met with hardness of heart on the part of the children of Israel, were linked to a tightening of the divine law, as though subjection of the children of Israel to a theocracy was a substitute for the chastisement of being exterminated. This was the basis for the divine decree among the children of Israel "that if anyone slays a human being, unless it be [in punishment] for murder or for spreading corruption on earth – it shall be as though he had slain all mankind..." (*Sūrah al-Mā'idah* 5:32). Hence, such a person had to be put to death without the possibility of either pardon or the payment of bloodwit, for example.

The Qur'an draws Muslims' attention to the connection between the rejection of God's miraculous signs and subsequent divine chastisement, and it was because of this very connection that God did not grant concrete miracles such as the raising of the dead, healing the sick, multiplying food and the like to the people of Muhammad's time. As we saw in *Sūrah al-Isrā'* quoted above, "And nothing has prevented Us from sending [this message, like the earlier ones,] with miraculous signs [in its wake], save [Our knowledge] that the people of olden times [only too often] gave the lie to them" (17:59) or, like "the people of olden times," such individuals were simply looking for an excuse to reject faith in Muhammad, his message, or the afterlife. As we read in *Sūrah al-Furqān*:

> And [even] before you, [O Muhammad,] We never sent as Our message-bearers any but [mortal men] who indeed ate food [like other human beings] and went about in the marketplaces: for [it is thus that] We cause you [human beings] to be a means of testing one another. Are you able to endure [this test] with patience? For [remember, O man,] your Sustainer is truly All-Seeing! (25:20)

Whenever people raised an objection to the Prophet's message, the Qur'an would refute it with a stronger argument. Thus, for example, when people complained about the Qur'an's being sent down piecemeal, the response came in *Sūrah al-Furqān*, where God declared:

> Now they who are bent on denying the truth are wont to ask, "Why has not the Qur'an been bestowed on him from on high in one single revelation?" [It has been revealed] in this manner so that We might strengthen your heart thereby – for We have so arranged its component parts that they form one consistent whole, and [that] they [who deny the truth] might never taunt you with any deceptive half-truth without Our conveying to you the [full] truth and [providing you] with the best explanation. (25:32-33)

We have a plethora of verses which offer cogent arguments for the Qur'an's being the greatest and most irrefutable of all signs. However, even though no prophet or apostle had produced a sign like the Qur'an before, the people of the Prophet's day were steeped in narratives of physical miracles that had been performed by previous messengers. As a consequence they viewed the absence of such miracles on Muhammad's part as a denigration of his message and his station. People compared him to Moses, at whose hands plagues were visited on the people of Egypt under Pharaoh and who parted the Red Sea, causing his enemies to be drowned in their pursuit of the children of Israel, and Jesus, who raised the dead and healed the sick. Of course, these mighty signs and miracles weren't enough to prevent the people of Israel from worshipping a golden calf in the wilderness not long after they crossed the Red Sea. Nor were they enough, after they saw other peoples of the land bowing down to idols, to deter them from demanding that Moses make them an idol to worship. Clearly, then, these miracles had failed to address the people's minds and hearts.

Nevertheless, narratives such as these led some people to attribute physical miracles to the Prophet Muhammad and, as a consequence, to preoccupy themselves with miracle stories rather than focusing their attention on the Qur'an. Meanwhile, they set aside the Qur'an's intellectual proof of its own message, which addresses human beings everywhere in all stages of their cultural, scientific and academic development, in favor of miracle stories attributed to the Messenger of God. This was followed by attempts to reconcile such stories with the Qur'anic verses which state unequivocally that the one and only sign, or miracle, associated with the Islamic messages is the Qur'an. All miracle accounts attributed to the Messenger of God must be judged in light of what the Qur'an has to say on this topic. Otherwise, the Muslim's mind is turned into a hotbed of superstition. The Qur'an's position on this matter is clear, and the position of Muslim scholars must conform itself to that of the Qur'an. The momentous, lasting miracle of the Qur'an was sufficient for the Messenger of God, and it should be sufficient for the Muslim community as well. And God knows best.

10. *The Final Message and its Distinguishing Features*

The Qur'an has been preserved by God Himself: in its arrangement, its style, and its uniqueness and inimitability, whereas the task of preserving earlier revealed books had been entrusted to scribes and clergy, who forgot, distorted and lost parts of their scriptures. In the Prophetic

Sunnah, we have been given a complete, integral body of literature that works in harmony with the Qur'an on the levels of explication and application, the role of the Qur'an being to confirm and "watch over" the Sunnah in the sense that it serves as the criterion on the basis of which we determine what is valid, or invalid, of the Sunnah as it has come down to us. Along with the Qur'an, the Prophetic Sunnah plays a role in shaping Islamic legislation. Rules have been set down to regulate the role the Sunnah plays in this process, which is founded upon a combination of rational evidence, secondary evidence, and evidence around which some disagreement exists. Given the comprehensive, rounded nature of this process and its ongoing universal relevance, it has rightfully survived and thrived.

CONCLUSION

The Prophet Muhammad's Sunnah is the Summation of the Examples and Experiences Left by the Prophets Before Him

The life story and example of the Prophet merit the attention of people everywhere, as they bring together the experiences and teachings of all other prophets and messengers. In him we see, for example, Noah with his patience and perseverance. We see Abraham with his struggle to find truth, his piety, and his obedience. We see Moses, his toil, and his keen concern for his people. We see Jesus, his self-denial, and his striving to ground his people in the deepest, most essential truths of their religion. For the Qur'an constitutes the substance of the divine revelation, while the Sunnah is the quintessence of the experiences of earlier prophets with their respective people and the examples they have left us. God commanded the Prophet:

> Say: "I am not the first of [God's] apostles; and [like all of them,] I do not know what will be done with me or with you: for I am nothing but a plain warner." Say: "Have you given thought [to how you will fare] if this be truly [a revelation] from God and yet you deny its truth? ..." (*Sūrah al-Aḥqāf*, 46:9-10)

Seen from this perspective, the Qur'an and the Sunnah are capable of empowering worshippers from all times and places, protecting them from the attempts of Satan and his followers to bring such worshippers into the ranks of those who refuse to bow down. Partial, decontextualized readings of the Qur'an and the Sunnah are dangerous unless they are bound firmly to the universal principles and values set forth in the Qur'an and its higher purposes. The Prophetic Sunnah must be tied inextricably to the Qur'an in a way that allows for no contradiction or conflict between the two but, rather, combines them into a seamless structural unity. The preservation of the Prophet's example (Sunnah) and life story (*sīrah*) depends on the Qur'an, and everything said or written by Muslim scholars, be they earlier or later, that indicates otherwise is not worth discussing.

2

Sunnah as Concept and as Technical Term

[FIRST]
The Concept of the *Sunnah* and its Historical Development

I VIEW the word *sunnah* not as a technical term, but as a concept.[1] In fact, it is a highly precise and subtle legal concept that has had a far-ranging and significant impact on the Islamic intellectual tradition overall. The word *sunnah* encompasses a network of related concepts, such as "way" or "path" (*ṭarīqah*), custom (*ʿādah*), social and natural law (*al-qānūn al-ijtimāʿī wa al-ṭabīʿī*), and the like. Hence, whether in its pre-Qur'anic use among Arabs, its Qur'anic usage, its use by the Prophet Muhammad, its various uses by those living in the first generation of Muslims (who witnessed the Qur'anic revelation), or its uses among Muslim scholars, be they scholars of the fundamentals of jurisprudence (*uṣūl scholars*), jurists, scholastic theologians, or hadith transmitters, the word *sunnah* signifies a full-fledged, fully rounded concept that spans a number of disciplines. Hence, the transmutation of the word *sunnah* into a mere technical term that could be used however one liked depending on the context led to a confusion and vagueness that Muslims could well have done without.[2]

Consequently, it is important to investigate, analyze and reformulate this concept in order to rescue it from the misunderstanding that now plagues it. What I aim to do here is not to further define the already numerous terms now in use in discussions of the Sunnah. Rather, my aim is to clarify the relationships among these various terms and, in so doing, to demonstrate the validity of viewing them as a single overarching concept that represents a unified legal entity (*ḥaqīqah sharʿiyyah wāḥidah*) rather than a technical term that scholars can bandy about however they wish, investing it with whatever meanings suit their fancy on the pretext that specialists in every field are entitled to their own jargon.

1. *The Notion of "Concept" (Mafhūm) and its Formulation*

Approached morphologically, the Arabic noun *mafhūm*, generally translated as "concept," is a passive participle derived from the triliteral root *f-h-m*, meaning to understand. As such, its literal meaning is "understood." Logicians define it as a perception, realization or cognition (*mudrak*), as what takes place, and might take place, in the mind, whether in the form of action or speech, whether through direct experience or someone else's verbal description. *Uṣūl* scholars (experts in the fundamentals, or *uṣūl*, of Islamic jurisprudence) define the word *mafhūm* in contrast to *manṭūq*, that which is uttered or pronounced. That which is uttered or spoken consists of a pronouncement on what has been spoken of, and on one or more of its properties. An example of a *manṭūq* might be, "I ate the apple," which indicates both the fact that I ate a particular apple, and that apples are edible (edibility is one of their properties).

The notion of *mafhūm* is then divided into two categories: (1) what might be termed "harmonious meaning" (*mafhūm muwāfaqah*), which is what is understood directly from what someone says either by way of exact correspondence or by way of implicit content, and (2) "divergent meaning" (*mafhūm mukhālafah*), which is what a statement or expression communicates by way of association, or through what has not been said in contrast to what has been said.

The word *sunnah* is a broad, multifaceted category – a universal, if you will – to which different expressions might apply based on a variety of considerations. The individual instances of this universal are related to the word *sunnah* in numerous disparate ways. Hence, we might amend the expression to read homonym (*mushakkik*).[3] However, it is agreed upon among *uṣūl* scholars and logicians that if the individual instances of the universal are not disparate, then they are to be viewed as synonymous.

Arab linguists have associated four meanings with the word *sunnah* – manner or way (*ṭarīqah*), habit or custom (*ʿādah*), conduct or way of life (*sīrah*), and nature, disposition, or character (*ṭabīʿah*). Although these four meanings, being fairly disparate, render the word *sunnah* closer to being a homonym, they are, nevertheless, quite close to each other as well. However, I prefer to classify them as more or less synonymous due to links among them that reduce their dissimilarities and mitigate the effects of such dissimilarities. Thus, for example, the words *ṭarīqah* (way or manner) and *sīrah* (conduct, way of life) are quite close in meaning. Similarly, the words *ṭarīqah* (way, manner), *sīrah* (conduct, way of life) and *ʿādah* (habit, custom) have a shared semantic field. As for the fourth meaning, namely, that of disposition or character (*ṭabīʿah*), it has elements in common with the notion of law, that is, stability, continuity, and agreement on origins and principles.

When we examine the ways in which *uṣūl* scholars, jurists and hadith transmitters have used the word *sunnah*, we need to identify each group's particular epistemological framework. And in order to do this, we need first to look to the Qur'an.

2. *The Concept of Sunnah in the Qur'an*

The triliteral root *s-n-n* occurs nine times in Meccan surahs, and ten times in Madinan surahs. This root and its derivatives are used in the Qur'an to refer to phenomena that have occurred with such regularity in the cosmos and in society that they manifest predictable, unchanging laws. God warns polytheists and those who have gone astray from His path that, given the unchanging nature of the moral laws at work in the universe and in human society, they will never escape the outcomes of their waywardness and defiance. He says, "Tell those who are bent on denying the truth that if they desist, all that is past shall be forgiven them; but if they revert [to their wrongdoing], let them remember what happened to the like of them in times gone by" (*Sūrah al-Anfāl*, 8:38), and:

> ...now that a warner has come unto them, [his call] but increases their aversion, their arrogant behavior on earth, and their devising of evil [arguments against God's messages]. Yet [in the end,] such evil scheming will engulf

> none but its authors: and can they expect anything but [to be made to go] the way of those [sinners] of olden times (*sunnat al-awwalīn*)? Thus [it is]: no change wilt you ever find in God's way (*sunnat Allāh*); yea, no deviation wilt you ever find in God's way (*sunnat Allāh*)!" (*Sūrah Fāṭir*, 35:42-43)

The word *sunnah* is thus used in the Qur'an in the sense of "way." According to linguist and Qur'an commentator al-Rāghib al-Iṣfahānī (d. 502 AH/1108 CE):

> When we speak of God's *sunnah*, we are speaking of the way of His wisdom and the way of obedience to Him, as in the verse where He warns, "And [now,] if they who are bent on denying the truth should fight against you, they will indeed turn their backs [in flight], and will find none to protect them and none to bring them succor, such being God's way (*sunnat Allāh*) which has ever obtained in the past – and never wilt you find any change in God's way (*sunnat Allāh*)" (*Sūrah al-Fatḥ*, 48: 22-23; see *Sūrah Fāṭir*, 35:43 quoted above).

The ageless nature of God's way may be seen in the fact that however many branches there may be of the divine laws, and however different these branches may appear, they all share a common, unchanging purpose, which is to purify people's hearts, thereby making them worthy of divine reward and prepared to dwell in the divine presence.

3. *The Word Sunnah From a Linguistic Perspective*

From a purely linguistic point of the view, the word *sunnah* refers to conduct or way of life, be it good or bad. The Messenger of God said:

> If someone comports himself well as a Muslim (*man sanna fī al-islām sunnatan ḥasanah*) and others follow this good example, he will be granted the same reward as those who followed his example, yet without these people's rewards being diminished in the least. Conversely, if someone comports himself badly as a Muslim (*man sanna fī al-islām sunnatan sayyi'ah*) and others follow this bad example, he will bear the same burden of guilt as that borne by those who followed his example, yet without these people's burden being alleviated in the least.

As we have seen, the Messenger of God used the word *sunnah* to refer to the act of setting an example, whether good or bad. Al-Khaṭṭābī

(d. 388 AH/988 CE) wrote, "The original meaning of the word *sunnah* is a laudable way of life. If it is used in an unqualified manner, it is the positive sense that prevails. It can, however, be qualified by a negative descriptor, as in the phrase, *man sanna sunnah sayyi'ah* (to set a bad example, comport oneself in a bad way)." Al-Shawkānī quotes al-Kisā'ī as saying that "the word *sunnah* means constancy, continuance, perseverance (*al-dawām*)." Al-Shawkānī comments on this statement, saying, "Perhaps what he [al-Kisā'ī] was speaking of was 'something that is done habitually, or on a regular basis' (*al-amr alladhī yudāwamu ʿalayhi*). Alternatively, he might be referring to the regular practices of bygone generations."

The derivation of the word sunnah

Fakhr al-Dīn al-Rāzī cites three possible derivations of the word *sunnah*. (1) It may be viewed as a noun on the *fuʿlah* pattern, which bears the sense of the passive participle, *mafʿūlah*. In this case, the verb *sanna* is understood to mean "to pour continuously," or, "to pour in a continuous stream." Arabic speakers have likened a straight path to a stream of water being poured out, since, once one has begun pouring water, the water molecules follow each other in succession, and in a single direction, thus forming a single entity. (2) The verb *sanna* may be understood to mean "to sharpen," as one does with a knife blade. Hence, as used to describe the actions attributed to the Prophet, the word *sunnah* bears the sense of something that has been sharpened or refined. (3) The noun *sunnah* might also be derived from the verb *sanna* as in the phrase *sanna al-ibl*, that is, to graze one's camels generously. Similarly, the actions that were performed regularly by the Prophet were referred to as sunnah in the sense that he persevered in the practices he established.

Does the word *sunnah* refer to a custom or habit? According to al-ʿAḍud and many other *uṣūl* scholars, the word *sunnah* simply refers to a way of life, habit, or customary practice. In his commentary on *Sūrah Fāṭir* 35:43, al-Zamakhsharī states that the words, "can they expect anything but [to be made to go] the way of those [sinners] of olden times?" refers to these people's expectation of a fate similar to "the unleashing of chastisement against earlier peoples who had given the lie to their messengers." Al-Zamakhsharī explains that God's "custom" (*ʿādah*), which is to inflict retribution on those who give the lie to His messengers – is not subject to change. Hence, he understood the word *sunnah* to be synonymous with *ʿādah*, or customary practice, which is the position taken by a number of other scholars as well.

However, though it may be acceptable to use the word *ʿādah* in relation to human beings, it is not appropriate to use it in relation to God. Perhaps it would be more fitting to understand the word *sunnah* in relation to God as meaning "law" (*qānūn*), and this despite the use of the word *ʿādah* in a supplication relating to deniers of the truth that reads, "O God, [forget not] Your customary ways in relation to the likes of them!" It should be remembered here that scholars might adopt a given meaning and cite textual evidence in its support simply because it is more consistent with their particular epistemological model.

Nowhere does a dictionary state explicitly that the word *sunnah* is synonymous with the word *ʿādah*, nor that the word *ʿādah* is synonymous with way of life (*ṭarīqah*) or conduct (*sīrah*). What the dictionary does tell us is that the word *ʿādah* is derived from the verb *ʿāda/yaʿūdu*, meaning "to return." As such, it refers to an action to which one returns over and over again. Some scholars have defined *ʿādah* as "the repetition of something, all or some of the time, in the same way, and in a mindless fashion." According to ʿAbd al-Ghanī, the words *ʿādah* and *ʿurf* are synonymous, where the word *ʿādah* refers to customary or habitual actions, while the word *ʿurf* refers to customary or habitual statements. He states, "To discuss *ʿādah* from a linguistic point of view is one thing, and to discuss the *sunnah* is another. Nevertheless, the word *ʿādah* has been treated as though it were synonymous with *sunnah* when it is not."

If we examine all meanings of the word *ʿādah*, we find that they converge around the notions of continuation and persistence. Those who take *sunnah* to be synonymous with *ʿādah* seem to be basing this position on al-Kisāʾī's statement, quoted above, that *sunnah* means continuation, persistence (*inna al-sunnah al-dawām*). If, moreover, we look at the dictionary definition of *ʿādah* as something that "becomes established in people's psyches" (*mā yastaqirru fī al-nufūs*), its definition in *al-ʿAyn* as "persistence or perseverance in something," as well al-Iṣfahānī's explanation of the word *ṭabīʿah*, meaning nature or disposition, it becomes apparent that the word *ʿādah* may be used in the same sense as *ṭabīʿah*; however, as we have had occasion to note, the word *ʿādah* is synonymous with neither *ṭabīʿah* nor *sunnah*. Given the aforementioned definition of *ʿādah* as the repetition of something, whether some or all of the time, and the view of it as synonymous with *ʿurf*, meaning custom or more, it becomes apparent that it also bears the sense of *ṭarīqah*, meaning manner or way of life. Hence, it conveys the notion of continuation and repetition. In his book entitled *al-Furūq al-Lughawiyyah* (Linguistic Distinctions), Abū Hilāl al-ʿAskarī mentions differences between *ʿādah* and *sunnah*. He states, "*ʿĀdah* is something someone does continuously of his/her own accord while *sunnah* is something one does based on a previous example."

In sum, the meanings of the terms *ʿādah, ṭabīʿah, ṭarīqah* and *dawām* share an element of commonality which, although it falls short of synonymity, may nevertheless be classified as a kind of semantic integration or homonymity.

4. *The Concept of Sunnah in the Prophetic Sunnah Itself*

Qubayṣah ibn Dhu'ayb said:

> A certain grandmother came to Abū Bakr the Upright and asked him for her inheritance. He said to her, "According to the Book of God, you are due nothing, and I can ascertain nothing from the *sunnah* of the Messenger of God. So go back [home] until I have inquired of others." He then asked the Prophet's other Companions. Al-Mughīrah ibn Shuʿbah said, "I once came to the Messenger of God, and he gave her[4] one-sixth." Abū Bakr asked him, "Is there anyone else who agrees with you?" Muḥammad ibn Maslamah al-Anṣārī rose and said the same thing al-Mughīrah ibn Shuʿbah had said. So Abū Bakr gave it to her.

Similarly, Jābir ibn ʿAbd Allāh related that "The Messenger of God established the practice of [offering] a slaughter camel and a cow on behalf of seven people."

In his book entitled, *Naẓarah ʿĀmah fī Tārīkh al-Fiqh al-Islāmī* (A General Look at the History of Islamic Jurisprudence), Ali Hasan Abd al-Qadir states:

> In Arab circles of olden times, the word *sunnah* was used to refer to the proper way of life for both the individual and the community...This meaning carried over into Islam in the early schools in the Hejaz, and in Iraq also, where it referred to current or prevalent action. In Islamic circles the term was used to mean that which was generally agreed upon, and the ideal of correct behavior, yet without any specific reference to the example set by the Prophet himself. It was not until the late second century AH that the meaning of the word *sunnah* narrowed to the point where it referred solely to the practices of the Apostle. This narrowing occurred under the influence of Imam al-Shāfiʿī, who went against the word's original agreed-upon usage.

[SECOND]
Later Use of the Term *Sunnah*

During the first century AH, the term *sunnah* was associated with a number of different meanings. The following meanings were gleaned from al-Ṭabarī's *Tārīkh* (History) by D. S. Margoliouth:

1. Based on a conversation that took place in 34 AH between ʿAlī ibn Abī Ṭālib and ʿUthmān ibn ʿAffān in which mention was made of someone who "established a known practice and eliminated a little-practiced innovation," it can be gathered that the term *sunnah* was used in the sense of legitimate, generally approved action as opposed to unfamiliar or suspect innovation. A similar usage is found in a quote attributed to Ṭalḥah ibn al-Zubayr during the war against ʿAlī in 36 AH. He said, "This is a situation concerning which, since it has never arisen before, we have neither a Qur'anic revelation nor a precedent set by the Messenger of God."

2. In 35 AH, the Caliph ʿUthmān ibn ʿAffān delivered a speech to the people of Makkah in which he spoke of "the laudable practice introduced by the Messenger of God (*al-sunnah al-ḥasanah allatī istanna bihā rasūl Allāh*) and the first two Caliphs."

3. In the year 38 AH, ʿAlī ibn Abī Ṭālib entered into a discussion with al-Khirrīt, who had opposed ʿAlī over the arbitration at the Battle of

Ṣiffīn and wanted to distance himself from him. In this context, he said, "Come, let us study the book [the Qur'an] together and debate over the *sunan* (plural of *sunnah*)," where the word *sunnah* is used simply to denote people's customary actions. Another example of this use of the word *sunnah* is found al-Muhallab's instructions to his sons in the year 82 AH, saying, "Read and recite the Qur'an, and teach the *sunan* and the rules of etiquette adhered to by the righteous."

4. The word *sunnah* has been used to refer to a variety of concepts and entities, including the way of Islam (*sunnat al-Islām*) (34 AH), the way of the Muslims (*sunnat al-muslimīn*) (36 AH), and the way of God (*sunnat Allāh*) (38 AH).

5. It has been used to refer to the actions of the Prophet and the two first Caliphs, Abū Bakr and ʿUmar ibn al-Khaṭṭāb; an instance of this use is found in ʿUthmān ibn ʿAffān's statement in 35 AH, quoted above, in reference to "the laudable practice introduced by the Messenger of God (*al-sunnah al-ḥasanah allatī istanna bihā rasūl Allāh*) and the first two caliphs."

6. The word *sunnah* has been used to refer to things over and above the actions of the Prophet, as in the statement made by Zayd ibn ʿAlī in 122 AH, "We invite you to the Book of God and the *sunnah* of His Prophet. We call upon you to maintain laudable practices (*sunan*), and to extinguish [useless] innovations (*bidaʿ*)."

7. The word has been used to refer to Muhammad himself as the one who led them to engage in laudable action. The source for this usage is found in a discourse attributed to ʿAlī in the year 36 AH, in which he stated, "He taught them the Book, wisdom, their religious duties and the *sunnah*. The Muslims then appointed, as his successors, two righteous leaders in keeping with the Book and the *sunnah*. These two leaders exhibited good conduct and did not go beyond the Sunnah. We owe it to you to act on the Book of God and the Sunnah of His Messenger."

8. The word *sunnah* may refer to the action called for in the Qur'an. This usage is found in a speech delivered by the founder of the Abbasid state (ʿAbd Allāh al-Saffāḥ) in 129 AH, in which he stated, "God revealed His Book to [the Prophet] from on high, permitting what is permissible and forbidding what is forbidden. In it He enacted His law and established its practices (*wa sanna fīhi sunanahu*)."

Confusion among meanings

Confusion relating to the meaning of the word *sunnah* arose among scholars of certain schools of Islamic jurisprudence. Such scholars cited the use of the word *sunnah* in statements made by the Prophet, his Companions, and his Companions' Successors, as evidence of the exemplary nature of actions which they sought to encourage as desirable; however, they were using the word *sunnah* in the strictly terminological sense that developed in the second century AH. In other words, they had begun associating the word *sunnah* specifically with the precedents set by the Prophet rather than understanding it in its broader sense as any conduct worthy of emulation. This narrowed conceptualization was mistaken, since, as we have noted, the term *sunnah* as employed in the narratives about the life of the Prophet and statements made by his Companions and their Successors was meant in the more comprehensive sense to which we have made reference. This broader sense of the word *sunnah* included beliefs, acts of worship, day-to-day transactions, morals, rules of etiquette, and the like. It is clear from the accounts of events in the life of the Prophet and from the ways in which his Companions used the word that it refers to some practice that had met with acceptance on the part of "the people of opinion" (*ahl al-ra'y*) and leading, influential figures (*ahl al-ḥal wa al-ʿaqd*) either because it had been established by their forebears or senior opinion leaders, or because it was a custom or tradition that had been passed down among them and which, having met with acceptance on the part of trusted authorities, was viewed as sound and worthy of maintaining.

1. *The Sunnah in the Late First Century and the Early Second Century* AH

When ʿUmar ibn ʿAbd al-ʿAzīz became governor over Madinah in 86 AH, the people stood before him and he said, "O people, if you rise, we rise, and if you are seated, we will be seated. The only One for whom we should all rise is the Lord of the Worlds. God has imposed obligations and established practices (*wa sanna sunan*). Those who fulfill these obligations and adhere to these practices will endure, and those who neglect them will be blotted out."

A careful reading of the exchanges that took place between ʿUmar ibn ʿAbd al-ʿAzīz and his administrative officers and governors indicates that the understanding of the Sunnah embraced by ʿUmar ibn ʿAbd al-ʿAzīz was the one he had received from the residents and scholars of Madinah, who played a major role in his intellectual formation when he served as governor over the city. The people of Madinah understood the word *sunnah* to mean the actions that had been performed by the Messenger of God and by his Companions after him. This is the understanding which Imam Mālik adopted and applied in his book *Al-Muwaṭṭa'*. Mālik took care not to include in his *Al-Muwaṭṭa'* any practice that was not adhered to by the people of Madinah, who had inherited the guidance of the Prophet. If he received a report that he considered to be valid but which did not form part of the Madinans' practice, he would include it his book; however, he would state explicitly that the report in question was in conflict with the practice that prevailed among the city's scholars and was not to be adhered to. At that time, therefore, the word *sunnah* had not yet been used to refer to a mere statement or narrated account. Rather, it was used to refer to the ongoing practices prevalent in the Madinan community. However, actions or practices that had gained such prevalence would undoubtedly have had their origins in the Qur'an, which had been revealed to the Messenger of God so that he, in turn, could teach his people its wisdom, purify their hearts and minds, and strive mightily against God's enemies.

2. *Sunnah and Hadith*

In more than one passage of the Qur'an, God uses the word *sunnah* in relation to Himself. We read in *Sūrah al-Aḥzāb*, for example, "Such has been God's way (*sunnat Allāh*) with those who [sinned in like manner and] passed away aforetime – and never will you find any change in God's way (*sunnat Allāh*)!" (33:62) By "God's way" is meant the unchanging divine laws that manifest themselves in the cosmos, the human soul, and society. The word *sunnah* is likewise used in relation to human beings, as in *Sūrah al-Nisā'*, which reads, "God wants to make [all this] clear unto you, and to guide you onto the [righteous] ways of life (*sunan*) of those who preceded you, and to turn unto you in His mercy: for God is All-Knowing, Wise" (4:26). The phrase "the [righteous] ways of life of those who preceded you (*sunan alladhīna min qablikum*)" refers to their predecessors' repeated and consistent striving to follow the guidance of the prophets. When the word *sunnah* is used in relation to the Messenger of God, it refers to practices through which he was applying the teachings of the Qur'an, and in which he engaged so repeatedly that they became a predictable, unchanging pattern of conduct. This phenomenon is best expressed in the words of ʿĀ'ishah, who, when asked to describe the Prophet's character, said, "his character was that of the Qur'an" (*kāna khuluquhu al-Qur'ān*). In other words, the teachings of the Qur'an had so permeated his being that they had become second nature to him on the levels of daily conduct and worship. This being so, we are called upon to obey him. In this case, the Sunnah finds its origin in the Qur'an and expresses itself through the Prophet's conduct and behavior.

As for the hadith literature, it emerged as people began relating to others accounts of the things the Messenger of God had done, their purpose being to communicate these things to people who had not witnessed these events or actions themselves. Hence, a hadith (the word *ḥadīth* meaning "conversation," "talk") is an account in which one informs others of some aspect of the Prophet's Sunnah, that is, his practices and habitual ways of conducting himself. In other words, the hadiths are not the sunnah as such but, rather, a collection of accounts that describe the sunnah. Each such account was documented via a chain of narrators that reassured believers of its veracity. The body or text (*matn*) of the hadith might reflect the narrator's own understanding of the practices being described. Questions might then arise as to whether a given action or statement by the Prophet was an example that Muslims were expected to emulate. Was the action the example to be emulated, with the words being subordinate to the action and serving simply to confirm or reinforce it, or was it the other way around? This, of course, is a matter that may concern only *uṣūl* scholars, whose job it is to identify the sources of Islamic legislation and their levels of priority. *Uṣūl* scholars should have given the Prophet's actions a higher place than they did. Be that as it may, we place priority on actions accompanied by words, such as we find in the hadiths, "Pray as you have seen me pray," and, "Take from me your rites of worship." Following this we have actions of the Prophet that are not accompanied by words, which come closer to the concept of *sunnah* as traditionally understood. And lastly, we have words alone.

All controversies that have arisen among scholars have had to do with the reports concerning the Sunnah (understood as what the Prophet did, said, and approved), not with the concept of *sunnah* itself (the notion of emulating what the Prophet did and said), since no true believer in God and His Messenger would reject the idea of emulating an action that can be documented as having been performed by the Prophet, either because it is supported by the Qur'an, or because it was transmitted in a sound and trustworthy manner. In sum, controversy has been limited almost entirely to the question of whether the Prophet's Sunnah has been transmitted accurately. And God knows best.

3. *The Word Sunnah as Understood by Scholars in Specialized Fields*

The meanings scholars have attributed to the word *sunnah* can be categorized based on the epistemological models peculiar to their respective disciplines.

a) ***Uṣūl*** **scholars (scholars of the fundamentals of jurisprudence)**: The epistemological model adopted by these scholars rests on working "to prove that what serves as valid evidence in the realm of jurisprudence is also valid as evidence overall." The *uṣūl* scholars' focus on this aspect led them to define the Sunnah as "the second source of Islamic legislation." Since they wanted to show the Sunnah to be an independent type of juristic evidence and one of the fundamental sources for Islamic jurisprudence, they clothed the word *sunnah* in this particular definition. Among the various possible meanings of the word *sunnah*, they chose that of way or manner (*ṭarīqah*). As for the alternative meanings that others had adopted, they did not see themselves as obliged to address them given their conviction that as specialists in a given field, they were entitled to the use of their own mutually agreed-upon terminology.

b) **Jurists:** The implicit epistemological model among jurists is informed by the discourse of accountability (*khiṭāb al-taklīf*), which aims to assess and classify the actions of the morally accountable individual. Seeing that the *uṣūl* scholars had relegated the sunnah to second place among the various kinds of recognized legal evidence, jurists decided to assign the word *sunnah* a similar place within the discourse of moral accountability by defining it as a desirable action whose value has been established on the basis of conjectural evidence and which, therefore, cannot be classified as a duty or obligation. Following this line of reasoning, jurists identified *sunnah* as an action for the commission of which one will be rewarded, but for the omission of which one will not be punished; or alternatively, as an action whose performer merits praise, but whose non-performer merits no blame.

c) **Hadith transmitters:** The entire epistemological model of hadith transmitters revolves around the twin poles of narrative (*riwāyah*), and chain of transmission (*isnād*). Hadith transmitters have thus defined the Sunnah as everything that has been attributed to the Prophet by way of actions, words, or affirmations of others' actions or words.

When we examine the definitions that these various groups have assigned the word *sunnah*, we note a lack of common denominators among them due to the disparate models which they use as their starting points. Classification of the Sunnah as a secondary type of juristic evidence (by the *uṣūl scholars*), for example, has nothing to do with whether the commission or omission of the related action merits reward or punishment (as per the jurists' definition of sunnah). Besides, one might question the validity of defining the Sunnah as all actions, words, or affirmations attributed to the Prophet. Consequently, these three definitions of *sunnah* are disjointed and mutually irrelevant. Hence, rather than treating the word *sunnah* as a technical term whose meaning can be captured in a precisely formulated definition that pertains to a particular, limited field of specialization, it should be treated as an integral, flexible concept that emerges from a comprehensive theory which embraces all the meanings applicable to the word *sunnah*, whether on the levels of dictionary definitions, Qur'anic usages, or the way it was used by the Prophet. Rather than remaining lost in a maze of specialized jargon, we need to place the term *sunnah* within an agreed-upon framework that gives it the flexibility it needs in order to accommodate all the meanings with which it has been associated in the past, as well as whatever meanings will emerge in the future.

[THIRD]
Semantic Evolution of Notions Relating to the Concept of *Sunnah*

1. *Semantic Evolution of the Term Fiqh*

The term *fiqh* generally rendered nowadays as "jurisprudence" simply means understanding or realization. The word *fiqh* has been used to refer to knowledge gained through vision and observation, since vision or seeing represents the most potent form of knowledge. The triliteral root *f-q-h* occurs approximate twenty times in the Qur'an, most of these instances being the present tense of the verb in the sense of "understand." The most precise form of understanding, which is the understanding of the heart – the heart being the organ of discernment – is seen in the Qur'anic usage of the word *fiqh*.

The word *fiqh* continued to bear the sense of understanding throughout the early days of Islam. With the development of Islamic society and changes in day-to-day interactions among people, religious authorities needed sharper powers of understanding, which required a keenness to grasp the text under study and its subtle nuances of meaning. ʿUmar ibn al-Khaṭṭāb wrote to Abū Mūsā al-Ashʿarī, "When something is presented to you, exercise your powers of understanding." Commentators have understood this statement to mean that correct understanding is a light that God casts into the servant's heart. Moreover, a mufti or ruler will only be able to issue a legal ruling or govern justly by virtue of two kinds of understanding. The first is an understanding and discernment of reality and the ability to ascertain the true nature of what has taken place based on evidence, signs and interrelations. The second is an understanding of the ruling appropriate to this reality based on the contents of the Qur'an or a statement by the Messenger of God. One of these kinds of understanding is then applied to the other. The knower is the person who, through knowledge and study of reality, determines the rulings of God and His Messenger.

The step-by-step process involves reading, then knowledge and understanding, where the understanding may either accompany knowledge or follow it. Herein lie the beginnings of the use of *fiqh*. This same order of events may be found in al-Ṭabarī's commentary on *Sūrah al-Baqarah*, 2:269, which speaks of God's "granting wisdom unto whom He wills." Al-Ṭabarī cites various narratives in support of different interpretations of the word *al-ḥikmah*, or wisdom. He speaks of recitation and study of the Qur'an (*al-Qur'ānu wa al-fiqhu fīhi*), or the study of the Qur'an (*al-fiqhu fī al-Qur'an*), or the Book and the study of it (*al-kitābu wa al-fiqhu fīhi*), or the Qur'an, knowledge and understanding (*al-Qur'an wa al-ʿilmu wa al-fiqh*). Knowledge, when spoken of in conjunction with the Qur'an (the Book), is that which has been narrated (the hadith or the sunnah), while *fiqh*, or understanding, accompanies or follows knowledge.

When we compare this progression of meanings with the progression of dictionary definitions for the word *fiqh*, a clear parallel emerges between the linguistic and social evolution of the term. Those charged with issuing legal rulings for people, whether as judges or as muftis, passed through a progression of stages: (a) Reading a written text, an activity undertaken by people known as readers, or reciters (*qurrā'*, plural of *qāri'*); (b) knowledge passed down in a rote manner in the form of a sunnah or religious obligation (*farīḍah*) that clarified the meaning of the Qur'an. Those who undertook this activity were known as *ʿulamā'* (plural of *ʿālim*, meaning "knower"), while the *sunnah* was referred to as knowledge, or *ʿilm*. (c) Reflective understanding and comprehension enlightened with insight. Those who engaged in this activity were known as *fuqahā'* (plural of *faqīh*), that is, jurists or legists.

It should be borne in mind, however, that up through the second century AH, the word *fiqh* was still not understood in the later sense just mentioned, or in the way it is understood today. This may be seen from the fact that Abū Ḥanīfah (d. 150 AH/767 CE) understood the word *fiqh* to refer to a comprehensive knowledge of the soul: its virtues and vices, its strengths and weaknesses, a person's beliefs, moral character and behavior. The understanding involved was an insight so all-encompassing that it was worthy to be classed as the wisdom that God grants to whom He wills (cf. *Sūrah al-Baqarah*, 2:269). In the days of Imam Mālik (d. 179 AH/795 CE), the term *fiqh* was still being used in a sense that was broader than its modern-day definition, which is restricted to a concern with people's behavior and social interactions. The further narrowing of the word's import to the realm of action would come in the following stage.

This next stage of development took place in a class of scholars who concerned themselves more with meanings, technical terms and their definitions, the division and classification of the sciences, and other such pursuits which were not widespread in the Hejaz, and which would not have been expected to have a great impact there. Iraq, by contrast, was marked by an environment more conducive to such a development. The word *fiqh* was not in circulation in its more specialized sense during the days of the Prophet's Companions, although it began to emerge toward the end of this period and during the era of the Companions' successors. Imam Mālik joined the procession of religious culture at a time when the word *fiqh* had not been set apart as a distinct technical term. Instead, muftis concerned themselves with knowledge, or *ʿilm*, urging others to gain a profound understanding (*fiqh*) of what they knew. Nevertheless, the word *fiqh* had yet to acquire the semantic dimensions with which it is associated in our day.

2. *Evolution of the Concept of Ra'y*

The triliteral root *r-'-y*, from which the noun *ra'y* is derived, refers most basically to the physical act of seeing. Since knowing something with the mind is analogous to seeing something with the eye, the derivative meanings of *r-'-y* include that of perceiving, discerning, considering, and adopting or expressing a point of view or opinion (*ra'y*), all of which involve the act of seeing with the "eye" of the mind. This sense of the word is reflected in numerous words, such as *ru'yā*, or vision, as what one sees in a dream, and which might be termed a vision of the heart, that is, belief. It might also be understood to refer to a waking vision, such as that mentioned in *Sūrah al-Isrā'*, 17:60. The Qur'an uses the root *r-'-y* in the sense of sight more than it does in any other sense. Its use in the sense of belief is rare except as one possible interpretation, as in the case of *Sūrah al-Nisā'*: "We have bestowed upon you from on high this divine writ, setting forth the truth, so that you may judge between people in accordance with what God has taught you (*arāka*, that is, caused you see or believe)" (4:105). Moreover, the noun *ra'ī*, which occurs infrequently in the Qur'an, conveys only the general sense of understanding or consideration.

The word *ra'y* in the sense of opinion or point of view is an outcome of knowledge and understanding, which are indispensable when there is a need for a legal ruling on a given situation. In the context of the successive roles that have been played by muftis – that of reader/reciter (*qāri'*), scholar (*ʿālim*) and jurist (*faqīh*) – they have to form an opinion or point of view whatever their level of culture or education happens to be (from the ability to read, to the reception of narrated accounts, to reflection on narrated accounts that have been passed down from one generation to the next). Consequently, the stages through which the term *ra'y* passed socially speaking parallel the stages through which religious leaders passed (from readers/reciters, to scholars, to jurists). We know that no sooner had the Apostle fallen silent then reciters began reflecting on the contents of the Islamic message, deepening their understanding of it and forming opinions. After the Prophet's death, his Companions met to discuss, debate and defend their respective points of view before arriving at the decision to pledge their allegiance to Abū Bakr as the first Caliph. Later they discussed and debated what to do in response to the apostasy of certain tribes on the Arabian Peninsula. They were clearly striving for the best understanding of the situation at hand, and of how to apply the text of the Qur'an to said situation.

In the face of such trials, the Companions sought out the opinions of individuals known for their knowledge and insight. They would even use the word *ra'y* as a title of appreciation and respect. Al-ʿAbbās, for example, was referred to as Dhū al-Ra'y, that is, "The One with the Opinion." In other cases they would precede the word *ra'y* with a person's name, as in Mughīrah al-Ra'y (Mughīrah of the Opinion, that is, Mughīrah the Perceptive), Rabīʿah al-Ra'y (Rabīʿah the Perceptive). Used in this manner, the word *ra'y* refers to the disclosure of a problematic issue and the discovery of a solution to it. The word *ra'y* was also appended to the names of some jurists, as in the case of Hilāl al-Ra'y, where the word *ra'y* meant simply penetrating insight.

The city of Madinah was home to those who had received knowledge from the Prophet himself and whose perspicacity and observation served as the basis of their governance. Madinah may thus have preceded other Islamic regions in its use of the word *ra'y* with this general meaning, which draws no distinction between one jurist and another, or between one *mujtahid*, or scholarly interpreter, and another. Imam Mālik himself once spoke of some opinion as "not worthy of consideration," describing it as *ra'yun mā huwa ra'yun*, which indicates that Imam Mālik viewed himself as qualified to give and evaluate opinions. Ibn Qutaybah also viewed Mālik as qualified to give informed opinions. Ibn Rushd, in fact, termed Imam Mālik "the commander of the faithful" among those in the field of opinion-formation and application of the principle of *qiyās*, or analogical reasoning.

This, then, is an explication of the word *ra'y* in the realm of understanding and knowledge. An opinion or point of view will differ depending on one's mindset, environment, and the culture that forms one's understanding, sets its orientation, and determines the precision with which one thinks.

3. *Evolution in the Concept of Naṣṣ*

a) Traditional uses of the root n-ṣ-ṣ

The word *naṣṣ*, the verbal noun derived from the triliteral root *n-ṣ-ṣ*, has been used with numerous meanings, of which the following are the most important:

- **Lifting or raising** in both the physical and nonphysical senses. Hadith transmitters, for example, used the term *naṣṣ* to speak of the process of tracing ("lifting") a narrative back to the Prophet, or attributing a saying to the person who had uttered it. In praise of al-Zuhrī, ʿAmr ibn Dīnār once said, "Never have I encountered a man more conscientious about tracing his hadiths back to the Prophet (*mā ra'aytu rajulān anaṣṣa li al-ḥadīthi minhu*)."
- Used in an unqualified sense, the word *naṣṣ* has been used to refer to something's **end or goal**.
- **Interrogation**. One might say, *naṣṣ al-rajulu naṣṣan*, meaning roughly, "The man thoroughly questioned, or examined (his interlocutor)."
- The act of **specifying or appointing**.
- The act of **informing**. To say, *naṣṣahu ʿalayhi naṣṣan*, would mean roughly, "He informed him of the matter."
- The act of **manifesting or making clear**. One might say, *naṣṣ al-shay'a naṣṣan*, meaning, "He made it clear."

These, then, are the overall traditional uses of the Arabic root *n-ṣ-ṣ* and its derivatives.

b) Naṣṣ as used by Imam al-Shāfiʿī

In paragraph 56 of *al-Risālah*, Imam al-Shāfiʿī wrote, "The Apostle established no sunnah but that it was based on a ruling contained in a text from the Qur'an (*naṣṣun ḥukmun*)." In paragraph 97 he spoke of "religious obligations clearly set forth (*al-farā'iḍ al-manṣūṣah*) in the Book of God...," and in paragraph 100 he spoke of rulings "which [God] has manifested through the sunnah of His Prophet without the presence of an explicit text from the Qur'an (*bilā naṣṣ al-kitāb*)." In this final passage, Imam al-Shāfiʿī was speaking of a practice that had been clarified by the sunnah, but which was had not been explicated by the Qur'an in any explicit text. In paragraph 298 he stated:

> The *sunan* of the Messenger of God are of two types. The first consists of an action in which he was applying an explicit teaching of the Qur'an (*naṣṣ kitāb*), while the second consists of an action in the course of which he showed the specific practical meaning of a teaching stated in general terms (*bi al-jumlah*) in the Qur'an. In both of them, however, he was applying the Book of God.

The phrase *bi al-jumlah* (translated above as "stated in general terms") does not mean vague or obscure, but simply undetailed. Hence, it is not being contrasted with clarity, but with detail, although clarity is intrinsic to detail. What we are talking about, then, is a general, universal Qur'anic principle the meaning of which becomes clear through the particulars, details, and practical applications provided in the Sunnah. So, although the principle in question has not been stated explicitly, it has nevertheless been revealed by God. And God knows best.[5]

The reason I have presented the concept of *naṣṣ* as employed by al-Shāfiʿī prior to discussing the word *naṣṣ* as a technical term is that Imam al-Shāfiʿī was a linguistic authority whose usage of a word carried significant weight with regard to how it was to be defined. He is also the founder of the discipline that came to be known as *ʿilm uṣūl al-fiqh*, or the fundamentals of jurisprudence. Al-Shāfiʿī is recognized by the majority of Muslim scholars both ancient and modern as the person who raised the status of what are known as *āḥād* – 'solitary' hadiths, a term that applies to any hadith which is not *mutawātir* (a report narrated by a group of individuals sufficiently large and disparate that it would be impossible for them to have colluded in falsification) – by making a defense for their usefulness and reliability. In addition, it was al-Shāfiʿī who raised the Sunnah overall to a status parallel to that of the Qur'an. However, as will be seen clearly from the quotes above, al-Shāfiʿī viewed the Qur'an alone as the foundational text for Islamic teaching and practice. He stated in no uncertain terms that any hadith classified as authentic and reliable must have a clear origin in the Qur'an.

c) The meaning of the word naṣṣ in customary usage, and as a technical juristic term

Scholars use the word *naṣṣ* in its most unqualified sense to mean simply "all intelligible speech." Intelligibility is a necessary component of the meaning of *naṣṣ*. It is in the nature of a *naṣṣ* for its meaning to be fully comprehensible and unambiguous. In other words, it is subject to one interpretation only; hence, its apparent meaning being its actual meaning.

If someone were to say, "this ruling is corroborated by the text" (*hādhā al-ḥukm thābita bi al-naṣṣ*), what this means is that the evidence for the ruling in question has been established based on the Qur'an or the Sunnah due to the fact that it can be traced back to the Prophet. Among the majority of *uṣūl* scholars (referred to as Shafiites or scholastic theologians), the term *naṣṣ* refers to any word or phrase that conveys a ruling in an explicit, unequivocal manner. An example of a *naṣṣ* in this sense is found in *Sūrah al-Fatḥ*, which states, "Muhammad is God's Apostle" (48:29) in a manner that leaves no room for doubt that divine apostleship was given to Muhammad, and which allows for no other interpretation. As for *uṣūl* scholars who were legists associated with the Hanafite school, they defined *naṣṣ* as "an expression that is rendered clearer by virtue of its linguistic context, and which, without this context, would not convey an obvious meaning." The example they provide of such a *naṣṣ* is in *Sūrah al-Baqarah*, which reads:

> Those who gorge themselves on usury behave but as he might behave whom Satan has confounded with his touch; for they say, "Buying and selling is but a kind of usury" – the while God has made buying and selling lawful and usury unlawful. Hence, whoever becomes aware of his Sustainer's admonition, and thereupon desists [from usury], may keep his past gains, and it will be for God to judge him; but as for those who return to it – they are destined for the fire, therein to abide (2:275)!

The text here has to do with the distinction between selling and usury, the former being permitted and the latter being forbidden. This distinction is understood based on the verse's verbal context, in which God states, "God has made buying and selling lawful and usury unlawful."

This context indicates that the intention of the text is to establish the distinction between selling and usury. Scholars maintain that this verse makes it plain that selling is permitted, while usury is prohibited. Nevertheless, the context mentioned above renders the verse still clearer in its import.

Each particular school of thought has sought to defend its view on this point. However, if we note what it means from a purely linguistic point of view, as well as the way al-Shāfiʿī uses it, the word *naṣṣ* clearly refers to the Qur'an alone, which enjoys primacy over all else and which is the ultimate goal and end. No other entity should be referred to or described as the *naṣṣ*. Scholars of the fundamentals of jurisprudence could have used some other word rather than diluting this term in the way that they have. Instead, however, other meanings have been associated with it, which has obscured the nature of the relationship between the Qur'an and the Sunnah. By translating the term *naṣṣ* simply as "text," thereby indicating that it can be used to refer to virtually any statement or discourse, hadith scholars have sown confusion.

In sum, the term *naṣṣ* applies properly only to the Qur'an and to nothing else. As for the *sunan*, plural of *sunnah*, their purpose is to clarify the Qur'anic *naṣṣ* that requires explication. The Sunnah is subordinate to and inseparable from the Qur'an, revolving in its orbit. However, the use of the term Sunnah in a manner that departs from the meaning with which it was invested by the Prophet and his Companions, and which differs from one sect or juristic school of thought to another, has turned the Sunnah from a legacy that provides us with unifying guidance, to a source of misunderstanding and sectarian divisions.

3

The Qur'an as Creative Source and the Sunnah as Practical Clarification

THE PROPHET forbade his Companions to mix the Qur'an with his own words, and his rightly guided Caliphs wisely adhered to his instructions in this regard. Hence, the relationship between the Qur'an and the Sunnah was set down by God with the utmost precision, and was explained by the Messenger of God with the utmost clarity. The Qur'an is the creative source and revealer of divine ordinances, as well as the explanation of everything relating to them. It is the Qur'an that sets down the general principles and constants of the religion brought by all the prophets.

Muslims have always agreed on the Qur'an's centrality and supremacy. This agreement extends to those who hold that the Sunnah can stand alone as a source of legislation, since what such people propose as the basis for legislation is, upon closer examination, traceable to the universals set forth in the Qur'an itself. Hence, the dual process of establishing and clarifying God's laws takes place through the Qur'an in keeping with God's declarations: "Judgment rests with none but God" (*Sūrah al-Anʿām*, 6:57), and: "We have bestowed from on high upon you, step by step, this divine writ, to make everything clear" (*Sūrah al-Naḥl*, 16:89).

The Messenger of God recited the Qur'an, followed its teaching, taught it to others, and showed them how to translate its words into a concrete way of life, that is, into an ethical system that would govern their actions, their conceptualizations, their morals, their dealings, and their relationships. Hence, what is referred to as the Sunnah of the Messenger of God is, in reality, a clarification and application of what the Book of God had communicated. Therefore God said:

> But nay, by your Sustainer! They do not [really] believe unless they make you [O Prophet] a judge of all on which they disagree among themselves, and then find in their hearts no bar to an acceptance of your decision and give themselves up [to it] in utter self-surrender. (*Sūrah al-Nisā'*, 4:65)

This was because the basis of his decisions would be the rulings of the Qur'an. This fact is stressed as follows in *Sūrah al-Mā'idah*:

> And unto you [O Prophet] have We vouchsafed this divine writ, setting forth the truth, confirming the truth of whatever there still remains of earlier revelations and determining what is true therein. Judge, then, between the followers of earlier revelation in accordance with what God has bestowed from on high, and do not follow their errant views, forsaking the truth that has come unto you. Unto every one of you have We appointed a [different] law and way of life. And if God had so willed, He could surely have made you all one single community: but [He willed it otherwise] in order to test you by means of what He has vouchsafed unto you. Vie, then, with one another in doing good works! Unto God you all must return; and then He will make you truly understand all that on which you were wont to differ. (5:48)

[FIRST]
The Concept of *Waḥy*

In order for us properly to define the concept of *sunnah* and understand the relationship between the Sunnah and the Qur'an, it is essential that we arrive at a precise definition of "revelation" (*waḥy*) as well. Only then will we succeed in avoiding the excessive leniency that has allowed people to classify as "revelation" other than the Qur'an everything passed down on the authority of the Prophet including simply statements attributed to him in narrated reports traced back to his Companions and their Successors. It should be borne in mind that according to *uṣūl* scholars, the Qur'an is defined as "the speech of God, which is to be followed and recited in a reverent, worshipful spirit, whose opponents were unable to meet the challenge to produce the likes of even its shortest surah, and which was thus shown to be beyond the capacity of any mere human being to imitate." As such, the Prophet's only role in relation to the Qur'an was to follow the angel Gabriel in its recitation, and to relate it to others as he had received it.

For the present discussion, *waḥy* will be defined as the divine speech which God sent down from on high into the heart of His Servant, Messenger and Prophet, which opens with *Sūrah al-Fātiḥah* and concludes with *Sūrah al-Nās* (thus consisting of one hundred fourteen chapters, or surahs). As for all other statements, actions, or affirmations of others' words or actions attributed to the Prophet, it is unanimously recognized that they emerged based on a variety of considerations. Among the things the Prophet did, some were simply actions that would be engaged in by any human being by virtue of being human; some involved application of the ordinances and principles laid down in the Qur'an; and some he engaged in within the context of his functions as a religious and political leader, judge, mufti, teacher, guide and legislator. Some of these actions will undoubtedly fall into the category of "relativities" that applied exclusively to his personal circumstances and which were appropriate to his and his Companions' specific environment, time and place. Still others, by contrast, must be viewed as the basis for enduring legislation that derives its timeless nature from the Qur'an. Until or unless these distinctions are recognized, there will be ongoing debate over the relevance of the Prophet's life to modern times, and an ongoing failure to determine even where the points of contention lie.

By identifying what "revelation" (*waḥy*) is vis-à-vis the Qur'an, the Sunnah and the affirmation of God's oneness and its implications (*ʿilm al-tawḥīd*), we will be able to clarify a fundamental aspect of the question at hand – how to relate properly to the Sunnah of the Prophet. Then, in the light of this clarification, it will become possible to correct a number of other concepts as well.

1. *What is the Meaning of Waḥy?*

Al-Iṣfahānī wrote, "The root meaning of *waḥy* is a rapid signal." Since its definition includes the element of speed, the word *waḥy* has been used to describe communication that involves symbol and allusion, nonverbal sounds, bodily gestures, or writing. This sense of the word is found in *Sūrah Maryam*, which tells us that Zakariah came "out of the sanctuary unto his people and signified to them [by gestures] (*awḥā ilayhim*): 'Extol His limitless glory by day and by night!'" (19:11).

Hence, one meaning of the verb *awḥā* is to motion or point. This verb appears in *Sūrah al-Anʿām*, where God states:

> And thus it is that against every prophet We have set up as enemies the evil forces from among humans as well as from among invisible beings that whisper unto one another (*yūḥī baʿḍuhum ilā baʿḍ*) glittering half-truths meant to delude the mind... (6:112)

In *Sūrah al-Anʿām* we read, "And, verily, the evil impulses [within men's hearts] whisper (*yūḥūna*) unto those who have made them their own that they should involve you in argument..." (6:121). The verb *awḥā* as used in such contexts has been viewed as synonymous with the verb *waswasa* used in *Sūrah al-Nās*, which is a prayer for God's protection "from the evil of the whispering, elusive tempter (*al-waswās al-khannās*) who whispers in the hearts of men (*yuwaswisu fī ṣudūr al-nās*)" (114:4-5).

The noun *waḥy* is also, however, used to refer to the message God conveys to His prophets and messengers through a variety of media. The word of revelation might be delivered through a visible messenger who communicates via audible speech; in another situation, the prophet might hear speech without seeing where it is coming from; in still another, the word from God might come in the form of the instinct that tells bees, for example, to build their nests here or there (as in *Sūrah al-Naḥl*, 16:68), through a dream, or through some other form of inspiration.[1]

***Ilhām* (inspiration) from a linguistic perspective.** The word *ilhām* has been defined as that which comes suddenly to a person's mind. It refers in particular to something that is poured out in abundance, and which comes from God and the heavenly realms. The word *ilhām* has also been defined as the act of casting into the heart something that brings a sense of tranquility, and which God grants to some of His pure-hearted ones. The verb *alhama* is used in *Sūrah al-Shams*, 91:8, which tells us that God has imbued the soul (*alhamahā*) with knowledge of both its moral failings and its God-consciousness. Ibn Sīnā defined the word *ilhām* as "that which the active intelligence casts into the human soul supported by an intense purity, clarity and serenity, and by intense contact with intellectual principles." In his *Jamʿ al-Jawāmiʿ*, al-Subkī defines *ilhām* as "that which is cast into the heart bringing solace and peace, and which God bestows specially upon some of His pure-hearted ones." It could not, however, serve as authoritative evidence given the impossibility of having complete confidence in someone who is not protected from sin in his inner thoughts. The Sufis define it as "transfusion, or breathing into the heart, soul or mind (*al-nafthu fī al-rūʿ*), and a casting into the heart of a knowledge not based upon evidential reasoning and inquiry." In this connection the Prophet is reported to have said, "The Holy Spirit breathed into my heart" (*inna rūḥ al-qudus nafatha fī rūʿī*)." As for Muhammad Abduh (d. 1905 CE), he defined it as "a sentiment of which the soul feels certain and whose promptings it follows without knowing whence it has come. It might be likened to a state of hunger, thirst, sadness or delight." Drawing a distinction between inspiration (*ilhām*) and divine revelation (*waḥy*), Rashid Rida (d. 1935) wrote of

> what some refer to as psychological suggestion or revelation (*al-waḥy al-nafsī*), a phenomenon which philosophers have interpreted as a kind of inspiration (*ilhām*) that wells up from within an individual's higher self. Our disagreement with such philosophers centers around the fact that, in our belief, legitimate revelation (*al-waḥy al-sharʿī*) comes from outside the soul of the prophet, having descended upon him from the heavens rather than having welled up from within him as they suppose. [Our difference with them also] revolves around our belief in the existence of a spiritual messenger who has descended on the Prophet from God. As God declares in *Sūrah al-Shuʿarā'*: "Now behold, this [divine writ) has indeed been bestowed from on high by the Sustainer of all the worlds; trustworthy divine inspiration has alighted with it from on high upon your heart, [O Muhammad] so that you may be among those who preach in the clear Arabic tongue" (26:92-95). As for inspiration, instinctual behavior (cf. *Sūrah al-Naḥl*, 16:68), visions in dreams, and Gabriel's delivery of messages to the Prophet by appearing in a particular form, these are spoken of in *Sūrah al-Shūrā*, where we read that "it is not given to mortal man that God should speak unto him otherwise than through sudden inspiration (*waḥyan*), or [by a voice, as it were,] from behind a veil, or by sending an apostle to reveal (*aw an yursila rasūlan fa yūḥī*), by His leave, whatever He wills [to reveal]: for, verily, He is Exalted, Wise." (42:51)

God speaks to the Prophet, saying, "before your time We never sent any apostle without having revealed to him (*illā an nūḥiya ilayhi*) that there is no deity save Me, [and that,] therefore, you shall worship Me [alone]!" (*Sūrah al-Anbiyā'*, 21:25). In so speaking, God is referring to a general kind of revelation, since the recognition of God's oneness and the necessity of worshipping Him is not found only in the revelation granted to God's messengers "endowed with firmness of heart" (*Sūrah al-Aḥqāf*, 46:35). Rather, this is something that can be known through reason and human inspiration just as it can be known through special revelation. What the aforementioned passage is drawing our attention to is that it would be unthinkable for a messenger of God not to realize God's oneness and human beings' duty to worship Him. In a reference to the revelation that came to Jesus Christ, we read in *Sūrah al-Mā'idah*, "And [remember the time] when I inspired the white garbed ones[2]: 'Believe in Me and in My Apostle!' They answered: 'We believe; and bear You witness that we have surrendered ourselves [unto You]'" (5:111). See also *Sūrah Yūnus*, 10:87 and *Sūrah Ṭāhā*, 20:48.

In reference to the revelation the Prophet had been given, God instructed him, saying, "Follow you what has been revealed unto you by your Sustainer – save Whom there is no deity – and turn your back upon all who ascribe divinity to aught beside Him" (*Sūrah al-Anᶜām*, 6:106). Similarly, He said, "We have inspired you, [O Muhammad, with this message:] 'Follow the creed of Abraham, who turned away from all that is false, and was not of those who ascribe divinity to aught beside God'" (*Sūrah al-Naḥl*, 16:123).

In *Sūrah al-Anfāl* the word *waḥy* is used in association with the angels: "Lo! Your Sustainer inspired the angels (*awḥā ilā al-malā'ikah*) [to convey this His message to the believers]: 'I am with you !' (8:12)" Elsewhere the Qur'an speaks of God "revealing" to the heavens what their functions are to be, saying, "And He [it is who] decreed that they become seven heavens in two aeons, and imparted unto each heaven its function" (*wa awḥā fī kulli samā'in amrahā*) (41:12). If the revelation being referred to here is addressed to the inhabitants of the heavens, who are not mentioned explicitly, then we conclude that God revealed this to the angels. If, on the other hand, we view the entity to which the revelation was given as being the heavens themselves, then, for those who consider the heavens to be nonliving it falls under the category of revelation embodied in the laws of the cosmos, and for those who do view the heavens as a living entity, it falls under the category of a spoken command. In *Sūrah al-Zalzalah* we read about the Earth being the recipient of God's revelation or inspiration: "When the earth quakes with her [last] mighty quaking, and [when] the earth yields up her burdens, and man cries out, 'What has happened to her?' – on that Day will she recount all her tidings, as your Sustainer will have inspired her to do (*awḥā lahā*)!" (99:1-5). Speaking to the Prophet about his reception of the Qur'an, God says, "[Know,] then, [that] God is sublimely exalted, the Ultimate Sovereign, the Ultimate Truth and [knowing this,] do not approach the Qur'an in haste, ere it has been revealed unto you in full (*min qabli an yuqḍā ilayka waḥyuhu*), but [always) say: 'O my Sustainer, cause me to grow in knowledge!'" (20:114).

During the lifetime of the Prophet, his uncle Abū Jahl began a movement to deny his prophethood. At a later time, al-Walīd ibn al-Mughīrah headed a movement that aimed to place revelation on a par with non-revelation. Then, following the age of recording and translation there arose groups of freethinkers and atheists along with a variety of philosophical currents. There were those who, for example, discussed the nature of created entities, including human beings, animals, plants and inanimate objects, claiming that such entities had no true existence. Those who held such a view saw no difference between the miracles performed by prophets and the illusions produced by sorcerers and cult priests.

Early members of the Muslim community believed in divine revelation and prophethood as part of their faith in the realm of the unseen. Once they had witnessed the challenge to produce the likes of the Qur'an and it had become apparent how thoroughly inimitable the Qur'an was, they felt no need to explain revelation or to represent it in a way that would be acceptable to the philosophical mind or, alternatively, to those with empirical mindsets of the sort that prevail in our day and age.

2. *Qur'anic and Non-Qur'anic Revelation*

As we saw earlier in *Sūrah al-Shūrā*, 42:51, God speaks to human beings either "through sudden inspiration (*waḥyan*), or [by a voice, as it were,] from behind a veil, or by sending an apostle to reveal (*aw an yursila rasūlan fa yūḥī*), by His leave, whatever He wills [to reveal]." The "apostle" spoken of here is "the faithful spirit," while the "faithful spirit" who revealed the Qur'an to the Messenger of God has been shown to be the angel Gabriel. The Prophet had been prepared psychologically and intellectually to receive the revelation in some ways that are known only to God. However, we find indications of what these ways were in some verses of the Qur'an, in the form of either a question in the Prophet's mind, a thought that occurred to him, or an aspiration on his part to receive a decisive word from the Qur'an concerning some situation that required a response or decision. As God said to the Prophet when he was seeking clarity on the matter of Muslims' direction for prayer, "We have seen you [O Prophet] often turn your face towards heaven [for guidance]" (*Sūrah al-Baqarah*, 2:144). We also know that at one point, one of the Prophet's wives divulged a confidence he had related to her. The Qur'an speaks of this saying, "And lo! [It so happened that] the Prophet told something in confidence to one of his wives; and when she thereupon divulged it, and God made this known to him, he acquainted [others] with some of it and passed over some of it" (*Sūrah al-Taḥrīm*, 66:3).

Since the Prophet's function was to convey to others the message he had received from God, he was not permitted to forbid or sanction anything unless he had received God's command to do so. The Qur'anic revelation that was given is what God willed to be included in His Book by way of details, situations and events from the era of revelation. Through the Qur'an we are informed of situations and events pertaining to the period of revelation and the completion of the Islamic religion. God revealed what people need to know about such matters in the recited text of the Qur'an, which He promised to compile, clarify and preserve from all distortion or conflicting accounts until the Day of Judgment (*Sūrah al-Ḥijr*, 15:9).

In this respect the Qur'an differs from all other historical records or accounts, not included in the divine promise, with which people have tampered in one way or another. *Sūrah al-Najm* reads:

> Consider this unfolding [of God's message], as it comes down from on high! This fellow-man of yours has not gone astray, nor is he deluded, and neither does he speak out of his own desire: that [which he conveys to you] is but [a divine] inspiration with which he is being inspired (*in huwa illā waḥyun yūḥā*) – something that a very mighty one has imparted to him. (53:1-5)

One might ask: When was the Messenger of God, who was well-known in his community, accused of being deluded? He was never faced with this accusation until he began conveying the words of the Qur'an and announced that he was God's messenger to all people. In the passage just quoted, God defends His messenger against this charge, asserting that the words he is uttering are none other than "[a divine] inspiration with which he is being inspired (*in huwa illā waḥyun yūḥā*)." Being familiar with his accustomed manner of expressing himself, the members of the Prophet's community accused him of straying into error when he began giving voice to the Qur'an. In his defense, God declared that he was neither "deluded," nor was he speaking "out of his own desire."

Some people have interpreted the phrase that reads, "neither does he speak out of his own desire: that [which he conveys to you] is but [a divine] inspiration" as applying to everything the Prophet ever said. However, this interpretation fails to take into account the context of the verse in question. It should be remembered that God is not speaking here to those who believe in the Qur'anic message, telling them that they are obliged to act on every word that came out of the Prophet's mouth. Rather, He is addressing those who are giving the lie to the Qur'an. Nor, on the other hand, does this mean that there is no evidence for the authoritative nature of the Sunnah. As we read in *Sūrah al-Nisā'*, "Whoever pays heed unto the Apostle pays heed unto God thereby" (4:80). The behaviors in which the Messenger of God engaged in his daily life other than those directly related to the Qur'anic revelation were subject to the same human laws to which all other people's behaviors are, although on the highest planes of perfection. The Qur'an makes reference to this in numerous verses addressed to the Apostle. *Sūrah Āl ʿImrān* (3:161), for example, reads, "And it is not conceivable that a prophet should deceive – since he who deceives shall be faced with his deceit on the Day of Resurrection, when every human being shall be repaid in full for whatever he has done, and none shall be wronged."

In some situations the Messenger of God would do something for which he was corrected by a verse of the Qur'an. In *Sūrah al-Aḥzāb*, for example, God says to the Prophet:

> And lo, [O Muhammad,] you did say unto the one to whom God had shown favor and to whom you had shown favor, "Hold on to your wife, and remain conscious of God!" And [thus] would you hide within yourself something that God was about to bring to light – for you did stand in awe of [what] people [might think], whereas it was God alone of Whom you should have stood in awe! (33:37)

In another situation God said to him, "No [other] women shall henceforth be lawful to you nor art you [allowed] to supplant [any of] them by other wives, even though their beauty should please you greatly -: [none shall be lawful to you] beyond those whom you [already] have come to possess. And God keeps watch over everything" (33:52). The Qur'an specifies the nature of the revelation that God has commanded His messenger to record and convey to others, and whether it includes only the Qur'anic revelation, or other types of revelation as well. God addressed the Prophet in *Sūrah al-Anʿām* with the words:

> Say: "What could most weightily bear witness to the truth?" Say: "God is witness between me and you; and this Qur'an has been revealed unto me so that on the strength thereof I might warn you and all whom it may reach." Could you in truth bear witness that there are other deities side by side with God? Say: "I bear no [such] witness!" Say: "He is the One God; and, behold, far be it from me to ascribe divinity, as you do, to aught beside Him!" (6:19)

This is a testimony from God and from His messenger to the fact that the Qur'anic revelation is the very message that the Prophet had been commanded to convey to people. The Qur'an is the true source of knowledge. Hence, we read in *Sūrah Fāṭir*:

> And [know that] all of the divine writ with which We have inspired you is the very truth, confirming the truth of whatever there still remains of earlier revelations for, behold, of [the needs of] His servants God is Fully Aware, All-Seeing. And so, We have bestowed this divine writ as a heritage unto such of Our servants as We chose: and among them are some who sin against themselves; and some who keep half-way [between right and wrong]; and some who, by God's leave, are foremost in deeds of goodness: [and] this, indeed, is a merit most high! (35:31-32)

In defining the divine message and the Prophet's role in it, God said to him:

> [You are but entrusted with Our message:] and so We have revealed unto you a discourse in the Arabic tongue in order that you may warn the foremost of all cities and all who dwell around it – to wit, warn [them] of the Day of the Gathering, [the coming of] which is beyond all doubt: [the Day when] some shall find themselves in paradise, and some in the blazing flame. (*Sūrah al-Shūrā*, 42:7)

Elsewhere He said to him:

> Thus have We raised you [O Muhammad] as Our Apostle amidst a community [of unbelievers] before whose time [similar] communities have come and gone, so that you might propound to them what We have revealed unto you: for [in their ignorance] they deny the Most Gracious!" (*Sūrah al-Raʿd*, 13:30)

And elsewhere:

> Is it, then, conceivable [O Prophet] that you couldst omit any part of what is being revealed unto you [because the deniers of the truth dislike it,- and] because your heart is distressed at their saying, "Why has not a treasure been bestowed upon him from on high?" – or, "[Why has not] an angel come [visibly] with him?" [They fail to understand that] you are only a warner, whereas God has everything in His care. (*Sūrah Hūd*, 11:12)

Hence, the revelation given to the Messenger of God was defined in terms of both quality and quantity such that he could distinguish the parts from the whole. For unlike the revelations the Arab community had inherited prior to it, the Qur'an was recorded and reviewed during the lifetime of the Prophet and under his supervision. We read in *Sūrah al-Isrā'*:

> And they will ask you about [the nature of] divine inspiration (*al-rūḥ*). Say: "This inspiration [comes] at my Sustainer's behest; and [you cannot understand its nature, O men, since] you have been granted very little of [real] knowledge." And if We so willed, We could indeed take away whatever We have revealed unto you (*mā awḥaynā ilayk*), and in that [state of need] you would find none to plead in your behalf before Us. [You are spared] only by your Sustainer's grace: behold, His favor towards you is great indeed! Say: "If all mankind and all invisible beings would come together with a view to producing the like of this Qur'an, they could not produce its like even though they were to exert all their strength in aiding one another!" (17:85-88)

This passage from the Qur'an specifies the source from which Muslims draw their religious knowledge and legal rulings, and which God has not willed to "take away." Rather, it is enduring, having been preserved by God's providence. The Qur'an itself is the divine sign which demonstrates the Prophet's truthfulness. God challenged the Arabs of the Prophet's day to produce something comparable to the Qur'an, but they were unable to do so. Doesn't this challenge by the Qur'an alone show that the text that was revealed to the Apostle and which he was commanded to deliver to others is none other than the Qur'an itself, God's final message?

God has made clear in numerous verses of the Qur'an that there is no way for us to determine the accuracy of historical reports and narratives dealing with the miraculous unless we have access to a source of knowledge that can be demonstrated indisputably to be of divine origin. After an account of miraculous events in the lives of Mary the mother of Jesus and of Zachariah, Mary's guardian and father of John the Baptist (*Āl ʿImrān*, 3:37-43), God told the Prophet that:

> This account of something that was beyond the reach of your perception We [now] reveal unto you: for you were not with them when they drew lots as to which of them should be Mary's guardian, and you were not with them when they contended [about it] with one another. (3:44)

God warns us not to fabricate lies against Him or to claim to have legal sources to which He has lent no authority. In *Sūrah al-Anʿām* God asks rhetorically, "And who could be more wicked than he who invents a lie about God, or says, 'This has been revealed unto me,' the while nothing has been revealed to him? – or he who says, 'I, too, can bestow from on high the like of what God has bestowed'?" (6:93). Similarly, He warns against following anything but that which has been revealed from on high, saying:

> Means of insight have now come unto you from your Sustainer [through this divine writ]. Whoever, therefore, chooses to see, does so for his own good; and whoever chooses to remain blind, does so to his own hurt. And [say unto the blind of heart]: "I am not your keeper." And thus do We give many facets to Our messages. And to the end that they might say, "You have taken [all this] well to heart," and that We might make it clear unto people of [innate] knowledge, follow you what has been revealed unto you (*mā ūḥiya ilayk*) by your Sustainer – save whom there is no deity – and turn your back upon all who ascribe divinity to aught beside Him. (*Sūrah al-Anʿām*, 6:104-106)

This Qur'anic revelation is the Law which God commanded His messengers, and all Muslims, to adhere to. Any interpretation of this Law must have a Qur'anic basis and be consistent with Qur'anic evidence. Additionally, no such interpretation will be acceptable or valid unless the person offering it is marked by godliness (*al-rabbāniyyah*), a quality that all God's messengers and prophets have exhorted their hearers to cultivate. It was this virtue that God was speaking of in *Sūrah Āl ʿImrān* when He declared:

> It is not conceivable that a human being unto whom God had granted revelation, and sound judgment, and prophethood, should thereafter have said unto people, "Worship me beside God"; but rather [did he exhort them], "Become men of God (*kūnū rabbāniyyīn*) by spreading the knowledge of the divine writ, and by your own deep study [thereof]." (3:79)

Herein lies an affirmation of the fact that the Qur'an contains everything God willed to convey to the created world until the Day of Judgment. God has affirmed this by making clear that the task assigned to His Apostle was to warn others based on the Qur'anic revelation he had received from on high. As God says in *Sūrah al-Anʿām*:

> Say [O Prophet]: "I do not say unto you, 'God's treasures are with me,' nor [do I say], 'I know the things that are beyond the reach of human perception'; nor do I say unto you, 'Behold, I am an angel': I but follow what is revealed to me." (6:50)

The Qur'an is the sign the Apostle was granted as evidence of his truthfulness:

> And [thus it is:] whenever Our messages are conveyed unto them in all their clarity, those who do not believe that they are destined to meet Us [are wont to] say, "Bring us a discourse other than this, or alter this one." Say [O Prophet]: "It is not conceivable that I should alter it of my own volition; I only follow what is revealed to me. Behold, I would dread, were I [thus] to rebel against my Sustainer, the suffering [which would befall me] on that awesome Day [of Judgment] (*Sūrah Yūnus*, 10:15)!"

Here we have clear evidence that the Messenger of God himself was commanded to convey nothing to people but a single legal source, that is, the Qur'anic revelation containing God's final, eternal message.

God has warned Muslims, and mankind, not to adopt legal texts other than those of the Qur'anic Law, which were recorded during the era of revelation under the supervision of the one to whom the revelation had been given. He has said:

> Hence, do notutter falsehoods by letting your tongues determine [at your own discretion], "This is lawful and that is forbidden," thus attributing your own lying inventions to God: for, behold, they who attribute their own lying inventions to God will never attain to a happy state! (*Sūrah al-Naḥl*, 16:116)

> So hold fast to all that has been revealed to you: for, behold, you art on a straight way; and verily, this [revelation] shall indeed become [a source of] eminence for you and your people: but in time you all will be called to account [for what you have done with it]. (*Sūrah al-Zukhruf*, 43:43-44)

From the foregoing we may conclude that the explication and

application of Qur'anic teachings that we find in the life of the Prophet, and which came later to be referred to as the Sunnah, are subject to the judgment of the Qur'an, as is the heritage left by all prophets and messengers of God. This is why we find the Qur'an correcting some of the Prophet's actions and applications of Qur'anic teachings, as in *Sūrah al-Anfāl*, where God declares:

> It is not fitting for an apostle that he should have prisoners of war until he hath thoroughly subdued the land. Ye look for the temporal goods of this world; but Allah looketh to the Hereafter: And Allah is Exalted in might, Wise. (8:67)

Elsewhere, when the Prophet had allowed certain fighters to stay back from a military expedition, God chided him, saying, "May God pardon you [O Prophet]! Why did you grant them permission [to stay at home] before it had become obvious to you as to who was speaking the truth, and [before] you came to know [who were] the liars?" (*Sūrah al-Tawbah*, 9:43). These are only some of the passages which demonstrate that it is the Qur'an that stands in judgment over the Prophet's actions. This was one of the ways in which God preserved, protected and corrected His Messenger, which in turn gives us all the more reason to have confidence in the Prophet's explications of the Qur'an. For this reason al-Shāfiʿī wrote saying, "No situation will ever arise for an adherent of God's religion but that he will find, in the Qur'an, a source of guidance relating thereto." In support of this statement he cites the first verse of *Sūrah Ibrāhīm*, which reads:

> Alīf. Lām. Rā. [This is] a divine writ which We have bestowed upon you from on high in order that you might bring forth all mankind, by their Sustainer's leave, out of the depths of darkness into the light: onto the way that leads to the Almighty, the One to Whom all praise is due. (14:1)

(See also *Sūrah al-Naḥl*, 16:44 and 89, and *Sūrah al-Shūrā*, 42:52). It follows that the actions and sayings which Muslims are called upon to emulate and which are viewed as divine revelation themselves have their roots in the Qur'an. If something lacks a Qur'anic foundation, it may still be drawn on as a source of wisdom and practical benefit. However, it will not have the character of divinely revealed legislation.

[SECOND]
The Sunnah and the Theory of Elucidation

The theory on which we base our concept of the Sunnah – one that delineates the nature of the relationship between the Qur'an and the Sunnah – we are terming "the theory of elucidation" (*naẓariyyah al-bayān*), where the word "elucidation" (*bayān*) is understood in the Qur'anic sense of clarification and explication. The Sunnah may be thought of as an applied, interpretative elucidation of the Qur'an. As such, it remains within the Qur'an's orbit and under its authority. The Sunnah is never autonomous of the Qur'an; on the contrary, it is inseparable from it.

The example set by the Prophet for the Muslim community is the summation of the life stories of all the prophets who preceded him and the guidance they brought. As God said to him, "Say: 'I am not the first of [God's] apostles; and [like all of them] I do not know what will be done with me or with you: for I am nothing but a plain warner'" (*Sūrah al-Aḥqāf*, 46:9). The actions of God's prophets and messengers embody the practical aspect of the revelations they have received so that their followers can emulate and obey them. As God declares in *Sūrah al-Mā'idah*:

> O People of the Book! Now, after a long time during which no apostles have appeared, there has come unto you [this] Our Apostle to make [the truth] clear to you, lest you say, "No bearer of glad tidings has come unto us, nor any warner": for now there has come unto you a bearer of glad tidings and a warner – since God has the power to will anything. (5:19)

The explanatory role the Prophet was intended to play is described in *Sūrah al-Mā'idah*, where God says:

> And unto you [O Prophet] have We vouchsafed this divine writ, setting forth the truth, confirming the truth of whatever there still remains of earlier revelations and determining what is true therein. Judge, then, between the followers of earlier revelation in accordance with what God has bestowed from on high, and do not follow their errant views, forsaking the truth that has come unto you. (5:48)

However, the Prophet's performance of these functions will only yield the knowledge, wisdom and purity of heart they are intended to if his followers abide by what he taught. As God reminded him:

> But nay, by your Sustainer! They do not [really] believe unless they make you [O Prophet] a judge of all on which they disagree among themselves, and then find in their hearts no bar to an acceptance of your decision and give themselves up [to it] in utter self-surrender. (*Sūrah al-Nisā'*, 4:65)

Unlike interpretation (ijtihad), analogical reasoning (*qiyās*) and their subsidiary disciplines, the Prophet's Sunnah is at once both explanatory and binding in nature. As God says in *Sūrah Ibrāhīm*:

> [This is] a divine writ which We have bestowed upon you from on high in order that you might bring forth all mankind, by their Sustainer's leave, out of the depths of darkness into the light: onto the way that leads to the Almighty, the One to whom all praise is due. (14:1)

And as He says to the Prophet in *Sūrah al-Naḥl*: "And upon you [too] have We bestowed from on high this reminder, so that you might make clear unto mankind all that has ever been thus bestowed upon them…" (16:44).

1. *The Concept of Bayān (Elucidation) as Understood by Imam Al-Shāfiʿī*

According to al-Shāfiʿī, the process of *bayān* involves clarification of the Qur'an through its application and interpretation in concrete circumstances. At the height of his conflict with the *Ahl al-Ra'y* (People of Opinion) and his defense of the *Ahl al-Ḥadīth* (People of Hadith), al-Shāfiʿī interpreted the concept of *bayān* as implying that there is a degree of vagueness or obscurity (*ibhām*) in the Qur'an, which contains passages that are general (*mujmal*) or ambiguous (*mutashābih*) as well as allusion (*kināyah*), figures of speech (*istiʿārah*), metaphor (*majāz*), and ellipsis (*ḥadhf*). It is due to the presence of such phenomena in the Qur'an that it requires elucidation, or *bayān*. Al-Shāfiʿī devoted an entire section of *al-Risālah* to a discussion of the process of elucidation, which he divided into five levels. The first and second levels involve the Qur'an's elucidation of itself, while the third level includes the ways in which the Messenger of God added specificity to passages of the Qur'an that were general in nature. So, for example, he detailed the command in *Sūrah al-Nisā'* to "be constant in prayer" (4:77) by specifying the number of prayers one is required to pray daily and the times at which they are to be performed.

The fourth level of *bayān* includes the elucidations provided by the Prophet's actions, that is, his Sunnah. The Sunnah makes clear those things which God left it to the Prophet to clarify. Al-Shāfiʿī stresses throughout his discussion that what the Messenger of God elucidated always had its source in the Qur'an. It was in affirmation of this point that he wrote, as mentioned above, "No situation will ever arise for an adherent of God's religion but that he will find, in the Qur'an, a source of guidance relating thereto, be it explicit or implicit." Anything that is not dealt with specifically and explicitly in the Book of God will be addressed through the general, universal principles it sets forth. Al-Shāfiʿī concludes his treatment of *bayān* with a lengthy discussion of its fifth level, which consists of clarifications that take place through linguistic cues, concrete phenomena or indications, and the like. It is here that al-Shāfiʿī helps us to see the relationship between *bayān* and language in particular.

Binding elucidation (al-bayān al-mulzim)

The Qur'an's self-elucidation is undoubtedly the highest level of *bayān*. Therefore, it is essential that Muslims familiarize themselves with it and give it precedence over all other types of elucidation. Of the remaining levels of elucidation, the Prophet's actions, words and affirmations are the only type that is binding on Muslims. The process of emulating the Prophet is related, of course, to belief in his sinlessness, that is, his having been protected by God from the commission of any sin, great or small, throughout his life. After all, if the Apostle was not sinless, then the divine injunction to obey and emulate him would entail a command to commit error and wrongdoing, which is unthinkable. Hence, all verses of the Qur'an that urge us to obey the Messenger of God may be seen within the framework of this structural unity, which commits us to observing both the Qur'an's elucidation of itself and its elucidation by the Prophet. All other forms of elucidation are said by *uṣūl* scholars to be the subject of disagreement. Hence, assuming they can be classed as valid forms of elucidation, they are non-binding in nature.

2. *Bayān as Understood by Uṣūl Scholars*

Imam al-Rāzī divided what he termed "generalities in need of elucidation" (*al-mujmal al-mubayyan*) into a number of categories. He then treated the second of these categories under a number of different headings, one of which was "types of texts which require elucidation" (*al-mubayyan wa aqsāmuhu*) as well as the types of elucidation (*aqsām al-bayānāt*). He also devoted a discussion to the question of how to rank that which requires elucidation (*al-mubayyan*) vis-à-vis that which elucidates it (*al-mubayyin*). A study and analysis of al-Rāzī's discussions shows that he made numerous additions to the theory of elucidation as set forth by Imam al-Shāfiʿī. Nevertheless, one senses a gap between that which requires elucidation – the Qur'an – and that which elucidates it – the Sunnah – because of the extent to which the theme of moral accountability dominates the juristic mindset. The majority of *uṣūl* scholars held that even an action unaccompanied by speech could be considered a means of elucidating the Qur'an, the question then being whether or not such an action constituted a basis for a legal ruling applicable to morally accountable individuals. For details on the four points of view taken on this question, see al-Rāzī's *al-Maḥṣūl fī ʿIlm al-Uṣūl*.

The complexity of the ensuing debate reveals the confusion that came to surround the concept of *sunnah*. Nevertheless, scholars' conversations were interspersed increasingly with the notion that the Sunnah revolves around the Qur'an, since that which elucidates (in this case, the Sunnah) should not go beyond or take precedence over that which is being elucidated (the Qur'an).

3. *The Word Bayān as a Technical Term*

The purpose in elucidating the Qur'an is to minimize disagreements over how it is to be understood and thereby help people to apply it more effectively (cf. *Sūrah al-Naḥl*, 16:44). As we have seen, this elucidation takes place through actions, words and the act of approving this or that idea or action (cf. *Sūrah al-Mā'idah*, 5:15). However, there are rules to which the process of elucidation must adhere. For example, it must not change the essential meaning of what is being elucidated or introduce anything extraneous into it.

The role played by the Qur'an in relation to the legacies left by earlier prophets is to affirm whatever truth they still contain, and to purge them of whatever distortion or manipulation they had been subjected to. Hence, the Seal of the Prophets was assigned a dual task: (1) to bring the "unlettered" Arabs of the Arabian Peninsula ("unlettered" in the sense of having no scripture of their own) into the fold of "the people of the Book," that is, those communities who possess a holy writ, by giving them the Qur'an, and (2) to show the Jews and Christians how the Qur'an conveys the truths found in earlier revelation through a corrective rereading of the legacy brought by earlier messengers and prophets.

Through the noble life he lived, the Messenger of God modeled the best possible way to preserve the prophetic heritage on the practical level and to apply the Qur'an's teaching to day-to-day reality. Hence, God has tirelessly preserved His final revelation for His own glory. As He said to the Prophet in *Sūrah al-Qiyāmah*: "Move not your tongue in haste, [repeating the words of the revelation:] for, behold, it is for Us to gather it [in your heart,] and to cause it to be read [as it ought to be read]. Thus, when We recite it, follow you its wording [with all your mind]" (75:16-18), and in *Sūrah al-Ḥijr*: "Behold, it is We Ourselves who have bestowed from on high, step by step, this reminder, and behold, it is We who shall truly guard it [from all corruption]" (15:9). Just as God involved no other being in revealing the Qur'an, He involved no other being in its preservation. In this way there came to be a single, authoritative point of reference for human beings in the Qur'an.

As the final revelation, the Qur'an enjoys primacy over not only the legacy left by earlier prophets; it also enjoys primacy over the words and actions of the Prophet Muhammad. As we have stated before, the Qur'an eliminated the distortion and falsification to which the heritage brought by previous prophets had been subjected by correcting uninformed interpretations and presenting the message anew in a true, purified form. However, in order for this process to reach completion, we must take one further step.

[THIRD]
Examining the Sunnah in Light of the Qur'an

By examining the Sunnah in light of the Qur'an, my intention is to follow in the footsteps of the majority of Muslim scholars from al-Shāfiʿī to Imam al-Shāṭibī (d. 790 AH1388 CE), as well as those who came after them, who held that every reliable, well-authenticated Sunnah must have its origin in the Qur'an. Al-Shāfiʿī wrote in *al-Risālah*:

> Since God required the Prophet to follow what He had revealed to him, ...the Sunnah could not possibly be in conflict with the Book of God. On the contrary, the Sunnah would be consistent with the Book of God by applying or clarifying the meaning that God had intended to convey through the Qur'an.....The Sunnah of the Messenger of God will never be in conflict with the Book of God. Rather, it elucidates it, both in its generalities and in its specifics ... The elucidation of the specific and the general alike falls under the category of exegesis ... Every practice established by the Messenger of God will be consistent with the Book of God, either as a concrete application of an unambiguous text or as a God-given clarification of something stated in the Qur'an in general terms.

Some scholars have divided hadiths into three categories based on the nature of their relationship to the Qur'an. The first category consists of hadiths that are in full agreement with the Qur'an, and which Muslims are obliged to emulate. The second category consists of hadiths that add something to the Qur'an, and which Muslims are also mandated to emulate. The third category consists of hadiths that conflict with the Qur'an, and which are to be rejected.

Most scholars of the Hanafite school made examination of the Sunnah in light of the Qur'an the foundation of their hadith criticism. Al-Sarakhsī (d. 286 AH/899 CE), for example, divided discontinuity in historical reports into two types: (1) discontinuity in wording by which he meant hadiths classified as *mursal*, and (2) discontinuity in meaning. Al-Sarakhsī then went on to explain that what he meant by discontinuity in meaning was for a hadith to be in conflict with the Qur'an.

Such a hadith would not be acceptable, nor would it be a valid basis for action, whether the verse in question is general in meaning or specific, and whether or not it is subject to more than one interpretation.

Al-Sarakhsī arrived at his conclusions based on both authoritative tradition (*al-naql*) and reason (*al-ʿaql*). As for the authoritative tradition, it consisted in the Prophet's statement that "every condition not found in the Book of God is invalid, since the Book of God is truer [than any other sources]." Al-Sarakhsī interpreted the phrase "every condition not found in the Book of God" to mean every condition which conflicts with the Qur'an. He also cited the Prophet's saying:

> After I am gone, you will have numerous accounts of things I said and did. If someone attributes some action or saying to me, compare it to the Book of God. If it agrees with the Book of God, accept it and know that it is from me. If it conflicts with the Book of God, reject it, and know that I had had no part in it.

Al-Sarakhsī's rational argument centers around a process of comparing the Qur'an to the report vis-à-vis its reliability, since the Qur'an is known to be fully trustworthy, whereas there is uncertainty surrounding whether a "solitary" hadith (*āḥād*) can be reliably traced back to the Messenger of God. When it is impossible to adopt both the report and the Qur'anic text, one must adopt the more certain and abandon what is subject to doubt. The same principle applies to both specific rulings and general principles. A general principle is a binding source for legal rulings in the area it addresses just as a specific text is. The same is true with respect to texts that can support more than one interpretation depending on the context, and those that can support only one interpretation and whose meaning is unambiguous without the need for clarification from the context. The reason for this is that the text of the Qur'an is of certain reliability, while the text of a hadith can never be deemed devoid of uncertainty due to the possibility that it was narrated not verbatim, but only paraphrased in terms of its overall meaning.

The text of the Qur'an enjoys greater reliability than a solitary report (*khabar āḥād*) based on the Qur'an's being classed as *mutawātir* that is, something that has been handed down through such a large number of narrators that it would have been impossible for them to conspire to deceive. Hence, if a solitary report conflicts with the Qur'an this indicates clearly that it has been fabricated.

Stressing the importance of examining hadiths in light of the Qur'an and the most widely circulating, well-recognized Sunnah, al-Sarakhsī praised Hanafite scholars for following this approach, saying:

> These two approaches to hadith criticism are based on significant knowledge and provide an effective means of preserving the religion. For unjustified innovations and caprice have their origins in the failure to examine solitary reports in light of the Qur'an and widely circulating sunnah narratives. There are people who have treated the Sunnah as authoritative despite the existence of uncertainty as to whether it actually originated with the Messenger of God, and even though it does not provide certain knowledge. Such people then proceed to interpret the Qur'an and the widely circulating sunnah narratives in light of such dubious reports. In so doing, they turn things on their heads by making the follower into the leader, and by treating that which lacks certainty as their foundation. As a consequence, they fall prey to whim, caprice, and harmful religious innovation no less than those who reject any solitary hadith for the mere reason that it is not *mutawātir* ....By contrast, those of our scholars who give each kind of evidence its proper weight are on the right path. These scholars treat the Qur'an and the widely circulating sunnah narratives as their authoritative foundation, interpreting solitary reports, which are of less certain reliability, in light of them. That which agrees with the widely accepted narratives, they accept; that which they find no mention of in either the Qur'an or the widely circulating sunnah narratives, they also accept and require people to follow; and as for that which conflicts with the Qur'an and the Sunnah, they reject it.

Among those who held the same view as the Hanafites, albeit with slight differences, was Imam Mālik, whose approach was similar to that of the jurists of Iraq who weighed solitary reports against the Qur'an. Jurists of the Malikite school deduced from their imam's practice that he gave precedence to the apparent meaning of the Qur'an over the Sunnah, especially if the Sunnah came into conflict with some other standard, such as analogical reasoning or the practice that prevailed among the people of Madinah, and on this basis he rejected a number of hadiths. Imam al-Shāṭibī also supported the Hanafites' insistence on the need to weigh hadiths against the Qur'an, and made mention of the fact that the earliest, most respected Muslim scholars had done the same.

As for hadith transmitters and others who attributed to the Sunnah as much authority as they attributed to the Qur'an, if not even greater authority, they did not weigh hadith narratives against the Qur'an. On the contrary, they vehemently denounced this practice, since they denied the mere possibility that any authentic hadith could conflict with the Qur'an in the first place. In expression of this point of view, Ibn Ḥazm (d. 456 AH/1064 CE) wrote:

> It would be impossible for an authentic report to conflict with the Qur'an to begin with. Every such report should be viewed as an authoritative source of Islamic law, since it will either be (1) an addition to what is in the Qur'an, providing an explanation of general statements found therein, or (2) a specification of exceptions to general rules set down in the Qur'an. There is no third possibility.

It appears that in the view of Ibn Ḥazm and those of his ilk, when God told the Prophet that he was to "make clear (*li tubayyina*) unto mankind all that has ever been thus bestowed upon them...," (16:44) this meant that the Prophet was to clarify what had been revealed in the Qur'an *through the Sunnah*. In fact however and as I have shown, what the Prophet was being told to do was to clarify the Qur'an through the Qur'an itself, by reciting it and teaching people its meaning.

In support of their position, hadith transmitters cited a particular hadith which indicates that the practice of comparing hadith narratives to the Qur'an is not required. Ibn Mājah (d. 273 AH/887 CE) related on the authority of al-Miqdām ibn Maʿdi Karib al-Kindī that the Messenger of God said:

> A time is coming soon when a man sated with worldly comforts will relate something I said or did. And he will say, "We have the Book of God among us [as a source of authority]. Whatever we find to be permitted therein, we declare permissible, and whatever we find to be forbidden therein, we declare prohibited. [However,] whatever the Messenger of God has forbidden, God Himself has forbidden."

According to al-Khaṭṭābī, this hadith warns us not to depart from practices established by the Prophet that are not mentioned in the Qur'an. This was in response to sects such as the Kharijites and the Rafidites, who clung to the apparent meaning of the Qur'an and ignored sunnah practices that served implicitly to elucidate the Qur'an. As a consequence, they fell into confusion and error. Al-Khaṭṭābī states:

> This hadith indicates that there is no need to examine a hadith narrative in light of the Book of God. Rather, whatever can be demonstrated to have been done or said by the Messenger of God serves, by itself, as authoritative evidence.

However, a statement such as this reflects serious confusion between what has, and what has not, been demonstrated to be reliable and trustworthy. As we have quoted al-Shāfiʿī and others as saying, a truly well-authenticated report of an action or statement by the Prophet cannot, in fact, conflict with the Qur'an. Ibn Mājah also relates on the authority of ʿUbayd Allāh ibn Abī Rāfiʿ, on the authority of the latter's father, that the Messenger of God said:

> Let me not find any of you sated with worldly comforts and, when presented with something I have commanded or forbidden, saying, "I do not know [whether this is valid or not]. Whatever we find in the Book of God is what we follow."

As for the hadith cited by those who hold that we *are* obliged to weigh hadith narratives against the Qur'an, hadith transmitters judge it to be weak. In fact, they hold that such hadiths are forgeries. In this connection, al-Khaṭṭābī quotes Yaḥyā ibn Muʿīn as saying, "This hadith was forged by atheists."

The hadith transmitters saw the practice of weighing the Sunnah against the Qur'an as dangerous because they feared it would lead to an abandonment of the Sunnah altogether and dependence on the Qur'an alone. Al-Khaṭṭābī wrote, "This is the opinion of people who have no share in the religion, and who have departed from the unanimous consensus (*ijmāʿ*) of the Muslim community." In so saying, al-Khaṭṭābī associated this point of view with the teachings of the Kharijites and the Rafidites. In defense of Imam Aḥmad [ibn Ḥanbal], Ibn al-Qayyim approves the hadith transmitters' view, saying:

> If everything that is required by the Sunnah but not required by the Qur'an were viewed as an abrogation of it [the Qur'an], then most of the practices established by the Messenger of God would be rendered null and void. People would say, "This is an addition to the Qur'an and should not be accepted or adhered to." However, this is precisely what the Messenger of God said would happen, and which he warned against.

The Kharijites, the Rafidites and other sects who were contemporary to this debate failed to reconcile their respective points of view. Jurists among the People of Opinion then introduced an additional barrier to acceptance of hadiths being weighed against the Qur'an. This barrier was termed "additions to the text," as these jurists rejected some hadiths simply because they contained legal rulings not found in the Qur'an. Such extreme positions aside, the idea of weighing hadiths against the Qur'an is a perfectly sound one; it is not an illegitimate innovation or later addition to the religion. On the contrary, the notion was in circulation during the days of the Prophet's Companions and was applied by both those who passed down numerous hadith narratives and by those who did not. At the same time, it should be noted that they did not compare hadiths to the Qur'an in all cases, but only in those situations where the reliability of a particular hadith had been called into question.

Shaykh Muhammad Abu Zuhrah (d. 1974) wrote:

> From this you will see that jurists representing the People of Opinion, who would not accept a hadith until they had examined it in light of the unambiguous verses of the Qur'an which require no elucidation, relied for their methodology on the Companions themselves, including Abū Bakr, ʿUmar ibn al-Khaṭṭāb, ʿĀ'ishah and others. Since these scholars modeled their approach on that of the Companions, they cannot be viewed as innovators in the negative sense of the word. On the contrary, they were "followers." The idea itself is a sound one, and controversy over it only arose due to particular circumstances and divergent ways of understanding it. This may be seen in the fact that the hadith transmitters themselves treated it, in practice, as fundamental to hadith criticism, and held that if a hadith

contradicted something found explicitly in the Qur'an, this indicated that the text of the hadith had been forged.

Methodological Difficulties in Dealing with the Sunnah

As we have seen, the task of formulating the relationship between the Qur'an and the Prophetic Sunnah with the requisite accuracy and precision presented a major challenge to Muslim thinkers, and it continued to raise numerous questions. Some scholars held that the Sunnah could be an independent source of Islamic legislation. As an outgrowth of this position, jurists and *uṣūl* scholars concluded that the Sunnah was the second source of Islamic legislation, the first source being the Qur'an. They then set about constructing their intellectual legacy based on the distinction between 'definitive' (*qaṭʿī*) and 'presumptive' (*ẓannī*). The Qur'an, being definitive in nature, ranked first as a source of legal rulings, while the Sunnah, being largely presumptive in nature, ranked second.

At the same time, some scholars referred to the Qur'an and the Sunnah as *al-waḥyayn*, or "the two divine revelations," the only difference being in the areas of inimitability (*iʿjāz*), and unquestionability (*taʿabbud*). The Qur'an was seen as having been revealed word for word, and the Sunnah as having been revealed on the level of meaning, but not literal wording. The verses of the Qur'an thus served as the basis for a challenge to others to produce something equal to them – a challenge no one was able to meet – whereas the Sunnah was seen to lack this quality of inimitability. Hence, it was held that the Qur'an must be recited verbatim, precisely as it was revealed, whereas it was permissible to narrate the Sunnah in paraphrase.

Conceptualizations such as these yielded a number of dangerous outcomes, for example, the assertion that the Sunnah and the Qur'an might contradict each other, in which case they would have to be reconciled via abrogation, alternative interpretations, or by some other means. This attitude led some to imagine or suppose that the only distinctions between the Qur'an and the Sunnah were merely formal, having to do with wording and status. In this way, the meanings of the Qur'an came to be so intimately associated with the historical context in which the Sunnah came into being and the interpretations linked with that context that it was believed that such interpretations could never be changed or breached. Consequently, it was deemed impermissible to explore any ways of understanding the Qur'an other than those that prevailed during the lifetimes of the Prophet and the first generation of Muslims.

Any understanding that can lead to the mistaken belief that the Qur'an is relative in nature rather than being a changeless document that accommodates all times and places should be avoided as a dangerous perspective. It does no good to speak of the general nature and inclusivity of the Qur'anic discourse if, at the end of the day, the Qur'an is going to be viewed as a relative text whose meanings are determined by time and place, since the upshot of this perspective is that the Qur'anic text is incapable of either accommodating or transcending the historical process of change. Such an outlook involves a disregard for the Qur'an-Sunnah relationship set forth in *Sūrah al-Naḥl*, where God says to the Prophet:

> And upon you [too] have We bestowed from on high this divine writ for no other reason than that you might make clear unto them all [questions of faith] on which they have come to hold divergent views, and [thus offer] guidance and grace unto people who will believe. (16:65)

> We have bestowed from on high upon you, step by step, this divine writ, to make everything clear. (16:89)

In the same vein God addresses the Apostle in *Sūrah al-Naml*, saying:

> [Say, O Muhammad:] "I have been bidden to worship the Sustainer of this City – Him who has made it sacred, and unto Whom all things belong: and I have been bidden to be of those who surrender themselves to Him, and to convey this Qur'an [to the world]." (27:91-92)

Verses such as these make it clear that the pivot and source of the message the Apostle was given is the Qur'an itself, and that the task of Prophethood was to deliver and elucidate this message and to present a concrete application of its values and precepts that people could emulate in all ages and places. There is no need for people to reconstruct this application, and if they imagine themselves required to do so, they are mistaken. However, until we have precise definitions that enable us to discern the subtle differences between the Qur'an and the Sunnah, there will be serious confusion among Muslims as to where their "authoritative points of reference" truly lie.

Islam's intellectual history in the areas of jurisprudence and hadith scholarship, among others, is replete with notions that have not been well understood and which, as a consequence, have obscured the nature of the Qur'an-Sunnah link. Among these notions are, for example, that "the Sunnah stands in judgment over the Qur'an," that "the Sunnah abrogates the Qur'an," or that "the Qur'an needs the Sunnah more than the Sunnah needs the Qur'an." All imprecise and irresponsible statements indicate how seriously the relationship between the Qur'an and the Sunnah has been distorted in people's minds.

Filled as it is with references to specific individuals and to concrete events and situations for which it is easy to find counterparts and analogues in later generations the Sunnah has proved to be more accessible than the Qur'an as a source of input for the process of inferring rulings from juristic particulars. This fact has, unfortunately, reinforced the notion of a separation between the Sunnah and the Qur'an.

Matters have been further complicated by attempts to challenge the authoritative status of the Sunnah or to undermine its importance. By undermining the Sunnah's importance, however, we undermine the complementary relationship between the Sunnah and the Qur'an.

1. *Difficulties Relating to the Legacy Left by Uṣūl Scholars*

Many contemporary Muslims have only a vague understanding of the various tasks that were involved in the Prophet's mission and the distinctions among them. The process of defining the boundaries among these tasks is a challenging one that requires thorough, in-depth study. The leading *uṣūl* scholars, who have made numerous statements about the variety that marked the Apostle's mission, have recognized the distinction between the kinds of actions and behaviors the Prophet engaged in simply as a member of society in keeping with his inborn human propensities, and the things he did in his capacity as Prophet, Messenger, teacher, religious leader, ruler, and the other functions he performed. However, they have not applied the same rigor in their treatment of the Prophet's statements.

Furthermore, *uṣūl* scholars made no distinction between the words and actions of the Prophet that were legislative in nature, and those that were not. When discussing Sunnah-related topics on which their respective imams had stated positions, they would modify the positions taken by hadith transmitters to agree with those of their imams, while accepting hadith transmitters' definitions for terms such as *ṣaḥīḥ* (authentic), *ḥasan* (good), *mashhūr* (famous), *muʿallal* (defective), *mudallas* (concealed), and *muʿanʿan* (containing the conjunction *ʿan* in its chain of narration). At the same time, they classed the various types of sunnah practices indiscriminately as "legislative." Even those spontaneous actions or statements of the Prophet that could be shown to have been performed or uttered out of simple habit, or in his capacity as a human being like other human beings, were treated as implicit sources of legislation.

Moreover, by promoting the view of the Sunnah as an independent source of authority alongside the Qur'an, such scholars opened the door to rulings that might be viewed as frivolous or unnecessary. Thus, for example, if a statement by the Prophet indicated that a given action was more or less neutral, it was classed as 'permissible' (*mubāḥ*). This stance led to a prolonged debate over the matter of permissibility (*ibāḥah*), the question being: Is something deemed permissible based on a legal ruling, or based on a rational judgment? The majority of these scholars insisted that permissibility is based on a legal ruling, and listed 'permissibility' as the fifth juristic category into which they classified actions. The list then became: (1) obligatory (*wājib*), (2) forbidden (*ḥarām*), (3) recommended (*mandūb*), (4) reprehensible (*makrūh*), and (5) permissible (*mubāḥ*). By classing permissibility as a legal ruling rather than a rational judgment, these scholars restricted the issue to that of demonstrating that a given hadith narrative was authentic. If this could be demonstrated, the matter was considered settled, since every hadith narration was assumed, *ipso facto*, to be a kind of legislation.

2. *The Juristic Method and its Dominance Over Approaches to the Sunnah*

Given the exclusively juristic focus on the Qur'an and the Sunnah as sources of legal rulings, Muslims began losing sight of the fact that, taken together, the Qur'an and the Sunnah are intended to build up human society and help us achieve a prospering civilization. Hence, there is a need to highlight the non-juristic aspects of the Qur'an and the Sunnah, which have not received the requisite attention.

For those engaged in formulating juristic rulings, the Sunnah was a more accessible reference than the Qur'an because it dealt directly with events, individuals and situations for which it was easy to find counterparts and analogues in later times. This fact further reinforced the notion of a separation between the Qur'an and the Sunnah, both of which were increasingly read and interpreted from an atomistic perspective that caused scholars to lose sight of the overarching structural, thematic and functional unity between them. This development served in turn to entrench the notion of a hierarchy between the Qur'an and the Sunnah which jurists upheld based on a forged hadith narrated on the authority of Muʿādh ibn Jabal.[3]

This hierarchy is based on a set of mistaken assumptions. The first of these is that the verses of the Qur'an are finite, whereas the number of situations and cases that might conceivably face human beings is infinite. But, we ask, how can the verses of the Qur'an be finite when God has said, "We have bestowed from on high upon you, step by step, this divine writ, to make everything clear" (*al-Naḥl* 16:89)? The two subsequent verses mention universals such as justice, kindness, generosity and faithfulness to one's word, which serves to show how the Qur'an encompasses everything that has happened, or ever will happen, among human beings. God has told us explicitly, in fact, that He has neglected nothing in the Qur'an (*al-Anʿām* 6:38).

The second mistaken assumption is that Muʿādh would only have looked for rulings in the Sunnah after despairing of finding what he was looking for in the Qur'an. Such an assumption runs contrary to the complementary relationship God established between the Qur'an and the Prophet's practical application of its teachings. Another problematic assumption of relevance here is that one only engages in ijtihad when one finds no ruling on the issue in question in either the Qur'an or the Sunnah. We know from abundant evidence in Islamic legal sources that human beings' foremost duty is to know God. However, such knowledge begins with rational investigation, followed by examination of the Prophet's claims and the miracle he was given, and ending with acknowledgment of and faith in what he brought.

When we realize this fact, we discover that most of the controversy that raged of old and which rages still, over the authority and autonomy of the Sunnah as a source of Islamic legislation and whether the Sunnah stands in judgment over the Qur'an or vice-versa has grown out of our limitations as human beings, who have to investigate and digest the more important things before going on to the less important ones. Someone might object at this juncture that someone who engages in ijtihad to resolve a question first gathers all the relevant hadiths at his disposal; he then sifts, classifies and studies them, determining which of them have abrogated others and which have been abrogated, which are of unqualified validity and which require qualification, which are general and which are specific, which are broad and which are narrow, and so on. This being the case, the reading being done is comprehensive. Why, then, is it described as being partial?

The answer to this question is that when we speak of a comprehensive or inclusive reading, we are not speaking of the approach described above. For although it may appear at first glance to be comprehensive and inclusive, it does not revolve around the universals of the Sunnah and the Qur'an as a whole. Rather, it revolves around a universal value as it applies to a particular situation or juristic inquiry. A comprehensive, inclusive reading of the Qur'an and the Sunnah is, by contrast, the discovery of overarching, unchanging values through an investigation of the Revelation's overall content and aim and human beings' purposes in relation to the entire cosmos. The overarching, unchanging values to which I am referring include for example the oneness of the Divine (*al-tawḥīd*), the need for self-purification (*al-tazkiyah*), and the goodness of progress and prosperity (*al-ʿumrān*). They also include the values of justice, freedom, and the fulfillment of human needs from the most basic material necessities to the level of more abstract, spiritual and esthetic needs. Recognition of these governing values leads naturally to the formulation of regulatory principles, the disclosure of unstated assumptions, and the identification of methodological determinants such as philosophical premises and assumptions.

Interpretations founded on the juristic model alone may have contributed to a failure to discern the need for a comprehensive approach that views particular situations and Qur'anic verses within the broader context of the overarching principles found in the Qur'an.

3. *Isnād Methodology in Isolation*

Isnād-based methodology has been viewed by some as an unrivalled means of demonstrating a hadith's authenticity and reliability. This view is based on the assumption that there is nothing about the actual content of a hadith that would render it inauthentic or unreliable. If this assumption is correct, then if the *isnād* is judged to be sound, nothing more needs to be said about the hadith in question. However, when the content of a hadith is critiqued based on exacting, knowledge-based criteria established by hadith transmitters themselves, these criteria can be fruitfully integrated with and complemented by *isnād*-based criticism. We then begin to see the Sunnah not as a collection of disjointed texts, but, rather, as a means of applying the values and teachings of the Qur'an.

The confidence placed in *isnād*-based methodology was based on the assumption that the Qur'an's unassailable authority was derived from its having been transmitted by significant numbers of reliable narrators from one generation to the next. In fact, however, the Qur'an had been preserved from within by God Himself so that no falsehood could infiltrate it regardless of how many, or few, individuals had been involved in transmitting its text. Hence, such external factors had nothing to do with the degree of reliability that could be attributed to the Qur'an, the completeness with which it had been preserved, its infallibility, or its definitiveness.

Would that hadith scholars, like many jurists, had committed themselves to the use of both methodologies. In this case, they would have first examined the *isnād*, or chain of transmission, to determine how reliable and authentic it is. They would then have subjected the *matn*, or main body of the hadith to rigorous standards of authenticity and reliability based on the governing values of Islam – the oneness of the Divine (*al-tawḥīd*), self-purification (*al-tazkiyah*), and progress and prosperity (*al-ʿumrān*). In this way, the two methodologies would have been allowed to complement one another and evolve together over time and as a consequence, we could have avoided the huge controversy that has arisen over what have come to be known as 'disputed hadiths,' or over the notion of 'authoritativeness' (*al-ḥujjiyah*) itself. Nor would we have witnessed the emergence of wayward sects such as those who refer to themselves as 'Qur'anists' (*al-qur'āniyyūn*) when, in fact, a true 'Qur'anist' would never spurn or judge the Sunnah based merely on his or her own thoughts, desires, or whims, keeping the parts that strike his fancy and rejecting that parts that he finds objectionable.

Most of the disagreements current today are a result of our having neglected one of these two methods of hadith criticism. There are some who adopt the *isnād*-critique method and who, if a hadith's chain of transmission is shown to be authentic, refuse to critique its *matn* since, in their view, the hadith has "passed muster" and nothing remains to be done. Others, by contrast, ignore the *isnād* altogether, since it makes no difference to them whether the hadith under scrutiny was passed down by al-Bukhārī, Muslim, al-Ṭabarānī, Ibn Mājah or whoever else. They simply critique the text of the hadith against the requisite criteria without regard for its chain of transmission. Others, by contrast, bypass these criteria, which no one has developed since the end of the first four centuries AH, and subject them instead to standards which others might view as capricious, arbitrary and subjective and, therefore, lacking in any academic or intellectual value. Needless to say, this is a practice that no self-respecting scholar should ever fall into.

The only way to resolve the present impasse is to undertake a thorough critique and analysis of both *isnād* and *matn* criticism. Both methodologies should be evaluated in light of the knowledge that was available during the historical periods in which they emerged. A study should be undertaken of hadith transmitters' use of these methodologies, whether separately or together, which hadiths were subjected to only one methodology and not the other, these methodologies' historical evolution, and the periods in which their use and development by jurists and *uṣūl* scholars were halted or interrupted. The study and analysis of specific texts might also facilitate the reappraisal and refinement of these methods.

4

The Expanding Role of Narrative – A Historical Overview

IF THE guidance brought by the Prophet had been followed after his death the way it was during his lifetime, the question of how the Qur'an relates to the Sunnah would simply never have arisen. We read in *Sūrah Āl ʿImrān*:

> Indeed, God bestowed a favor upon the believers when he raised up in their midst an apostle from among themselves, to convey His messages unto them, to cause them to grow in purity, and to impart unto them the divine writ as well as wisdom – whereas before that they were indeed, most obviously, lost in error. (3:164)

However, subsequent changes in people's attitudes and interpretations brought this question to the fore, which led in turn to difficulties in all sciences relating to the transmission of the Islamic revelation and tradition. It even impacted the language in which the Sunnah and other narrated reports were conveyed.

As we approach the second-most important formative influence on the Muslim community (the most important being the Qur'an), we need a clear historical perspective on succeeding Muslim generations' attitudes toward the Qur'an and its elucidation in the Prophetic Sunnah. For the purposes of this discussion, we will refer to these generations as (1) the generation that witnessed the Qur'anic revelation, (2) the narrative generation, (3) the generation of jurisprudence, and (4) the generation (or generations) of imitation or tradition (*taqlīd*).

[FIRST]
The Generation That Witnessed the Qur'anic Revelation

Given the clarity of perspective enjoyed by this first Muslim generation, the issue of the relationship between the Qur'an and the Sunnah was unlikely even to arise. Members of the Muslim community were accustomed to hearing the Messenger of God recite the verses of the Qur'an that were being revealed to him, his teaching, his understanding of the Qur'an, and his application of the wisdom contained in the Qur'an in such a way that it answered their questions, ordered their relationships, taught them what was permitted and forbidden, and helped them distinguish good from bad, true from false. Sometimes new verses would be revealed without having been triggered by a particular occasion or circumstance, while at other times they would come in answer to a question or in resolution of a difficulty. The Qur'an makes mention of fifteen situations in which the Prophet's Companions asked him for rulings on particular issues. In each of these places the Qur'an says, "They ask you....," and follows this with an answer to the question being raised. Of these questions, eight were juristic in nature. If the Messenger of God had known that he was authorized to legislate in response to these and related questions, he would not have waited for a ruling to be revealed to him, and would simply have answered the questions himself without delay.

There were also situations in which the Messenger of God was commanded to issue rulings on matters he had not been asked about. An example of such a situation is related in *Sūrah al-Anʿām*:

> Say: "Come, let me convey unto you what God has [really] forbidden to you: Do not ascribe divinity, in any way, to aught beside Him; and [do not offend against but, rather,] do good unto your parents; and do not kill your children for fear of poverty – [for] it is We who shall provide sustenance for you as well as for them; and do not commit any shameful deeds, be they open or secret; and do not take any human being's life – [the life] which God has declared to be sacred – otherwise than in [the pursuit of] justice: this has He enjoined upon you so that you might use your reason; and do not touch the substance of an orphan – save to improve it – before he comes

> of age. And [in all your dealings] give full measure and weight, with equity: [however,] We do not burden any human being with more than he is well able to bear; and when you voice an opinion, be just, even though it be [against] one near of kin. And [always] observe your bond with God: this has He enjoined upon you, so that you might keep it in mind. And [know] that this is the way leading straight unto Me: follow it, then, and follow not other ways, lest they cause you to deviate from His way. [All] this has He enjoined upon you, so that you might remain conscious of Him (6:151-154).

In the same vein we have *Sūrah al-Nisā'*, 4:2-59 and 92-94, as well as the rulings found in *Sūrah al-Isrā'*, 17:22-39. Numerous legal rulings are also found in *Sūrah al-Baqarah*, *Sūrah Āl ʿImrān*, and *Sūrah al-Mā'idah*, not to mention the many rulings scattered throughout the rest of the Qur'an in either explicit or implicit form. In short, all the jurisprudence that has served as the basis for the legislation instituted by the Muslim community has its origin in the Qur'anic Revelation. As for the Prophet, he submitted to this Revelation and conveyed it to others, clarifying it and teaching others how to translate it into concrete actions. This understanding was accepted without question, as no one of that generation viewed the Sunnah as anything more than a clarification of the rulings found originally in the Qur'an. Never once did the Prophet claim to have the right to legislate independently of the Qur'an, since the Qur'an had left nothing out, and because an elucidation is not the same as the formation of an autonomous ruling. Rather, whatever rulings were issued had been present already in the Qur'an. All the Prophet did was to make them clearer through his words, actions and applications.

On those occasions when the Messenger of God issued independent rulings, they all had to do with organizational matters and policies which he saw as being matters of opinion and which, therefore, it was appropriate for him to rule on as he saw fit. One such occasion had to do with the prisoners of war who were taken at the Battle of Badr, and in relation to whom a revelation came pointing out what the Prophet should have done; another had to do with the situation in which some of the hypocrites requested permission to stay back from the Battle of Tabūk. In these situations God made clear to people that He involves no one in His rule. Hence, it should be clear beyond a shadow of a doubt that the Prophet did not see himself as being authorized to issue legislation on his own. Rather, he was authorized to do nothing but convey God's laws to others and to be obedient to them. And, as we have explained, his elucidation of God's laws might take place in words, actions, or approval of others' words and actions.

The generation that witnessed the Qur'anic revelation was a pristine generation that had yet to witness the appearance of sects or factions, disagreements, juristic schools of thought, political struggles, or aspirations to power on the part of this or that member of the Muslim community. Those who possessed no political authority sought to acquire cultural authority, and those who were unable to satisfy their ambitions by stirring up tribal fervor that would elevate them to positions of leadership would assert their influence by creating philosophical, doctrinal or intellectual fervor.

1. Sunnah Methodology During the Era of the Rightly-Guided Caliphate

The Caliphs Abū Bakr and ʿUmar ibn al-Khaṭṭāb sought to verify narrated accounts by scrutinizing the content of any hadith that was narrated. Imam al-Dhahabī wrote:

> Abū Bakr was the first person to take precautions before accepting a report he had heard. Ibn Shihāb related on the authority of Qabīṣah ibn Dhu'ayb that a [certain] grandmother approached Abū Bakr requesting that she be included in someone's inheritance. In response, Abū Bakr told her, "According to the Book of God, you are due nothing, and I am unaware of the Messenger of God's having mentioned anything due to you." He then asked the Prophet's other Companions. Al-Mughīrah ibn Shuʿbah rose and said, "I once saw the Messenger of God giving her [a grandmother] one-sixth." Abū Bakr asked him, 'Is there anyone else who has a similar testimony?" Muḥammad ibn Maslamah al-Anṣārī then offered a similar testimony. So Abū Bakr gave it to her.

Abū Bakr thus established a way of dealing with any legal issue that might be raised. The first step in the process was to bring the issue directly to the Qur'an. Note that in taking this first step, the individual in need of an answer did not come to the Qur'an in search of proof texts to support this or that preconceived notion, supposition or claim.

This initial inquiry was then followed by a second step that involved searching for something the Prophet had said or done that pointed to a relevant Qur'anic principle that he had been applying or clarifying. In the event that something of relevance was found in the narratives about the Prophet, it was not treated as textual evidence in support of an already-established rule but rather as a clarification of the Qur'an's approach and its answer to the difficulty that had been posed. One of the most distinctive features of this early era of Islamic history was the insistence on keeping narratives about the Prophet to a minimum. At times, however, this step would be accompanied by a request for an additional witness in support of the first narrator, as we find in the incident related about Abū Mūsā al-Ashʿarī, who quoted the Prophet as having made a statement that one should knock three times before entering a house; if one was allowed entry, so be it; if no one answered, one was to withdraw. When Abū Mūsā quoted this statement to ʿUmar ibn al-Khaṭṭāb, ʿUmar insisted that he bring forth another witness to this statement before he acknowledged it as valid.

With regard to criticism of the *matn*, or text, of the hadith cited by al-Bukhāri, Muslim and others about Fāṭimah bint Qays, whose husband had divorced her irrevocably and to whom the Messenger of God supposedly allowed no housing or alimony, ʿUmar ibn al-Khaṭṭāb said:

> We will not disregard the Book of God and the Sunnah of our Prophet because of something said by a woman who, for all we know, has now forgotten [what she heard before], and who has both a place to live and material support. As God has said, "When you...divorce women...do not expel them from their homes; and neither shall they [be made to] leave unless they become openly guilty of immoral conduct" (*Sūrah al-Ṭalāq*, 65:1).

We also have accounts of situations in which ʿĀ'ishah took exception to the Companions by checking narratives against the Qur'an and correcting them on this basis. For example, she objected to a hadith according to which deceased individuals are said to be tormented by their families' weeping over their loss. The basis for ʿĀ'ishah's objection was the verse that tells us that "whatever [wrong] any human being commits rests upon himself alone; and no bearer of burdens shall be made to bear another's burden" (*Sūrah al-Anʿām*, 6:164).

2. The Prophet's Actions are Divided into Two Categories

The first category consists of actions which were necessary in order for the Prophet to carry out unambiguous Qur'anic directives, such as, "be constant in prayer, and spend in charity" (*Sūrah al-Baqarah*, 2:43). Such general commands, which are found scattered throughout the Qur'an, were detailed later by the Prophet through his actions and words, as when he said, "Pray as you have seen me pray," and, "Take your rites of worship from me." In fact, Imam al-Ghazālī went so far as to say that no actions of the Prophet should be viewed as having a general application except those that served to clarify an unchanging legal ruling. This category of actions forms part of the Prophet's mission to convey the Divine Revelation he had received.

The second category consists of actions which the Prophet engaged in on his own personal initiative in response to the situation at hand. This category, to which scholars have referred as the Prophet's "states and traits," stands in contradistinction to the divine message he had been commissioned to deliver. This category might include interpretations offered by the Prophet based on his personal appraisal of a situation, as well as things he did out of habit or as expressions of his natural temperament.

As for the notion that the Prophet was authorized to legislate independently of the Qur'an, it had not even been suggested at this stage. Ibn al-Qayyim and others stated explicitly that the Messenger of God's task was to detail the rulings already found in the Qur'an and to spell out the conditions, limitations, times and other qualifications associated with some of its injunctions; these were referred to by *uṣūl* scholars as "situational rulings" (*al-aḥkām al-waḍʿiyyah*). The Prophet's Companions attempted to make the Prophet's applications into a "Prophetic jurisprudence of the Qur'an" that would make it possible to formulate an approach to addressing events and situations such as the one that arose in relation to the grandmother who sought out Abū Bakr with a request for a share in an inheritance.

[SECOND]
The Narrative Generation is Born

The vacuum left by the Prophet's passing was not one to be filled easily. However, the edifice he had erected with the Qur'an as its foundation was sufficiently sturdy that it was able to endure and preserve the unity of the Muslim community despite the apostasy of a number of desert Arab tribes after the Prophet's death. Foremost among the leaders of the generation that witnessed the Qur'anic revelation were Abū Bakr, ʿUmar, ʿAlī, ʿĀ'ishah, and the remaining Companions. Islam maintained clear teachings concerning what was permitted and what was forbidden, and when dealing with actions that appeared ambiguous, it was possible with a bit of informed study and reflection to classify such actions properly in light of the universal values taught in the Qur'an and its explicit teachings. The Muslim community's heartfelt love for the Prophet also had a significant impact, both on early Islamic legislation and on the subsequent development of Islamic jurisprudence.

With the Islamic conquests, however, a variety of different peoples began entering the Islamic fold. Islam was now being practiced in new environments quite different from that of the Arabian Peninsula; hence, new questions were being raised and new problems were being faced. The intermingling of cultures began manifesting its effects, both positive and negative, while ideas, opinions and claims unknown to the generation that witnessed the Qur'anic revelation began to gain currency. As the first Muslim generation began to die out, people felt a need for sources of guidance over and above the Qur'an to help them address newly arising questions and problems. It was only natural, then, that the Muslim community would begin interpreting the verses of the Qur'an and, in some cases, reading into them meanings that would help to meet their legislative and intellectual needs. Nevertheless, there were still numerous questions that could not be answered simply by formulating opinions on the basis of informed or creative interpretations. Consequently, people began collecting narratives and reports in an attempt to trace everything of relevance to the life of the Apostle.

ʿUmar ibn ʿAbd al-ʿAzīz and the Recording of Hadiths

One of the first systematic attempts to set the hadiths down in writing was made by Caliphs Abd al-ʿAzīz ibn Marwān (d. 86 AH/705 CE) and ʿUmar ibn ʿAbd al-ʿAzīz (d. 101 AH/740 CE) – his son – together with the jurists of their day. Noting the numerous disputes that had arisen over where religious authority lay, these men sought to adopt the Sunnah as a substitute for the various juristic schools of thought. ʿAbd al-ʿAzīz and his son ʿUmar believed that if they collected all hadiths relating the words and deeds of the Prophet and placed them in people's hands alongside the Qur'an as the means of elucidating the Qur'an's meanings and how they were to be applied, this would prevent Muslims from dividing themselves into sects, schools, factions and denominations. The result was the emergence of what we are terming here "the narrative generation," which differed in significant ways from the generation that had preceded it.

As Caliphs ʿAbd al-ʿAzīz and his son ʿUmar viewed things, the purpose behind the collection of narratives about the Prophet's life was not to create a corpus of additional or autonomous legislative evidence that would stand alongside the Qur'an, since the Qur'an's relationship to the Sunnah was such that it would not have allowed for this kind of understanding. However even the best of medicines can have unwanted side effects, and the side effect that accompanied the collection of oral narratives was that – just as the leaders of the first Muslim generation had feared and cautioned against – people became so preoccupied with these narratives that they lost their focus on the Qur'an. It was for fear of this eventuality that the first Caliph, Abū Bakr, had hesitated to collect hadiths, and that ʿUmar ibn al-Khaṭṭāb, soon after collecting a number of hadiths, had them erased.

[THIRD]
Legists and the Generation of Jurisprudence

The concept of fiqh, or jurisprudence, came into circulation in the year 40 AH/660 CE in response to the spread of narratives about the sayings and actions of the Prophet. However, rather than being treated as a means of resolving disputes among scholastic theologians and jurists, these narrated accounts evolved into a new weapon in the war between proponents of different religious points of view, with each side defending its sect, school or denomination with whichever narratives served as grist for its own mill. No sooner had the recording process begun than people began relying on hadith narratives not simply as a way to understand and apply the Qur'an as the Prophet had done but, rather, as a source of Islamic legislation parallel to the Qur'an. There may even have been some who gave the Sunnah priority over the Qur'an itself. Consequently, the Qur'an lay abandoned or, at the very least, was largely neutralized. This took place on the pretext that "the Qur'an is subject to numerous interpretations" and, being miraculous and inimitable in its linguistic style, was seen as beyond the ken of all but a very few select individuals. Meanwhile, people turned their attention to fiqh and the Sunnah.

There then spread an erroneous notion that, by most estimates, the Qur'an contained no more than around 500 verses comprising legal rulings, and that it was these verses that should occupy most of scholars' attention. Among these verses, scholars tended to restrict themselves to those that begin with a clear positive or negative imperative (do's and don'ts). According to this view, the rest of the Qur'an had been revealed in order to describe the afterlife and to relate parables, stories, exhortations and the like. As a result, the only parts of the Qur'an for which there was an urgent need were found in an estimated 330 verses: 140 dealing with rites of worship, around 70 containing rulings on the family, around 70 on daily transactions, 30 dealing with legal penalties, and approximately 20 on the judiciary, legal testimony and the like. As for the hadiths containing legal rulings, they were estimated at a maximum of 1,100 representing the core hadith narratives. According to one scholar:

> [T]he number of hadiths containing legal rulings is equal to the number of Qur'anic verses containing such rulings; hence, each such verse is associated with a single hadith that explains how to apply its content: 70 verses on daily transactions, 20 verses on criminal offenses and penalties, and 90 verses on personal status.

Overall, the Sunnah was to be the pivotal text for Muslims, since it was from this text that one could both deduce the fundamental principles of the religion and issue fatwas on specific situations. In short, the Sunnah was viewed as the self-sufficient guidebook to Islamic life.

Then some began going so far as to classify all hadiths as sources of legal rulings, including even those that contained no rulings in explicit form. Thus, as mentioned earlier in our discussion, some scholars reasoned that any report of something the Prophet had done, allowed, or approved could be viewed as evidence that the act performed, allowed or approved was to be classified as 'permissible' (*mubāḥ*). On this basis, these scholars treated permissibility (*ibāḥah*) as a juristic category in and of itself. It was at this point that the dividing lines among Muslim scholars began to be drawn, ending in an actual split that led to the formation of the two schools that came to be known as "the people of opinion" (*ahl al-ra'y*) and "the people of hadith" (*ahl al-ḥadīth*). Each of these two schools developed distinctive features and its own arsenal of proof texts.

At this juncture we will pause to examine the critical developments that grew out of the notion that the Qur'an and the Sunnah are parallel sources of religious authority.

a) Gone was the extreme care that had been taken by those in the first Muslim generation to ensure that the Qur'an not be tainted by anything else whatsoever. Instead, people became engrossed in reports of things the Prophet had done or said until the Qur'an was nothing more than a source of proof texts to be cited by scholastic theologians, *uṣūl* scholars, jurists and others. If someone argued for or against something based on evidence from the Qur'an alone, someone would object, saying: "The Sunnah stands in judgment over the Qur'an. The Qur'an does not stand in judgment over the Sunnah." Notions such as these were adopted even by religious leaders and scholars of note. Saʿīd ibn Manṣūr narrated on the authority of ʿĪsā ibn Yūnus on the authority of al-Awzāʿī on the authority of Makḥūl, who said: "The Qur'an needs the Sunnah more than the Sunnah needs the Qur'an." The same statement was related by al-Awzāʿī on the authority of Yaḥyā ibn Abī Kathīr. In the same vein, al-Faḍl ibn Ziyād said:

I once heard Abū ʿAbd Allāh (that is, Aḥmad ibn Ḥanbal) being asked about the hadith according to which the Sunnah stands in judgment over the Qur'an, and he replied, "I would not dare make such claims. Rather, I would say simply that the Sunnah explains and clarifies the Qur'an."

Al-Faḍl also said: "I heard someone ask Aḥmad ibn Ḥanbal whether the Sunnah abrogates anything in the Qur'an, to which he replied, 'Nothing abrogates the Qur'an but the Qur'an itself.'" As for Abū ʿUmar, he said:

The position taken by al-Shāfiʿī, God have mercy on him, was that the Qur'an can be abrogated by nothing but something else in the Qur'an, since God has said, "And now... We replace one message by another" (*Sūrah al-Naḥl*, 16:101) and, "Any message which We annul or consign to oblivion We replace with a better or a similar one. Do you not know that God has the power to will anything?" (*Sūrah al-Baqarah*, 2:106)

Whatever the status enjoyed by these jurists and the circumstances under which their ideas developed, such statements indicate that tragedy had struck, and that the Muslim community was in crisis. They were now legislating based on narratives other than the Qur'an and claiming that the Prophet had brought both the Qur'an "and something equal to it." This was based on a hadith narrated by al-Miqdām ibn Maʿdi Karib al-Kindī on the authority of the Messenger of God, whom he quoted as saying:

Verily, I have been given the Qur'an and something else equal to it. Verily, a time is coming soon when a man sated with worldly comforts will say: "You must abide by this Qur'an. Whatever you find permitted therein, you also shall permit, and whatever you find forbidden therein, you also shall forbid." [But] verily, the flesh of donkey and fanged predators may not be eaten. Nor, if a Jew or Christian living under Muslims' protection should drop some money in the street, are you permitted to pick it up and keep it for yourself unless its owner has no need of it.

b) The majority of scholars during the period in question held that the Sunnah could abrogate the Qur'an even if it took the form of a solitary report (*khabar āḥād*). Hence, they assumed that between the Qur'an, the original source of the entire religion, and the Sunnah, the applied commentary on the Qur'an, there was an inconsistency that could only be eliminated by claiming that one had abrogated the other. Realizing, with his accustomed foresightedness, the dangers inherent in such a claim, Imam al-Shāfiʿī categorically rejected the possibility that the Qur'an could abrogate the Sunnah, or vice-versa. In an attempt to propose a compromise, al-Shāfiʿī proposed the idea of "support" (*al-ʿāḍid*). According to this idea, the Qur'an can only be abrogated by the Qur'an, but the Sunnah may serve as evidence in support of the Qur'an's abrogation of itself. Conversely the Sunnah cannot be abrogated by the Qur'an, but only by something else from the Sunnah; however, this self-abrogation of the Sunnah may find support in the Qur'an.

c) The aforementioned scholars circulated other statements as well in justification of their position, all the while disregarding the fact that the Qur'an is a book that has been guarded from all falsehood (*Sūrah Fuṣṣilat*, 41:42). One of them stated, "The Qur'an can bear numerous interpretations." Consequently, it was concluded, there was a need for the Sunnah to provide evidence specifying which of these numerous interpretations should be adopted. However, this contention flies in the face of all the assertions to the contrary in the Qur'an, which describes itself as being clear and easy to understand (12:1; 16:89; 19:97; 24:34; 36:69; 44:58; 54:17, and so on). The Qur'an also describes itself as having been conveyed to people "in a well-guarded divine writ" (*fī kitābin maknūn – Sūrah al-Wāqiʿah*, 56:78).

The Arabic word *maknūn*, meaning "hidden" or "concealed," implies that the Qur'an conveys meanings that are only disclosed little by little. As time passes, then, the Qur'an is shown to be capable of addressing all of humankind's needs, at all times and in all places. This is why we are told by al-Suyūṭī and others that many of the Companions, when they recited a verse of the Qur'an whose meaning eluded them, would say, "This is something whose interpretation has yet to be provided." In other words, they recognized that the Qur'an contained aspects that, being "well-guarded," bore meanings that would not be made clear to them in their lifetimes given the fact that the realities to which the verses related had not yet come into being. The words of the Qur'an thus transcended the era in which they were revealed, being intended to address the problems of another age. The Companions who knew the Qur'an well understood that they should not suspect the Qur'an of being obscure or overly general, thereby confusing its readers or hearers as to which of its many possible meanings was correct. Instead, they held the Qur'an blameless and committed themselves to seeing it as it portrays itself: as clear, easy to comprehend, and a means of understanding other things more clearly as well.

d) Some claimed that whereas the verses of the Qur'an are finite, the situations the Qur'an is required to address are infinite. Consequently, they concluded, more evidence was needed in order to fill what they mistakenly imagined to be a legislative vacuum. In so claiming, however, they were overlooking the fact that, as we are told in *Sūrah Maryam*, "never does your Sustainer forget [anything]" (19:64). Given that, as the Qur'an itself tells us, it has come to make everything clear, and God has neglected nothing in its pages, this must mean that in the Qur'an we find universal principles that are applicable to untold numbers of specifics and in light of which we can address whatever new issues or problems happen to arise. In short, the Qur'an is capable of accommodating virtually all the details of human life. On this basis God assured the Prophet that "they [who deny the truth] might never taunt you with any deceptive half-truth without Our conveying to you the [full] truth and [providing you] with the best explanation" (*Sūrah al-Furqān*, 25:33). The Qur'an is thus capable of leading us to the best solutions in relation to all of life's affairs.

The Qur'an has it own distinctive language and unmistakable style. However, like communities before them, the Muslim community exhibited a faulty understanding of what true piety entails, as well as an urge to innovate and add their own 'embellishments' to the religion. After belittling the Qur'an, supposedly in favor of narrated accounts, they proceeded to abandon the Qur'an and to neglect their narrated accounts as well, occupying themselves instead with self-devised rules to which they referred variously as "jurisprudence" (*fiqh*), "principles of jurisprudence" (*uṣūl al-fiqh*), "interpretation" (*tafsīr*) and "exegesis" (*ta'wīl*). They discussed the Qur'an based on interpretations not supported by the text, while at the same time adopting such a lenient stance on narrated accounts that they stood in violation of the method established by al-Bukhāri, Muslim, and the Companions who had recited the Qur'an. They were likewise in violation of the approach that had been adhered to by leaders of the generation that witnessed the Qur'anic revelation, who would not accept a report from a single individual even if he was one of the Companions themselves, unless he could bring forth another narrator to testify to the accuracy of what he had related. (We are told that when a Companion who had narrated a report individually was unable to provide another witness to the same event, ʿAlī ibn Abī Ṭālib would require him to take an oath). This approach was adhered to until 40 AH.

1. *The Contradiction Between the Claim That the Sunnah is Subject to the Qur'an, and the Practice of Giving the Sunnah Priority When Deducing Legal Rulings*

When this generation adopted the position that the Sunnah has a status inferior to that of the Qur'an, they viewed this as a solution to the problem of how to relate the Qur'an to the Sunnah. All they were doing, however, was to highlight the inseparable link between the Qur'an and the Messenger of God's obedient application of it through what he said and did. In their attempt to demonstrate the Sunnah's autonomy from the Qur'an, scholars mentioned only three issues, each of which is encompassed by the universals set forth in the Qur'an. These were: (1) the prohibition against a man's marrying the paternal aunt of the woman he is already married to, (2) the prohibition against consuming donkey meat, and (3) the prohibition against consumption of fanged predators, none of which is mentioned in the Qur'an. Scholars fell into inconsistencies by claiming that the Sunnah, while being an autonomous source of evidence for legal rulings, nevertheless occupies a lower status than the Qur'an. At the same time, they gave even solitary reports priority over the plain meaning of the Qur'an, which they had likewise designated 'a solitary report.' These scholars maintained that the Sunnah qualifies the Qur'an's unqualified statements and specifies its general statements. However, this assertion no longer had significant impact on how the Qur'an-Sunnah link was defined.

2. *The Emergence of Isnād Methodology*

It was after 140 AH/757 CE that the *isnād* emerged as a means of resolving doubts concerning the reliability of narrated reports, and most scholars date the first uses of the *isnād* method of hadith criticism back to the second half of the second century AH. What this means is that the reports that were collected and the narrators who passed them down prior to 140 AH were not subjected to close scrutiny. When scholars engaged in hadith criticism prior to this time, if they did so at all, they might simply conduct a cursory examination of the *matn* alone to ensure that it did not conflict with other hadiths on the same topic that had been passed down either by trustworthy narrators, or by a larger number of narrators than the report in question. When hadith transmitters began focusing on *isnāds*, they did their best to trace the hadith under study back to someone they knew and had met and from whom they had heard reports directly. They would then leave it to this person to vouch for the person on whose authority he had narrated the account, and so on.

To those who placed confidence in it, the *isnād* appeared to be an ingenuous way to eliminate doubts that might arise concerning whether a given report could actually be traced back to the Messenger of God. As for the Qur'an, people saw no need for an *isnād* to demonstrate its reliability, since the Qur'an's authority was seen as an outcome of its internal structure and style, its dazzling impact on its hearers and its way of speaking to their hearts, as well as its inimitability and its opponents' failure to produce anything comparable to it.

Hence, people's point of departure in relation to the Qur'an has been one of either faith or disbelief. In relation to hadiths, by contrast, people's starting-point has been to doubt whether they can be traced back to the Messenger of God. Until one can feel relatively confident that the Prophet actually did or said what has been attributed to him, a given report will be equally subject to belief or disbelief. Hence, the chain of transmission – *isnād* – is indispensable if one is going to achieve a reasonable degree of certainty concerning the report in question.

Attention was focused initially on the first person mentioned in the chain of transmission, as if hadith scholars were depending on each other to vouch for their respective narrators. This is why, after the end of the second century AH, narratives began receiving more lenient treatment. An example of this more lenient approach is the assessment of narrators through a process referred to as *al-sabr*, that is, an in-depth study of a narrator's previous reports. If it was found that previous reports passed down by a given narrator had been deemed sound, he was judged to be trustworthy. If this same narrator then related reports that were suspected of being forged or defective, they might still be accepted based on the soundness of other hadiths associated with his name.

It has been observed that people began providing *isnāds* for some or all of their narratives after the *fitnah*. However, there are numerous understandings of what is meant by the term *fitnah*. Does it refer to the revolt associated with the martyrdom of Caliph ʿUthmān ibn ʿAffān (d. 36 AH/656 CE), or to the discord that resulted from the new preoccupation with hadiths? Does it refer to the unrest associated with the uprising in Madinah led by ʿAbd Allāh ibn al-Zubayr in 63 AH/683 CE? To the persecution that targeted those who held that the Qur'an was uncreated under the Caliphate of al-Ma'mūn between 197-218 AH/813-833 CE, or to the division that arose over the stance of the Murji'ite sect? There were, quite clearly, numerous times of *fitnah*, that is, unrest, uprisings, divisions and disturbances, the beginnings of which were sparked by the assassination of Caliph ʿUmar ibn al-Khaṭṭāb in 23 AH/644 CE.

Be that as it may, there came a time when the Muslim community found itself drowning in a sea of narrated reports and traditions. Al-Khaṭīb al-Baghdādī (d. 463 AH/1071 CE), whose work spanned the midpoint of the evolution of the People of the Hadith, wrote the following critique of the scholarship of his day:

> Certain of our contemporaries have exerted great efforts in the study and collection of hadith narratives. However, they have not adhered to the methods followed by early hadith transmitters, who investigated the trust-

worthiness of both the narrator and that which was narrated, distinguished the bad from the good, derived legal rulings from the practices recorded in the Sunnah, and raised questions based on hadiths' contents concerning what is permissible and impermissible.

These contemporary scholars, by contrast, content themselves with the mere name of the hadith in question and do nothing but put it in written form. Gullible and simpleminded, these men are like donkeys bearing loads of books on their backs. Stoic and persevering, they have endured many a hardship, travelled far braving land and sea and, overcoming fear and trepidation, spent unstintingly of self and substance. They have done all of this in single-minded pursuit of the most trustworthy possible chains of transmission. So set are they on their aim, however, that they accept accounts from individuals of questionable integrity. They quote from people who should not be trusted, and pass on narrations from people whose accounts may or may not be accurate and reliable. They base their arguments on the authority of those who fail to do a proper reading of the sources at their disposal, and who do nothing to ensure that their accounts fulfill the conditions for soundness and trustworthiness. Such individuals make no distinction between someone who has simply heard an account or report from someone else, and someone who has been granted official permission to pass on narrated accounts. Similarly, they make no distinction between different classes of hadiths: between *musnad* and *mursal*, or between *maqṭūʿ* and *muttaṣil*. They do not even know the name of the shaykh from whom they received a hadith, and have to ask others to confirm this information for them. They see it as permissible to pass on accounts from individuals whose behavior is immoral and who are not well looked upon by other adherents of their own schools of thought, and from innovators whose religion has no sound root due to their corrupt beliefs. They see such a practice as permissible; in fact, they view themselves as obliged to act on the accounts related by such people as long as it has been established that they did, in fact, relate the narrative in question and provided that the narrative is accompanied by a lengthy *isnād* ...When their *isnād*s are in disagreement, they do nothing to correct or amend them, and when one of them relates an account, he will have derived it from written sources without having heard it directly or gone to the effort to collect it himself, and without any knowledge of the character of the person who passed it on. If such a scholar memorizes something, he mixes the lean with the fat, the sickly with the healthy. Moreover, if there is confusion in the order of the narrators in a report's chain of transmission or if he is asked about the circumstances surrounding a hadith narrative, he gets flustered, and so begins fiddling with his beard and clearing his throat to conceal his ignorance, being little better than a braying donkey...

Al-Khaṭīb al-Baghdādī was attempting to be fair toward the People of Hadith, criticizing only some of them and making clear why some of the People of Opinion were so critical of them. However, through this statement he paints us a picture of the full-blown crisis into which both factions had fallen.

[FOURTH]
The Imitator Generations

When the schools of jurisprudence had crystallized into their final forms, traditionalists (*al-muqallidūn*) began devoting themselves slavishly to the teachings of their respective imams, extolling their virtues and working to recruit new adherents to their schools of thought. In fact, there were some who went so far as to treat the statements of their imams as though they were holy writ, discussing whether they were subject to contradiction, whether some should be given preponderance over others, whether some of their assertions could abrogate others, and the like. Hence, there were many who concerned themselves more with the Sunnah than they did with the Qur'an on the pretext that the Sunnah encompassed the Qur'an and was intimately linked to it. They then began using hadiths as proof texts in support of the teachings of their imams, which led in turn to more attention being devoted to their imams' juristic teachings than to the Sunnah. As time went on, these imams' juristic writings came to be circulated and expounded so widely that one would have thought Islamic Law consisted of nothing but their teachings. This mode of thinking is illustrated in the following statement by Hanafite scholar Abū al-Ḥasan al-Karkhī:

> The principle we adhere to is that every verse of the Qur'an that conflicts with the teachings of our imams should be thought of either as having been abrogated, or as being of lesser weight than the imams' teachings. However it is preferable for such verses to be interpreted in such a way as to reconcile them with what our imams say.

Impertinent statements of this nature indicate that doctrinal bigotry had spread to such a pathological degree that the trunk was being treated as an offshoot of the branch! When, at the turn of the third century AH, commitment to the practice of ijtihad relating to jurisprudence and its principles waned, *isnād* methodology was supplanted by a dependence on written versions of hadiths found in books. Hence, hadiths might be spread through individuals who had not received official permission to pass them on to others; they might also be recited before a shaykh in an instructional setting and be passed on in this way.

Some hadiths were undoubtedly forged within the context of political struggles and competing claims to legitimacy, including the disputes that arose between Arabs and non-Arabs over status, recognition and influence. These conflicts naturally yielded efforts by the warring sides to bolster their positions with narratives and reports. After all, one would have been hard pressed to find anything in the Qur'an to support or reinforce such controversies. Consequently, contenders turned for support to narratives and reports, some of which were forged in praise of particular cities, tribes, peoples, imams or scholars, and then circulated widely. Examples of such forgeries include accounts extolling the virtues of Imams al-Shāfiʿī and Abū Ḥanīfah, the Kharijites, the Qadarites, and others. This phenomenon merits attention from critics, who would make a valuable contribution by sifting through such narratives, distinguishing the authentic from the inauthentic, and alerting people to their content.

Narratives Enjoy No Superiority Over the Qur'an

God has set the Qur'an apart through its distinct arrangement, style and structural unity, as well as through its contents, the ease with which it can be memorized, its impact, and the inability of its contemporaries, or anyone else for that matter, to meet the challenge to produce something comparable to it. He has declared the Qur'an above doubt and suspicion, free of contradiction and, hence, of indisputable reliability, its verses clear and unambiguous. God describes it in *Sūrah Hūd* as "a divine writ...with messages that have been made clear in and by themselves, and...distinctly spelled out" (11:1). The Qur'an's authenticity does not depend, nor should it depend, on any narrative, however well-attested it might happen to be. Its definitive certainty is founded on the fact that it is the speech of God to which no falsehood can gain access in any way whatsoever (*Sūrah Fuṣṣilat*, 41:42). The Prophet received it through Gabriel, and as he began reciting it to others at God's command, he inspired in them the desire to memorize and recite it, to teach it and circulate it both orally and in writing. Yet it was God who undertook to gather it together in the Prophet's mind, causing him to recite it properly, making its meanings clear, and preserving it (*Sūrah al-Qiyāmah*, 75:16-19; *Sūrah al-Ḥijr*, 15:9).

However, wanting to elevate the status of narrative and related methods, some of the People of the Hadith stressed the fact that the Qur'an had also been narrated. In so doing, they sought to gain legitimacy for what came later to be known as 'recitations' (*al-qirā'āt*) and the science of recitations (*ʿilm al-qirā'āt*), since it is these recitations which actually do depend on narrative. Our position on these recitations is that the Prophet permitted their use by individuals who had difficulty pronouncing some of the letters found in the Qur'an. Hence, those who had trouble pronouncing the letter *ḍād* were allowed to replace it with a *zā'* or a *sīn*, while those who were unable to pronounce the *ḥā'* could replace it with the letters *ʿayn* or *hā'*. However, in light of the two final reviews of the Qur'an which the Prophet received from Gabriel within days of his passing, this concession was not meant to extend beyond his lifetime.

The necessity of discontinuing this concession was confirmed after ʿUthmān ibn ʿAffān compiled the Qur'an in what came to be known as the Master Copy (*al-muṣḥaf al-imām*) which won the Muslim community's unanimous approval. Nowhere do ʿUthmān or those who assisted him in compiling the Qur'an mention a single word of this Master Copy being recited in several different ways. Hence, reversion to this concession after the death of the Prophet and after the Muslim community's unanimous acceptance of ʿUthmān's Master Copy is a most peculiar development that should not have happened. It has been supported on the basis of various narratives, including the hadith dealing with 'the seven dialects' (*al-aḥruf al-sabʿah*). However, these accounts are themselves in need of review and critique on the level of both their chains of transmission and their content.

Let me reaffirm here that the Book of God needs no validation via narratives passed down from one generation to the next. It is likewise independent of all the recitations, be they canonical or otherwise, which have been associated with it. Nor is the Qur'an subject to self-abrogation.

The Qur'an and everything relating thereto are a divine concern alone. If the Qur'an were dependent for its certainty on human narratives, as are hadiths and other historical reports, it would not have been possible for God to challenge both human beings and the jinn to produce something comparable to it. The Qur'an stands above all mere narrative. As such, it stands above all human methods of preserving texts, and it should not be subjected to the critical methods to which we would subject some other discourse. Consequently, it is shameful for some to say, as some in fact have said, that next to the Qur'an, *Ṣaḥīḥ al-Bukhārī* is the most well-authenticated book of the Islamic heritage. It would be perfectly valid for us to compare *Ṣaḥīḥ al-Bukhārī* to some other book of the same type. One might say, for example, that *Ṣaḥīḥ al-Bukhārī* is better authenticated than *Ṣaḥīḥ Muslim*, *Musnad Aḥmad*, or Imam Mālik's *Al-Muwaṭṭa'*. But to compare it to the Qur'an itself evinces an audacity and a lack of reverence for the Qur'an that I would not have expected of a respectable Muslim scholar. For the Book of God is without equal, and it would be unthinkable to view it as comparable, parallel, or subject to being measured against any other entity whatsoever. It is nothing but truth and unquestionable, unchanging certainty.

However, as the People of the Hadith and the People of Opinion were transmuted into political parties in every sense of the word, and as the issue of the relationship between the Qur'an and the Sunnah was dealt with in the midst of the tug-of-war taking place between them, the juristic scene became a battlefield. In this context, 'the Hadith Party' adopted certain narratives (which were themselves in need of thorough examination on the level of both *isnād* and *matn*) in an attempt to prove their claim that the practice of weighing the Sunnah against the Qur'an would never be demanded by believers, but only by atheists, freethinkers, hypocrites, libertines and others of their ilk.

5

The Chronicling of the Sunnah and its Historical Context

AN UNDERSTANDING of the historical context in which the Sunnah was chronicled will help us to understand many of the defects that plague the Islamic narrative heritage, as well as the impact this has had on the formation of the Muslim mindset.

Prior to the coming of Muhammad ibn ʿAbd Allāh, the Arabs living on the Arabian Peninsula had never witnessed the emergence of a prophet and apostle in their midst. However as the revelation descended upon him over a period of twenty-three years, those around him witnessed its effects on a regular basis. They perceived the light that surrounded the Prophet as Gabriel descended and reascended on so many occasions that it became a kind of 'given' in their experience. The effect of this experience was so profound that ʿUmar ibn al-Khaṭṭāb even denied that the Prophet had died. It was not easy for anyone, in fact, to believe that he had died, especially given the great love people had had for him and the faith of which this love was such an important expression.

Not surprisingly, then, the incredulity with which the news of the Prophet's death was met served to catalyze the formation of three groups. The first of these three consisted of political figures who expressed their ongoing love for the Prophet by establishing a caliphate patterned on his mission, which was seen as having manifested itself in his every move, his every action and word, and even his every silence. Perhaps the best illustration of this can be seen in the way Abū Bakr responded to the chaos that was unleashed by the widespread apostasy (*al-riddah*) that took place after the Prophet's death. Determined to foil those who now treated all the instructions the Prophet had left them as though they had never existed, the Caliph acted with unaccustomed resoluteness and forcefulness. Other political figures went even further than this by insisting on the need to transfer the authority that had been invested in the Prophet to the religious leaders of the Prophet's family in order to concretize the Prophet's ongoing presence in the Muslim community.

The second group consisted of Muslim mystics and ascetics who believed that the Apostle's Prophetic mission should continue in the form of sainthood. In this view, the saint is the Prophet's successor, or caliph, standing in for the Prophet by performing miracles as he did during his lifetime. Representatives of this perspective circulated a large number of hadiths, as they considered the Prophet's life to be a clearer, more powerful embodiment of otherworldliness and asceticism than the Qur'an was. Through their love for the Messenger of God, they sought to embody his presence in their gatherings by singing his praises in their poetry and prose. They also felt themselves justified in attributing to him sayings for which there was no chain of transmission on the pretext that he had revealed these to them by supernatural means. They had no hesitations about placing sayings in his mouth that supported their thinking, and they interpreted verses from the Qur'an in ways that harmonized with their own perceptions. One such verse is in *Sūrah al-Shuʿarā'*, where God refers to the Prophet's movements "among those who prostrate themselves [before Him]" (*taqallubaka fī al-sājidīn*) (26:219). Muslim mystics saw this verse as a confirmation that the 'Muhammadan reality' circulated among them in their *dhikr* circles.

As for the third group, it was comprised of those who came later to be known as the *ʿulamā'* (*al-ʿulamā'*, or "those who know"), including scholastic theologians, jurists, and hadith scholars. It was the members of this group and that of the Muslim mystics who changed the meaning of the term *sunnah* such that, rather than referring simply to application of and obedience to the Qur'an in people's daily lives, it now came to refer to virtually everything the Prophet was reported to have done or said. To this expanded definition of the term *sunnah* was then added a further element, as the Sunnah was said also to include everything the Prophet knew others to have done or said without condemning or disapproving of it. The Prophet's silence in response to others' actions or words was viewed as his tacit affirmation of their correctness, and this silence itself was classified into different levels and degrees.

When the Companions dispersed among various cities, hadith transmitters began traveling from place to place in order to continue compiling and recording hadiths. At this point, the Sunnah was no longer sought after as a clarification and application of the Qur'an, but for its own sake, that is, for the simple reason that it had originated with the Apostle. There was now a Sunnah-based corpus of legislation alongside the Qur'an-based legislation. What the Prophet had not done as a way of expounding the meaning of the Qur'an, he had done as a way of drawing nearer to God. Out of these acts of devotion there emerged what came to be known as 'confirmed Sunnah practices' (*sunan mu'akkadah*) which were almost on the order of religious obligations. So influential was this trend of thought that jurists spoke of the duty to fight against those who neglected to perform the two 'voluntary' sets of bows and prostrations prior to the dawn (*fajr*) prayer, or the odd number (*witr*) performed after the final evening (*ʿishā'*) prayer.

In this way, the Sunnah became the basis for a kind of 'self-regulation' that left nothing, large or small, to chance in the believer's daily life. The Sunnah imposed itself by virtue of the religious duty to obey and emulate the Prophet, whose every word, whose every move, indeed, whose every pause – whether in the privacy of his own home, or in public space – was treated as a law to be obeyed and enforced with rigorous and loving devotion. The duty to conform to the Sunnah remained in force regardless of whether or not the Prophet's words and actions were seen as an explanation and application of the Qur'an – that is, as having been uttered or performed in his capacity as Prophet – or as self-expressions that grew out of his role as one human being among others.

[FIRST]
The Chronicling of the Sunnah and the Impact of Jewish and Greek Culture

The Jewish presence was significantly smaller in Makkah than it was in

Khaybar or in Madinah and its environs, in part because the predictions of their awaited prophet pointed to his coming to these latter regions, and in part because they were largely engaged in agriculture during that historical period. Hence, when the Messenger of God received his calling and the Qur'anic revelation began descending upon him, he attempted, in keeping with the guidance of the Qur'an, to draw the Jews' and Christians' attention to the common ground they shared with Islam. He stressed the fact that he had come in part to correct and in part to confirm the previous revelations, and that the revelation he had brought was an extension of the message that had been brought by Abraham, the father of the prophets, who had been neither Jewish nor Christian but, rather, committed to the worship of the one true God. According to a narrative circulated by some writers on the authority of Abū Hurayrah (although we do not find it in sources recognized to be authoritative) Abū Hurayrah would narrate reports on the authority of the Apostle, while Kaʿb would narrate reports on the authority of the Jews. Those who heard such reports may have mistakenly related that they had heard a report from Abū Hurayrah when, in fact, they had heard it from Kaʿb.[1]

Once the Hebrew Scriptures (*al-tawrāh*) had been translated into Arabic, it became possible for Muslims to analyze these documents, which enabled them to see how much had been introduced into them by Hebrew storytellers. Some men of learning then wrote books warning Muslims to beware of such lore; one such book is al-Suyūṭī's *Taḥdhīr al-Khawāṣṣ min Akādhīb al-Qaṣṣāṣ*. In his *Kitāb al-Ḥawayān*, al-Jāḥiẓ quotes Kaʿb al-Aḥbār as saying, "It is written in the Hebrew Scriptures that Eve was punished in ten ways, and that Adam was likewise punished in ten ways." He then comments on this, saying:

> I suspect that much of what is related on Kaʿb's authority where he is quoted as saying, "It is written in the Hebrew Scriptures that..." is to be found in books (that is, the books of the prophets), and what they [the Israelites] have passed down from one generation to another from the books of Solomon, as well as writings such as the Book of Isaiah and others. If those who relate narratives on his [Kaʿb's] authority about ʿUmar ibn al-Khaṭṭāb and the like are telling the truth as they have heard it, and if the shaykh [Kaʿb al-Aḥbār] is not forging the reports, his words are to be understood in the manner I have described to you.

The interplay between the Arabs' lack of a sacred scripture of their own and the culture that prevailed prior to the coming of Islam lay the groundwork for the acceptance of ideas and conceptualizations that were foreign to Islam and which were bound to color our perceptions of it. One such idea was that of Determinism (*al-jabriyyah*), that is, the belief that human beings have no genuine free will and that everything we do is predetermined by Fate. Determinism is alien to an Islamic perspective, which places great importance on the moral code and people's accountability before God for their choices and actions. Islam does not acknowledge the notion that God controls human beings' decisions as one of its premises.

On the contrary, Islam is founded upon complete freedom of choice, and the relationship between human beings and their Lord is founded upon an ancient covenant. Human beings were offered a sacred trust and accepted it freely, as a result of which they were to be held morally accountable. As stated in *Sūrah Hūd*, God has allowed us this responsibility "in order to test you [and thus to make manifest] which of you is best in conduct" (11:7). Human beings' higher purpose is to be God's vicegerents, or representatives, on Earth, and it is in this capacity that they are put to the test. There is no place for Determinism in a religious teaching or law that rests on free human choices. Nevertheless, the prevailing culture read a deterministic doctrine into some passages of the Qur'an and treated them as evidence for this baseless doctrine despite its foreignness to Islamic teachings.

A series of philosophical and theological conundrums then emerged: from determinism (*al-jabriyyah*), to predestination (*al-qadariyyah*), to divine governance (*al-ḥākimiyyah al-ilāhiyyah*). Having differed to this extent over the Qur'an, the Muslim community was now divided and was unable to restore its unity with ease. The newly emerging philosophical-theological sects found themselves unable to resolve their disputes and divisions based on verses of the Qur'an. In fact, it was with the Qur'an as their weapon that some of these groups simultaneously launched attacks on one another and defended themselves. A favorite refrain was "the Qur'an is multifaceted" (*al-qur'ānu ḥammālu awjuh*), meaning that the same verses that are interpreted in one way might also be interpreted in the very opposite way. Another familiar refrain, also mentioned earlier, was that while the verses of the Qur'an are finite, there are infinite numbers of situations that human beings might conceivably face, as a result of which the Qur'an may not be able to provide us with all the guidance we need.

It was during this period, particularly following the translation movement initiated under the Abbasid Caliphate in the latter eighth and mid-ninth centuries CE, that work commenced to establish clearer distinctions and definitions in the Islamic sciences. Muslim scholars were influenced in this context by Aristotelian logic, which concerns itself with defining the essences of things. This type of logic exerted such dominance over the Muslim mind that, in the words of al-Ghazālī (d. 505 AH/1209 CE), it became "the standard of knowledge," the rule by which understanding was measured. It was believed that this system of logic would enable one to define the essences of things in a manner that was at once comprehensive and exclusive. However, al-Ghazālī and a number of other scholars contested this notion. Ibn Taymiyyah (d. 728 AH/1328 CE) in particular boldly contested Aristotle's system and sought to replace it with a Qur'anic approach to the definition of things.

Adoption of the Aristotelian approach to concept definition wreaked havoc on Islamic thought. It obfuscated the definitions of terms and concepts in virtually all fields of Islamic study, including the hadith sciences, whose later scholars failed to distinguish between the concepts employed by *uṣūl* scholars and jurists, and between commentators' and hadith scholars' understanding of the Sunnah. Among earlier scholars, by contrast, these concepts had been clearer, more precise, and more consistent with the Qur'an than the definitions around which such controversy raged later. Note, for example, the definition of the Prophetic Sunnah offered by al-Shāṭibī (d. 790 AH/1388 CE):

> The word *sunnah* is used to refer to that which has come down to us on the authority of the Prophet, particularly in relation to things about which there is no explicit Qur'anic text but which were addressed by the Prophet himself, whether as a clarification of something in the Qur'an or for some other purpose. The term is also used in contradistinction to the word *bidʿah*, or religious innovation. One might say, for example, "So-and-so is 'on the Sunnah' (*fulān ʿalā al-sunnah*)," meaning that he or she acts in

> keeping with the example of the Prophet, whether or not the person's action is explicitly called for in the Qur'an. Conversely, one might say, "So-and-so is 'on an innovation' (*fulān ʿalā bidʿah*)," meaning that he or she acts contrary to the example of the Prophet, whether or not such a person's action is explicitly prohibited in the Qur'an.
>
> This usage of the word *sunnah* appears to have been in specific reference to the actions of the one who brought the Law of Islam, even if these actions were applications of the Qur'an. The word *sunnah* was also used to refer to the practices of the Prophet's Companions (whether or not such practices were found in the Qur'an and the example of the Prophet, and whether or not they were passed down to us in the form of written accounts), or to interpretations on which the Companions or their successors collectively agreed. For their consensus was considered binding; their successors' practices were likewise based on this consensus and, hence, on an agreement to require people to adhere to these practices based on their view of what was in society's best interests.

What Imam al-Shāṭibī says here about the critical issues he raises conveys his personal understanding of the Sunnah. He may have arrived at this understanding in response to certain controversies raging at that time around Sunnah-related questions. Be that as it may, his statement reveals the depth of the chasm that had come to separate the thought and jurisprudence of earlier thinkers from that of later thinkers and, thus, the effects of time on ideas and concepts.

As we have seen, such boundaries and definitions are founded upon Aristotelian thought, which erroneously gives terms truth value irrespective of their meaning and significance on the concrete level. At the same time, they reflect the point of view of the individual engaged in the defining process and his or her way of understanding the entity to be qualified or defined. Such an individual will attempt to interpolate elements into the definition in order to make it unvarying, universal, preclusive, and beyond reproach. And since this was an impossibility, there was never-ending controversy over any definition that happened to be proposed. A cursory glance at any book from this era treating matters of jurisprudence, the fundamentals of jurisprudence, logic or scholastic theology will suffice as illustration of the wars that raged over virtually every definition proposed. Consequently, numerous concepts – including that of *sunnah* – were defined in ways that diverged from the Qur'anic understanding of them.

At this point we will examine the various stances that have been taken on the matter of chronicling the Sunnah. We shall begin by identifying the attitude adopted by the Messenger of God himself toward this process, which had serious implications for how the concept of *sunnah* would be approached.

[SECOND]
A Look at Hadiths That Address the Matter of Recording Narrated Reports in Writing

Hadiths That Regard the Chronicling of Reports as Undesirable

Abū Saʿīd al-Khudrī reported that the Messenger of God had said, "Write nothing down on my authority. Whoever records anything but the Qur'an on my authority must erase what he has written."

Another account reads, "We asked the Prophet for permission to write down [the things he said and did], but he did not grant it."

Zayd ibn Thābit once went to see Muʿāwiyah ibn Abī Sufyān and asked him about a certain hadith, whereupon Muʿāwiyah instructed someone to write it down. In response Zayd said to him, "The Messenger of God has commanded us not to write down any hadiths about him." There are also other hadiths with a similar purport.

Hadiths That Regard the Chronicling of Reports as Permissible

ʿAbd Allāh ibn ʿAmr ibn al-ʿAṣ said:

> I used to write down everything I heard the Messenger of God say, since I wanted to memorize it. However, members of the Quraysh tribe (that is, Muslims who had emigrated from Makkah to Madinah) forbade me, saying, "Are you writing down everything you have heard from the Messenger of God even though he is merely a human being who sometimes speaks in anger, and at other times speaks in approval?" So I stopped writing things down. But when I mentioned this to the Messenger of God, he pointed to his mouth and said, "Go on writing, for by the One who holds my soul in His hands, nothing but truth has ever passed these lips."

Abū Hurayrah once said, "None of the Prophet's Companions has related more accounts on his authority than I have. The only exception is ʿAbd Allāh ibn ʿAmr, who writes things down, whereas I do not." In a similar vein, Anas ibn Mālik said, "The Messenger of God said, 'Record knowledge in writing.'" Additional hadiths with a similar purport could be cited as well.

The Chronicling of Hadiths During the Lifetimes of the Prophet's Companions

During the era of the rightly guided Caliphs, it was clear to Abū Bakr, ʿUmar ibn al-Khaṭṭāb and other Companions and jurists well-versed in the Qur'an that it was not permissible to write hadiths down or to narrate excessive numbers of them lest people be distracted from the Qur'an, which should be the primary foundation upon which Muslim character is based on the levels of intellect, emotion and conduct. Al-Ḥākim related in his *sanad* on the authority of al-Qāsim ibn Muḥammad that ʿĀ'ishah said:

> My father (Abū Bakr) collected 500 hadiths that had been narrated on the authority of the Messenger of God. He tossed and turned that night, and the next morning he said to me, "Bring me all the hadiths in your possession." So I brought them to him, whereupon he called for a fire to be lit, and burned them. After this, ʿUmar ibn al-Khaṭṭāb addressed the people, saying, "O people, I have been informed that there are books among you. The books most pleasing to God are those that are the fairest and most accurate. Therefore, any of you who has a book in his possession must bring it to me so that I can make an assessment of it." Thinking that he simply wanted to examine the books and correct them in light of established facts, the people brought them to ʿUmar without hesitation. When he received them, however, he burned them..."

ʿAbd Allāh ibn Masʿūd said, "All we wrote down during the Prophet's lifetime was the prayer for guidance (*ṣalāt al-istikhārah*) and the testimony recited during the five daily prayers (*al-tashahhud*)." Similarly, Abū Mūsā did not like to have his son write down the things he had said for fear that he might have unintentionally added something to his accounts or omitted something from them. So he took water and rubbed out everything his son had written.

These and other accounts narrated on the authority of the Prophet's Companions make clear that the Companions were aware of the need to adhere to the Qur'an as the molder and shaper of Muslim character, and to view the guidance offered by the Prophet in proper relation to the Qur'an. They were to clarify the way in which the Prophet applied and recited the Qur'an and how he taught the Qur'an to others and used it to refine their characters. At the same time, they were to take care not to lead people away from the Book of God. It is a well-known fact that whatever is first established in one's mind, heart and behavior will take priority over any later influences. One's bedrock attitudes and behavior will then be the standard against which one measures and corrects everything else. Similarly, everything other than or subsequent to the Qur'an was to be accepted or rejected based on the extent to which it agreed, or disagreed, with the Qur'an's teachings, and was to be interpreted in light of the understanding gleaned from the Qur'an.

An analysis of the causes underlying divisions, sectarianism, and other ills that afflict the Muslim community today serves as a reminder of the fact that the weaker people's relationship to the Qur'an is, the greater will be their tendency to fragment their religion and to split into factions and parties. Those who cling to the Qur'an, perform regular prayers, and strive to keep the unity God has given them will fortify themselves against disputes and disunity. And conversely, those who abandon the Book of God and busy themselves with other things will never experience true unity in mind or in heart. Hence, we call upon the Muslim community to begin measuring everything other than the Qur'an against the Qur'an. For as they do so, they will be embracing the path of deliverance.

Chronicling of the Hadiths During the Lifetimes of the Companions' Successors

Some of the leading Successors of the Companions, including ʿUbaydah ibn ʿAmr al-Salmānī, Ibrāhīm al-Nakhʿī and others, refrained from writing down hadiths. ʿUbaydah in particular would not allow anyone to write things down in his presence; nor would he allow anyone to read to him. He once advised Ibrāhīm, saying, "Beware of passing down anything I have said in written form." Before his death,

ʿUbaydah had his books brought to him, and then burned them. Al-Shaʿbī said, "Never have I written anything down, nor have I ever heard a man narrate a hadith and wanted him to repeat it to me. Someone once told Jābir ibn Zayd, "They are writing down your opinions." Offended, he replied, "Will you record something that I might go back on tomorrow?" There are numerous other statements and events of relevance to this theme. However, we have cited these by way of illustration. Concerning the spread of the practice of recording hadiths in the late first and early second centuries AH, Abū Qilādah has been quoted as saying:

> ʿUmar ibn ʿAbd al-ʿAzīz once came out for the noon prayer carrying a piece of paper. Then he came out to join us for the mid-afternoon prayer carrying the same piece of paper. "O Commander of the Faithful," I asked, "what is that in your hand?" He replied, "It is a hadith that was narrated to me by ʿAwn ibn ʿAbd al-ʿAzīz which I liked and decided to write down."

However, no one before the reign of Caliph ʿUmar ibn ʿAbd al-ʿAzīz has ever been reported to have said that the Prophet abrogated the hadith in which he forbade others to record the Sunnah.

The Chronicling of Hadiths in the Second Generation of Successors

When, in the generation that followed al-Zuhrī (d. 124 AH/741-42 CE), the command to write down the Sunnah was officially announced, there were some who argued that this practice was undesirable. Al-Ḍaḥḥāk ibn Muzāḥim wrote forebodingly, "A time is coming when there will be so many hadiths in circulation that the Qur'an will lay forgotten and gathering dust." In a similar vein al-Awzāʿī lamented:

> Such knowledge was honorable when it flowed from the mouths of men who were receiving it and studying it amongst themselves. But when it was relegated to books, its light was extinguished, and it passed into the hands of people who were unworthy of it.

A practice common to some Successors of this generation was to write hadiths down temporarily in order to memorize them. Then, once the hadiths had been memorized, they would erase them. This practice had also been adopted by many of the earliest generations of pious Muslims such as Sufyān al-Thawrī, Ḥammād ibn Salamah and others.

Others by contrast are reported to have both collected and recorded hadiths. Among the first to collect hadiths were Ibn Jurayj (d. 150 AH/767 CE), al-Layth ibn Saʿd (d. 175 AH/791-92 CE), Imam Mālik (d. 179 AH/795-56 CE), Ibn al-Mubārak (d. 181 AH/797 CE), and Sufyān ibn ʿUyyaynah (d. 198 AH/813-814 CE). All of these men belonged to a single generation, and their method involved collecting hadiths passed down on the authority of the Messenger of God and combining them in a single book with sayings of the Companions and fatwas issued by the Successors.

Support For, and Opposition to, the Recording of Hadiths

God did not assign the task of preserving the Qur'an to any human being, not even to His Prophet. Rather, He took this task upon Himself, causing it be preserved through its own arrangement, inimitability and eloquence. This process I am terming "preservation from within." The Prophet stressed the importance of writing down the Qur'an, while placing equal emphasis on not writing down the Sunnah. Before writing down a hadith, the Companions were expected to request the Prophet's permission, which he might grant in one situation but not in the next.

The hadiths according to which it is permissible to record the Sunnah indicate that each situation must be judged on its own merits. The small number of individuals to whom the Prophet granted permission to write down hadiths were those whom he knew for certain to have absorbed the teachings, linguistic style and higher purposes of the Qur'an so fully into their minds and hearts that there would be no danger of them confusing the Qur'an with anyone else's statements.

However, the prohibition against recording hadiths was not simply due to the concern lest the Qur'an be confused with other sources of input, since the Arabs of that day had such a thorough command of the Arabic language on the levels of rhetoric, style and grammar that such admixture or confusion would have been virtually unthinkable. Indeed, they were keenly aware of the distinctiveness of the Qur'anic text from that of narratives and reports passed down from the Prophet himself. The concern to record the Qur'an at the very moment at which it was revealed served as clear evidence that the Qur'an was a text which was not to be subjected to any change whatsoever, whereas the Sunnah, by contrast, was for the most part simply a practical clarification that informed people of the ways in which the Prophet had applied the Qur'an and/or approved or explained particular actions. The Sunnah's purpose did not necessitate that its text be preserved word for word as in the case of the Qur'an. This is why the Companions and early Muslim scholars judged it permissible to paraphrase the Sunnah, and why they preferred that it be preserved not in written form, but in people's hearts and minds, since this would prevent it from becoming a sacrosanct text that might compete with the Qur'an for people's attention and allegiance. The focus at that time was therefore not on the Sunnah's linguistic structures, but on the meanings it conveyed.

As for those who held that it was, in fact, permissible to record the Sunnah, they were overgeneralizing the application of decisions the Prophet had made in response to certain exceptional circumstances, situations, and cases of urgent need. Given the unusual nature of such situations, they implied no change in the Prophet's stance against the adoption of another text alongside the Qur'an that would serve as a parallel source of authority, whether such a text was deemed equal in status to the Qur'an, or of a lesser status.

Those who classed the Sunnah as the second source of Islamic legislation hoped to refute this anticipated objection – that is, the question of how they could place alongside the Book of God another, parallel text that was independent of it and equal to it in authority. It was as if they wanted to say: "Since we have given the Sunnah second place rather than first, no blame should attach to this. For as can be seen, the matter has nothing to do with status per se. Rather, it has to do with textual reliability and the weight a text enjoys as evidence for or against this or that argument." In other words, it was a given that what could be shown to have originated with the Messenger of God was binding upon every Muslim. Hence, it was not a question of whether or not the Prophet's interpretations or applications of the Qur'an were authoritative but, rather, of how the narratives conveying these interpretations and applications had been handed down. Herein lies the wisdom exhibited by the Messenger of God, his Companions and his rightly guided Caliphs in adopting the bedrock principle that nothing but the Qur'an was to be written down.

Another purpose for the prohibition against narrating and recording hadiths was to prevent a confusion between divine ordinances, which the Prophet enforced on a practical level in other people's presence, and the human aspect of the Prophet's life, including his day-to-day conduct and the interpretations he arrived at in various capacities, including that of imam, judge, reformer, advisor and the like. As for divine ordinances, the Prophet's role was to convey them on God's authority as revealed to him in the Qur'an; he was also the first person to carry out whatever God had commanded him while urging his community to emulate his example in this connection. Hence, he was the model and exemplar in obedience to God, adherence to God's revelation, and inviting others to believe in it and obey it.

However, the Prophet's words, actions, or affirmations of others' words and actions were generally not witnessed by more than a few of his Companions who, none of them being infallible, might have remembered events inaccurately or related them in inconsistent ways. Add to this the fact that in keeping with the approach established by the Qur'an, the Messenger of God wanted to limit the number of required actions to the extent possible while maximizing the range of what was permitted. Hence, given the fact that over time, solitary accounts took on more and more binding authority, thereby increasing the burden of do's and don'ts in the process, it is better to allow everything other than the Qur'an simply to remain part of the oral culture of Islam and, as such, peripheral to the Qur'an.

The Emergence and Development of Hadith Narratives

a) The Circumstances Surrounding the Emergence of Hadith Narratives

Hadith narratives emerged in response to newly arising questions that called urgently for answers. As the era of the rightly guided Caliphs came to an end, there came about a hitherto unknown split between religious-intellectual leadership on one hand, and political leadership on the other. One of the most significant distinguishing features of the first four Caliphs' reigns, particularly during the lifetimes of Shaykhs Muslim and al-Bukhārī, was the inseparability of these two spheres of leadership – the religious-intellectual and the political. Not one of the first four Caliphs, political though his functions were, stood in need of a jurist or scholar to teach him his religion. Rather, each of them was at once a religious scholar and a political leader in his own right. It was he who guided his officials and judges, showing them what would, or would not, be consistent with the message of Islam in both letter and spirit, since he himself was an imam qualified to engage in ijtihad. The four rightly guided Caliphs had no need of scholars to issue religious rulings for them and tell them what would or would not be acceptable under Islamic law. But with the end of the rightly guided Caliphate, this union of political authority and religious-scholarly authority would likewise come to an end.

As positions of power were occupied by leaders of the Umayyad clan with plenteous stores of narratives to relate and with a fair understanding of Islamic jurisprudence, people were encouraged to narrate more and more accounts from the life of the Prophet and to glean legal rulings from them in response to newly emerging societal conditions. As a consequence, hadith narratives became increasingly intertwined with juristic and theological questions. This led in turn to the emergence of pointed disputes which were met with force on the part of the new caliphs.

In the midst of these events, Umayyad Caliph ʿAbd al-ʿAzīz ibn Marwān began considering the idea of collecting hadith narratives in the hope that they would provide an alternative to the conflicting juristic opinions and rulings that were now sowing division and anarchy among members of the Muslim community. The Sunnah was imbued with an air of authority that the views of jurists, however scholarly, lacked. For, being an explanation of the Qur'an, the Sunnah was, at least in the case of its well-authenticated narratives, inseparable from the Qur'anic text, whereas the same could not be said of the science of jurisprudence. Caliph ʿAbd al-ʿAzīz entertained the hope that as the Sunnah was joined with and confirmed by the Qur'an, it would clarify and resolve the issues over which individual members and factions of the Muslim community were in such disagreement. When ʿUmar succeeded his father ʿAbd al-ʿAzīz, restoration of the Muslim community's unity was his prime concern, as a result of which he initiated a serious dialogue with all of the factions against whom previous Umayyad Caliphs had declared war. Among these factions were the Kharijites and others. In addition, ʿUmar ordered the collection and examination of all hadith narratives and other traditions, his aim being to provide the Muslim community with a jurisprudence that would enable them to stop depending on jurists and their rulings, minimize the causes for the many disputes that had arisen among them, and bring them back to a focus on the Qur'an.

However, ʿUmar ibn ʿAbd al-ʿAzīz did not live long enough to complete these ambitious projects. Worse still, the hadith narratives the Caliph had set out to collect were exploited by his successors as an additional means of sowing discord. Some of these successors treated the Sunnah as parallel to the Qur'an. They lauded it as a text that not only contained everything found in the Qur'an, but was distinguished from the Qur'an by the fact that it offered more detail. Being both an exposition of the Qur'an and an application of its teaching, the Sunnah specified what was stated in the Qur'an only in general terms, and qualified matters couched by the Qur'an in absolute terms. With this in mind, al-Awzāʿī (d. 157 AH/774 CE) went so far as to assert that "the Sunnah stands in judgment over the Qur'an" and that "the Qur'an needs the Sunnah more than the Sunnah needs the Qur'an." As we saw earlier, it was in response to assertions such as these that Aḥmad ibn Ḥanbal declared, "I would not dare make such claims. Rather, I would say simply that the Sunnah explains and clarifies the Qur'an."

In response to unrest both internal and external, new societal and religious developments, pressures exerted by the confluence and interaction of varied cultures and civilizations, and acceptance of the peculiar maxim that "while the verses of the Qur'an are finite, the situations the Qur'an must address are infinite," there had arisen a certain atomistic mentality that could no longer see the organic unity between the Qur'an and the Sunnah, and which looked to the latter for the tools and mechanisms necessary to provide the juristic output required by changing circumstances.

Hence, the Sunnah was not a text that had been recorded in the generation that witnessed the Qur'anic revelation, nor had the Messenger of God mandated anyone to record it. In fact, when the Prophet learned of the portions of the Sunnah that some individuals had written down, he ordered them erased. It need not be concluded from this that the Prophet viewed his words and actions as carrying no weight as evidence in relation to juristic rulings and that, therefore, they had nothing to do with Islamic legislation and the development and guidance of the Muslim community. However, he wanted to ensure that Muslims' thoughts and attitudes would be shaped first and foremost by the Qur'an.

b) The Evolution of Narrative

The generation that was contemporary with the Prophet came to be known as "the generation of reception," the generation that followed it was known as "the generation of narrative," and the generation following it was known as "the generation of jurisprudence." In fact, however, there is overlap among these three generations. In the "generation of reception," which witnessed the death of the Apostle, narratives were already in circulation. However, most of those who heard these narratives were able to verify their accuracy through direct contact with the Apostle himself. Consequently, despite the circulation of narratives during that time period, people's emulation of the Prophet was still based for the most part on direct observation of him and his life. As for the generations of narrative and jurisprudence, they overlapped to a significant extent. Nevertheless, there remained issues and questions that related specifically to jurisprudence rather than to narratives. After all, scholars with the capacity to master both the field of jurisprudence (fiqh) and that of narratives (hadith) were limited in number, as a result of which there emerged a dangerous phenomenon that might be termed, "the fiqh-hadith rift." Manifesting itself initially in 40 AH/660 CE, this rift contributed to the formation of the schools that came to be known as "The People of Opinion" and "The People of Hadith." Despite the unwholesome effects to which this phenomenon gave rise, seekers of knowledge benefited from it in certain technical and educational respects.

In the beginning of the narrative phase, neither Islamic (religious) narratives nor historical and literary narratives were always treated with the greatest of care. Sometimes, for example, a narrative would have no *isnād*, or chain of transmission, but no one would ask about it until social conditions had drawn attention to its absence. Ibn Sīrīn (d. 110 AH/729 CE) tells us:

> No questions were asked about the chain of transmission until the time of the *fitnah*. At that point they said, 'Name your narrators for us.' If the narrators were found to be orthodox, the hadith in question would be accepted. If, on the other hand, the narrators were found to be unorthodox (religious innovators), their account would be dismissed.

It appears from the context that the *fitnah* mentioned by Ibn Sīrīn refers to the strife caused by the emergence of certain religious innovations and heretical claims. In his book, *Al-Imām Mālik*, Amin al-Khuli tells us that until the death of Imam Mālik in 179 AH/795 CE, the *isnād* was still not being used in a systematic fashion as we see it being employed by al-Bukhārī, for example, in the third century AH. Al-Bukhārī lived more than two generations later, and two strata of hadith scholars later. This may help to explain why, among the accounts passed down by Mālik and scholars before him, we find so many hadiths with chains of transmission that go only as far back as one of the Successors to the Companions. The plethora of hadiths in this category (referred to as *mursal*), whose reliability has been a subject of disagreement among *uṣūl* scholars appears to have resulted from the fact that in the generations that followed immediately upon the lives of the Companions, scholars saw no need to mention the specific Companion with whom an account had originated.

From the foregoing it may be seen that Islamic sciences have passed through three stages. (1) The "oral culture" phase: Oral traditions included Sunnah narratives, as well as the Qur'an itself, which was the only text at that time to have been committed to writing. Everything else, with a small number of exceptions, was being circulated orally at this stage. (2) The collection and recording phase, during which oral accounts began to be collected and written down. During this phase, hadiths and other traditions originating with the Companions were collected in books of Qur'anic commentary, jurisprudence, and the like. (3) The sorting and categorization phase. This phase was marked by a process of distinguishing among different types of knowledge, and by the appearance of what came later to be known as "the principles of the sciences" on the basis of which each science or academic discipline was recognized as having its own distinct definition and focus.

c) ʿUmar ibn ʿAbd al-ʿAzīz's Collection of the Sunnah in Historical Context

When ʿUmar ibn ʿAbd al-ʿAzīz became Caliph, the Muslim community was being racked by one division after another. Wanting to mend the rifts and regain the allegiance of factions that had broken with the larger community, he commenced his reform efforts by opening a dialogue with the Kharijites. He conceded their points on some issues while correcting on others, with the result that some of them returned to the fold.

Explaining what ʿUmar aimed to achieve through the collection and recording process, Abū Zurʿah al-Dimashqī wrote:

> ...ʿUmar ibn ʿAbd al-ʿAzīz sought to unify the people's understanding of things, be it in the form of legal rulings or scriptural interpretations...In each Muslim metropolis and army there were individuals who had been Companions of the Messenger of God. Among these were judges who issued rulings that had been approved by the Apostle's Companions as well as by the cities' inhabitants... To these rulings, then, they continued to adhere.

What this passage shows is that as the Muslim head of state at the time, ʿUmar ibn ʿAbd al-ʿAzīz's aim was, by having the Sunnah collected and written down, to make it into a law that would be binding on the members of the Muslim community. This view is supported by the fact that al-Zuhrī and others collected not only hadiths that were attributed to the Apostle but, in addition, biographies of the Companions, some of whom were among the rightly guided Caliphs and all of whom were qualified jurists. This approach which ʿUmar ibn ʿAbd al-ʿAzīz referred to in many of his sermons, points clearly to a practical understanding of the Sunnah as including the Companions' applications of the Qur'an.

ʿUmar ibn ʿAbd al-ʿAzīz and others at that time saw the need to collect hadith narratives in order to provide the Muslim community with a source of proper Qur'anic interpretation and application. The purpose in so doing was to clarify the way in which the Prophet had applied the teachings of the Qur'an so that Muslims would be able to emulate his example, and to settle disputes and disagreements and restore unity to the Muslim community. To this end, ʿUmar instructed Muslim scholars throughout his Caliphate to collect hadith narratives. He sent similar instructions to his regional governors, including Abū Bakr ibn Muḥammad ibn ʿAmr ibn Ḥazm (d. 117 AH/735 CE), saying, "Find hadith narratives relating the things done and said by the Messenger of God, as well as those describing the ongoing practice of the Muslim community. Then write them down, for I fear that knowledge will be obliterated with the disappearance of those who possess it."

The best example of the kind of Sunnah collection that ʿUmar ibn ʿAbd al-ʿAzīz hoped to carry out may be found in *Al-Muwaṭṭa'* by Imam Mālik ibn Anas. In what follows I present a description of the approach Imam Mālik followed in this work of his.

d) The Method Adhered to by Mālik ibn Anas in Al-Muwaṭṭa'

Imam Mālik's *Al-Muwaṭṭa'* is viewed as the earliest well-authenticated collection of Islamic learning in the fields of both hadith and fiqh. Concerning this work, Imam al-Shāfiʿī wrote, "I know of no scholarly book more correct than that of Mālik." Abbasid Caliph Jaʿfar al-Manṣūr (d. 158 AH/775 CE) once said to Imam Mālik:

> Write a book whose contents I can require people to adhere to... O Abū ʿAbd Allāh, compile this knowledge and record it in books. In so doing, avoid the austerities of ʿAbd Allāh ibn ʿUmar, the dispensations promoted by Ibn ʿAbbās, and the anomalous practices taught by Ibn Masʿūd. Strive instead for a path of moderation, encouraging people to adopt practices that were agreed upon by the Companions.

ʿUmar ibn ʿAbd al-ʿAzīz and Abū Jaʿfar al-Manṣūr were thus in agreement concerning the importance of compiling knowledge that went back to the time of the Companions in Madinah. ʿUmar had instructed Abū Bakr ibn Ḥazm to undertake such a collection, while Abū Jaʿfar al-Manṣūr instructed Imam Mālik to do the same. Given that Imam Mālik may already have seen the need to record knowledge from the Madinan community for fear of its being lost, the Caliph's request would have provided him with additional motivation to do so. Moreover, the caliphs who succeeded him held the same view. Hārūn al-Rashīd (d. 193 AH/809 CE), for example, required the judges under his Caliphate to rule in accordance with the teachings found in Mālik's *Al-Muwaṭṭa'*. In praise of Mālik's virtues, al-Suyūṭī relates that when Hārūn al-Rashīd requested that *Al-Muwaṭṭa'* be widely distributed, Mālik objected, saying, "O Commander of the Faithful, the fact that scholars hold differing opinions is a divine blessing upon the Muslim community."

Hence, one finds a visible common thread connecting what Umayyad Caliph ʿUmar ibn ʿAbd al-ʿAzīz sought to accomplish by collecting the Sunnah in his day, and what Imam Mālik did in *Al-Muwaṭṭa'* with encouragement from Abbasid Caliph Hārūn al-Rashīd. In both cases, their aim was to unify the judiciary by eliminating differences among the judges and governors in the various regions of the caliphate. In other words, they strove to standardize Islamic jurisprudence by providing judges with a written record of the actions and words of the Messenger of God, his Companions, the early Caliphs, and those who succeeded them – particularly those in Madinah who understood the Sunnah to be the practices they had inherited from the Prophet and his Companions. Governors and judges would thus have an authoritative point of reference in governance, administration of the judiciary, and issuance of legal rulings. The principle aim was thus not simply to undertake a haphazard collection of accounts but, rather, to organize the state legally and to encourage an insightful examination of the Prophet's actions and words that would guide people in emulating his example. It bears noting here that both ʿUmar ibn ʿAbd al-ʿAzīz and Imam Mālik were adherents of the Madinah school, which ultimately adopted a practical understanding of the Sunnah.

Mālik was among the best-attested narrators of hadiths originating in Madinah on the authority of the Messenger of God, with the most trustworthy chains of transmission. He was also among the most knowledgeable about the issues of concern to ʿUmar ibn al-Khaṭṭāb and the sayings of ʿAbd Allāh ibn ʿUmar, ʿĀ'ishah, and the seven jurists who served as advisors in Madinah to Caliph ʿUmar ibn ʿAbd al-ʿAzīz.[2] Together with a number of others, Mālik established the science of hadith narratives.

A question might arise as to how to categorize *Al-Muwaṭṭa'*: Does it belong to the realm of hadith, or fiqh? Different answers have been given to this question. Those who place emphasis on the numerous hadiths which Mālik cites in this work classify it as a book of hadith, whereas others classify it as a work of Islamic jurisprudence due to is juristic focus. In my view, *Al-Muwaṭṭa'* is best classified as a work dealing with what I would term the jurisprudence of the Sunnah (*fiqh al-sunnah*), as it attempts to answer juristic questions based on hadith narratives relating words and actions that would serve as the basis for juristic rulings.

In *Al-Muwaṭṭa'* Mālik has sought to bring together well-attested hadith narratives passed down by inhabitants of the Hejaz. These were combined with sayings by the Companions and their Successors, as well as the Successors' Successors. When he first wrote the book, it contained approximately ten thousand hadith narratives. Every year he would review it and delete some of its contents. Ibn ʿAbd al-Barr quotes Mālik as saying, "Here is a book that I took forty years to write, and which you have read in forty days. How little you understand of it!" Al-Suyūṭī wrote saying that "No *mursal* hadith is cited in *Al-Muwaṭṭa'* without at least one *ʿāḍid*, or support from another source."

e) Al-Muwaṭṭa' and Ṣaḥīḥ al-Bukhārī

In his introduction to *Ṣaḥīḥ al-Bukhārī*, Ibn Ḥajar (d. 853 AH/1449 CE) wrote:

> Some imams deem it problematic to ascribe the same authenticity to Mālik's book as they do to al-Bukhārī's even though both scholars imposed strict conditions for acceptance of a hadith as sound, and both went to great lengths to ensure the reliability of the hadiths they approved. The fact that al-Bukhārī included more hadiths in his collection than Mālik did does not mean that he should be given priority in terms of authenticity. Mālik, however, did not view a discontinuous chain of transmission as sufficient cause

> to call a hadith's authenticity into question. Hence, his collection includes hadiths that are classified as *mursal* and *munqatiᶜ*, as well as hadiths referred to as *balāghāt*, that is, hadiths whose chains of transmission contain the phrase *balaghanī min fulān* (meaning, "It came to my hearing through so-and-so…").

As for al-Bukhārī, he viewed a discontinuous *isnād* as a weakness which would disqualify a hadith from inclusion in his collection. He only listed hadiths with discontinuous *isnāds* in his introductory or marginal comments. Some hold that a hadith with a broken *isnād* may still be valid as legal evidence. However, hadiths with unbroken *isnāds* are still stronger provided that all the narrators in both cases are upright individuals known to have had reliable memories. On this basis, al-Shāfiᶜī rightly described *Al-Muwaṭṭa'* as being of greater authenticity than the comprehensive hadith collections of his day such as the *Jāmiᶜ* of Sufyān al-Thawrī (d. 161 AH/778 CE), the *Muṣannaf* of Ḥammād ibn Salamah (d. 167 AH/783 CE) and others. In this respect, al-Dāraquṭnī (d. 306 AH/918 CE) and others ranked *Al-Muwaṭṭa'* above the *Ṣaḥīḥ* compiled by Abū Bakr ibn Khuzaymah (d. 311 AH/924 CE). In his book *Al-Madkhal ilā Maᶜrifat al-Ṣaḥīḥ*, al-Ḥāfiẓ al-Ismāᶜīlī states:

> I have studied *Al-Jāmiᶜ* by Abū ᶜAbd Allāh al-Bukhārī, and I find it to be truly comprehensive, as its title suggests. In addition to containing numerous authentic hadith narratives, *Al-Jāmiᶜ* offers well-expressed interpretations that can only be properly understood by those with a solid knowledge of hadiths and their narrators, the science of narratives and their defects, and jurisprudence and language.

Al-Bukhārī recorded nothing but accounts which he deemed by his rigorous standards to be fully trustworthy and authentic. Consequently he avoided having to mention numerous hadiths that supported rulings that were inconsistent with his views. For, by virtue of his having demonstrated these hadiths' inauthenticity, they were rendered too weak to be used as evidence against his position.

Mālik wrote *Al-Muwaṭṭa'* after the manner of the Hejazis; as such, he set forth the sources of legal rulings derived from hadiths of agreed-upon authenticity and divided the material into chapters based on a variety of juristic topics. In explanation of his method and terminology, Imam Mālik wrote, "This book presents narratives from the life of the Messenger of God, sayings of the Companions, sayings of the Companions' Successors, and opinions that reflect the consensus of the Madinan scholars, from which I have not departed." He then expounds his method of reasoning from the evidence, saying:

> ...What I have written here reflects the practice of people in my region, and the contents of rulings issued among us which are known to the learned and ignorant alike. Similarly, it reflects statements which I have heard from men of knowledge in my region, and which I deem to be good and true. On matters about which I have heard nothing, I have formulated my own independent judgments by investigating matters in light of the juristic school adhered to by those whom I met. In the process I have sought to arrive at the truth, or a close approximation thereof, lest what I say be in violation of the views of the adherents of the Madinah school.

Memorizers of the Qur'an concerned themselves with learning hadiths' various paths and chains of transmission, "some of which are Hejazi, some of which are Iraqi, and some of which are from elsewhere." As for al-Bukhārī, he arranged hadiths by category and compiled the chains of transmission passed down by the Hejazis, the Iraqis, and inhabitants of the Levant, approving whatever hadiths they had agreed upon and omitting those over which they had differed. He would also cite and discuss the same hadith under a number of different headings, each time highlighting those aspects of the hadith in question that were relevant to the heading under which it was cited.

In his *Ṣaḥīḥ*, Muslim (d. 261 AH/875 CE) adopted the same approach as that of al-Bukhārī before him by including hadiths of agreed-upon authenticity; he omitted any repetitions, compiled their chains of transmission, and divided his material into chapters dealing with selected juristic themes. Nevertheless, al-Bukhārī's and Muslim's collections did not include all authentic hadiths, and for this they were criticized by those who asserted that their conditions for accepting a hadith as authentic were too strict. Abū Dāwūd, al-Tirmidhī and al-Nasā'ī then compiled their own collections, which included not only hadiths classified as authentic (*ṣaḥīḥ*) but, in addition, hadiths that fulfilled what are known as "conditions for practical application" (*shurūṭ al-ʿamal*), hadiths classified as "good" (*ḥasan*) and others as well. In so doing, these compilers set out to provide a complete guide to the Sunnah and its application, and their works are among the officially recognized classics in the realm of hadith collection.

f) Al-Bukhārī's Juristic Approach to the Formulation of Section Titles

In a discussion of al-Bukhārī's method of titling the sections of his hadith collection, Ibn Ḥajar wrote:

> Let us provide an overview of various types of section headings. Some of these deal with the surface meanings of the text, others with its underlying meanings. Our purpose here is not to focus on these types of headings. Rather, our intent is simply to ensure that whatever heading we use is consistent with the content of the text in question. The benefit to be derived from the heading lies in communicating the general content of what follows it without regard for specific details. Al-Bukhārī might state, for example, that a section contains such-and-such, or that it offers evidence for such-and-such a particular ruling.
>
> The section heading may use the same words found in the text being presented. Alternatively, it might employ only some of the same words, or simply be a loose paraphrase. When a loose paraphrase is used, it may indicate that the text to follow has more than one meaning, in which case the compiler identifies one of the two possible meanings as the more likely to be the correct one based on what is cited of the hadith that follows. The hadith might, on the other hand, contain words or phrases that support the very opposite interpretation, such that the possibility of more than one meaning inheres in the hadith, while the section heading specifies the meaning clearly. The section heading is thus a clarification of the underlying meaning of the hadith. As such, it plays the role of a jurist, for example, who might tell us that a hadith that appears to be general in nature is actually specific in its application or that a hadith that appears to be specific in nature actually has general application, thereby indicating that there is an element shared in common by the situation at hand and another, analogous, situation ruled on previously, or that the specific principle being conveyed by the hadith has a wider application than what appears on the surface... The same interpretative phenomenon that occurs in relation to the specific and the general may likewise occur in relation to the unqualified and the qualified, simplifying what is problematic, clarifying what is vague, revealing

the underlying layer of a text's apparent meaning, or detailing the undetailed. This situation is reflected in most of the section titles in this book.

According to a well-known statement by certain illustrious scholars, "al-Bukhārī's jurisprudence is found in his section titles." This is particularly the case in situations in which al-Bukhārī had found no unambiguous hadith meeting his conditions for authenticity in relation to a particular juristic topic or question. In order to provoke thought on the issue at hand and to reveal meanings hidden in a text, al-Bukhārī would frequently allude to a hadith cited elsewhere (earlier or later in the book) that explained a certain point. He also tended to phrase his section headings in the form of questions, his purpose being to show whether a given ruling was founded on the evidence or not. In some cases, the evidence would refute the ruling; in other cases it would support it, and in still others, it would lend support to two opposing views, but in differing degrees. Al-Bukhārī would deliberately leave room for further investigation by drawing attention to some uncertainty or contradiction that would require one to abstain from supporting one view over another. He might have believed, for example, that the hadith was unspecific in nature, or that what was understood from it would differ based on how one reasoned from the evidence. He frequently used a section heading which, at first glance, yielded little meaning. For example, one heading reads, "If a man says, 'We missed the ritual prayer (*fātatnā al-ṣalāh*, meaning literally, 'the ritual prayer passed us by').'" This section heading is an indirect response to those who deem it undesirable to use this phrase, and who prefer instead for one to say, "We failed to perform the ritual prayer on time" (*lam nudrik al-ṣalāh*). He would also use section headings that applied to specific situations, but whose meaning was not immediately apparent. One such heading reads, for example, "On whether an imam should clean his teeth with a twig in the presence of his congregation." At one time, cleaning one's teeth with a twig was considered something one shouldn't do in public. However, this view was reconsidered based on a hadith, first pointed out by Ibn Daqīq al-ʿĪd (d. 701 AH/1302 CE), in which the Prophet cleaned his teeth with a twig in others' presence.

Al-Bukhārī frequently uses a chapter heading in which he alludes to the meaning of a hadith that does not qualify as authentic according to his standards. At other times he makes explicit reference in the chapter heading to such a hadith. In the discussion that follows, he sometimes makes direct reference to the hadith's contents, and sometimes indirect reference. An example is the chapter entitled, "The Chapter on the Chieftains of Quraysh" (*bāb al-umarā' min quraysh*). This comes directly from a hadith narrated on the authority of ʿAlī ibn Abī Ṭālib which does not fulfill al-Bukhārī's conditions for authenticity. It is as if al-Bukhārī were saying, "There is nothing on this topic that meets my conditions for authenticity." And given that his readers might not have appreciated this fact, he left the book in draft form. Shaykh Nāṣir al-Dīn Aḥmad ibn al-Munīr, preacher of Alexandria, collected and discussed four hundred section headings from this work, which were also summarized by Badr al-Dīn ibn Jummāʿah (d. 733 AH/1333 CE). The topic was taken up briefly by Muhammad ibn Manṣūr ibn Jummāʿah, whose work entitled, *Fakk Aghrāḍ al-Bukhārī al-Mubhamah fī al-Jamʿ Bayna al-Ḥadīth wa al-Tarjamah* contains only around one hundred section headings. As for Zayn al-Dīn ʿAlī ibn al-Munīr (d. 695 AH/1296 CE), he discussed the matter at length in his commentary on al-Bukhārī (*Al-Mutawārī ʿan Tarājim al-Bukhārī: Sharḥ al-Jāmiʿ al-Ṣaḥīḥ li al-Bukhārī*). I have come across one volume of a work by Abū ʿAbd Allāh ibn Rashīd al-Sabtī entitled, *Turjumān al-Tarājim ʿalā Abwāb Ṣaḥīḥ al-Bukhārī*, which shares a similar aim, and which covers up to al-Bukhārī's chapter on Fasting. Given the quality of this man's work, he would have done us a great service had he finished this book.

It is clear, then, Mālik and al-Bukhārī each had distinct, cogent juristic views which revealed themselves through their respective works, *Al-Muwaṭṭa'* and *Al-Jāmiʿ al-Ṣaḥīḥ*. Similarly, from among the hadiths whose texts and chains of transmissions fulfilled their criteria for authenticity, each of these scholars cited those narratives that supported his juristic views. In this respect, Mālik and al-Bukhārī differed from most of their contemporaries. For while many other hadith transmitters' prime concern was simply to compile and record narratives, be they accounts handed down on the authority of the Apostle or the views of his Companions and Successors such as Ibn Abī Shaybah

(d. 235 AH/850 CE) and others, Mālik and al-Bukhārī approached hadiths from a legal perspective, viewing them as the foundations for a properly grounded Islamic jurisprudence.

CONCLUSION

The Outcomes of the Chronicling Process

The question that now arises is: Can the term *sunnah* be used to refer to what resulted from the process of recording the various accounts and reports attributed to the Prophet? This question, of course, has to do with the huge number of narratives that were compiled for us by Muslim scholars and recorded by hadith transmitters.

In answer to this question, it should first be remembered that the process of collecting the Sunnah was the fruit of a tremendous collective effort. However, it remains, in the end, a human effort subject to human limitations, uncertainties and a degree of speculation. No one can say for certain that the process encompassed every authentic hadith or that it prevented the recording of any weakly attested hadiths. Hence, it must be asked: How can people be expected to commit themselves religiously to something we may not be able to know in the first place, or which might turn out to be weakly attested or even a forgery? This question is rendered all the more pointed by the fact that the recording process we are talking about only began in earnest in the mid-second century AH, and was not completed until the third century AH.

The laborious enterprise which the chronicling process entailed had major consequences. For one thing, the number of Islamic legal rulings multiplied several times over, and this legacy, which was now passed down from one generation to the next, became the most salient component of every Muslim's religious instruction and upbringing. For another thing, narrators and transmitters had effectively turned the Sunnah into an investigation into which sayings could accurately be attributed to the Messenger of God, and which could not. In other words, whereas during the lifetimes of the Prophet and his Companions, the Sunnah had been comprised of the concrete practices of the Messenger of God in application of what had been revealed to him, the concept of the Sunnah then expanded to include everything the Prophet was reported to have said, done, or even approved. This modified and broadened understanding of the Sunnah, formulated by scholars of various academic disciplines based on the terminology proper to their respective fields of study, was a departure from the concept found both in the Qur'an and in Arabic lexicons. The revised understanding of the Sunnah reflected changing temporal and geographical factors that helped to define more precisely which of the practices and statements recorded in the hadiths contained binding legal rulings for the entire Muslim community, and which of them had been relevant only to those individuals to whom they were initially related or addressed. Similarly, it helped to clarify which accounts represented individual human responses on the part of the Prophet whose full dimensions would have been known only to those who had a direct role to play in them.

The things the Prophet said and did, he said and did in response to specific situations that arose in people's daily lives; none of them occurred in a vacuum. Hence, they were necessarily tied to practical situations of one sort or another. This is one of the most significant aspects of the distinction that must be made between the Qur'anic text, which for the most part contains universal principles, and the 'prophetic text,' which issued for the most part from concrete, changing circumstances.

When the hadith narratives portraying the life of the Prophet came to be viewed as themselves constituting the Sunnah, messages that had once been specific to defined situations came to be viewed as though they were intended for general application. However, most of the things the Prophet did and said were not only responses to specific, concrete situations, they were also, and no less importantly, reflections of his humanness. The Qur'an commanded the Prophet on numerous occasions to declare openly that he was only a human being. And in fact, he took care to emphasize this fact. As we noted in the incident related earlier by ʿAbd Allah ibn ʿUmar, who would write down everything he heard the Prophet said in order to memorize it, he was chided for this by fellow Muslims, who reminded him that the Prophet's words might be influenced by human emotion.

Consequently, the Prophet's humanness disqualifies many of his words and actions from being treated as the basis for binding legislation. He made this point explicitly clear in the well-known incident in which he expressed the view that the pollination of palm trees was not a useful practice, after which he reconsidered what he had said in light of his lack of knowledge about such matters, saying, "I am only human. So if I instruct you to do something relating to your religion, do as I say. But if I instruct you to do something based on my opinion, then remember that I am a mere human being." In another version of the same account, the Prophet was quoted as saying, "You all know best how to handle your worldly affairs." And in still another we read, "If I have supposed something to be true, do not take me to task for a mere supposition. But if I tell you something on God's authority, then act on it, for I would not lie about God."

Herein lies the greatness, and earthiness, of this religion. Herein lies its fitness for all times and places. For here we find the Prophet himself drawing a decisive distinction between his abilities as Prophet and his abilities as mere human being, between personal opinion and religious instruction, between human attempts to discern truth and divine revelation, between worldly affairs and spiritual affairs, between what he says on his own behalf and what he says as God's representative. There exists, then, both revelation from God, which is binding as a religious duty, and earthly matters about which experts in the field concerned know best.

What we might term the 'methodology of transmission' (*manhajiyyat al-naql*) has dominated not only the field of hadith studies, but virtually all of the sciences relating to Islamic tradition and law. *Isnād* methodology was thus seen as the ideal means of purging the hadith collections of all that was inauthentic, since it would make it possible for people to place their full confidence in accounts that had been passed down via well-attested chains of transmission. What many failed to realize was that, applied in isolation, the *isnād* method cannot provide complete certainty. On the contrary, certain individuals made it their profession to fabricate hadiths' chains of transmission just as they fabricated their texts. If they heard a statement they approved of, they would simply create an *isnād* for it. As Saʿīd al-Dimashqī once said, "If someone says something laudable, what is wrong with manufacturing an *isnād* for it?"! Such people knew, of course, that reputable hadith scholars would only approve a hadith for inclusion in their collections if it had what they thought to be a sound *isnād*.

Most of those who worked so diligently to collect the sayings of the Prophet were, no doubt, motivated simply by the desire to preserve the Apostle's legacy, to pass on knowledge they had been entrusted with, and to use these narratives as a kind of substitute for the Prophet's physical presence to which they no longer had access. Be that as it may, once the hadith corpus came into being, it became the subject of a science in its own right, and the basis for Islamic jurisprudence. With this development, the Muslim community entered the phase of 'juristic production' in which Muslim legal scholars had to sift through thousands upon thousands of hadith narratives. Their task now was to ascertain which hadiths were reliable and, therefore, valid as the basis for Islamic legal rulings. If a hadith was judged to be reliable, one was required to adhere to it as law, and if any jurist objected to or rebelled against such a conclusion, the sincerity of his faith would immediately be called into question. In fact, he might even be accused of outright unbelief.

The Muslim scholarly community was thus split into two camps: the 'People of Opinion' and the 'People of Hadith.' At the same time, the three groups comprised respectively of political figures, ascetics/mystics, and *ʿulamā'*, or academics, intensified their efforts to flesh out the life of the Apostle in a way that would attenuate the harsh reality of his absence. The Qur'an had prepared the way for the Prophet's loss in the following words, which were addressed to the stunned and grieving ʿUmar ibn al-Khaṭṭāb and his fellow Companions: "Muhammad is only an apostle; all the [other] apostles have passed away before him: if, then, he dies or is slain, will you turn about on your heels? But he that turns about on his heels can in no wise harm God – whereas God will requite all who are grateful [to Him]" (*Sūrah Āl ʿImrān*, 3:144). The same state of affairs was addressed by Abū Bakr, who declared, "To anyone who worships Muhammad, let it be known that Muhammad is dead, and to anyone who worships God, let it be known that God is alive forevermore." Hence although these factions grudgingly resigned themselves – at least theoretically – to the Prophet's absence, they seem to have reserved the right to reject it in their hearts. As a result, jurists, *uṣūl* scholars, and scholastic theologians alike attempted to compensate for the Prophet's absence by reiterating, circulating, and passing down accounts of events from his life.

As the Muslim community began committing its oral cultural memories to writing in the mid-second century AH, the Qur'an was largely marginalized. As far as the Muslim laity were concerned, the Qur'an was ambiguous and susceptible to numerous interpretations. Hence, although the Qur'an was viewed as a major miracle, the only portion of it which was viewed as vitally important consisted in somewhere between 240 and 340 verses. Apart from these, the recorded Sunnah of the Prophet now became the primary text in dialogue with which the Muslim community's "cultural memory" was to be molded. It was the hadiths that now served as the source from which the principles of Islamic jurisprudence were to be gleaned and as the basis for legal rulings on specific situations. So pivotal had the hadiths become that it was now possible to rely on them to the exclusion of all else, and impossible to dispense with them in favor of anything else.

In consequence, the Qur'an's role in Muslims' lives was greatly diminished, their relationship to it now being restricted to recitation for the purpose of earning heavenly reward and gleaning moral lessons. The hadiths thus became the actual material out of which the Muslim mentality was shaped – until, that is, the hadiths themselves were superseded by a preoccupation with still other sources, about which we will have more to say in what follows.

6

The Authoritativeness of the Reporting of the Sunnah

The Authoritativeness of the Sunnah

IN ITS CAPACITY as the binding elucidation of the Qur'an through the words and actions of the Prophet as heard and witnessed by the first generation of Muslims, the Sunnah is viewed as authoritative by necessity, and this authoritativeness is beyond dispute among Muslims everywhere. However, controversy has arisen over the authoritativeness of the Sunnah *as reported*. The question is: Should a communication or report concerning an action or statement by the Prophet be granted the same legal status as the action or statement itself? Can such a report or communication be the basis for a binding legal ruling originating with God?

The Muslim community would agree unanimously that God is the sole Lawgiver and Governor, and that the authority to promulgate laws for human beings is one manifestation of His divinity. Hence, when we affirm the authoritativeness of the Prophet's Sunnah and Muslims' obligation to recognize this authority, we are acknowledging implicitly that in order to be truly authoritative, a report or communication of something the Prophet did or said must be shown beyond reasonable doubt actually to have been done or said by him. This does not mean, however, that the Prophet himself was the source of his own authority, or that he was the actual promulgator of the laws he established through this words and deeds.

So how is it that obedience to the Prophet can be said to be tantamount to obedience to God? Since God requires us to obey the Apostle, as when He states in *Sūrah al-Nisā'*, "O you who have attained to faith!

Pay heed unto God, and pay heed unto the Apostle" (4:59; see also 5:92, 47:33 and 64:12), does this not mean that the Apostle is a ruler as well, and that the commands and prohibitions which he issues are not from God, but directly from him? When God commands us to "pay heed unto the Apostle," He is commanding us to do whatever the Prophet tells us to do. From these observations we might derive two principles. The first is an obligation imposed by God to surrender to the Apostle, while the second is the obligation to act, which is imposed by the Apostle. Therefore, one might conclude, the Apostle is a ruler in his own right.

Not so, however. Rather, the Ruler requiring action in obedience to the imperatives issued by the Apostle is God alone; the Prophet is merely the conduit through which the imperatives come. The words, "pay heed unto the Apostle" mean that if the Apostle issues a command or a prohibition, it is God who requires the Muslim to do what the Apostle has commanded or to refrain from what he has prohibited. An example of such a situation is the Prophet's statement: "When the sun crosses the meridian at your location on earth, I require you to perform the noon prayer." Were it not for God's command to obey the Apostle, his injunctions would not be binding upon us. For although he may appear to be a ruler and commander in his own right, the actual Ruler and Commander is God alone.

[FIRST]
The Authoritativeness of the Sunnah and Reports Thereof in the Generation Contemporary to the Prophet, and the Narrative Generation

Muslim scholars agree that the validity of the use of a hadith narrated on the Prophet's authority in support of a religious doctrine or legal ruling depends on two things. The first is the ability to demonstrate with certainty that the account in question did, in fact, originate with the Messenger of God. And the second is the ability to demonstrate that the account in question was passed down from the Messenger of God in an unquestionably reliable manner. The first condition applies to all generations without exception. As for the second condition, it applies only to those generations that rely on accounts that have been passed down from person to another – that is, the generation of the Companions' Successors and all generations since. The "narrative generations" include the Companions who had not yet reached puberty at the time of the Messenger of God's death. As for the Companions who were adults during the Prophet's lifetime, some of them may have heard the Prophet say certain things with their own ears, or seen him perform certain actions with their own eyes. In such cases, the second condition cited above would have no relevance, since the person citing the statement or action had witnessed it directly. As for those who were the Prophet's contemporaries but who were not present in Madinah at the time of a given incident, they would have needed to verify their occurrence through accounts they had heard from eye witnesses. So in this sense, they would be in the same position as the Companions' Successors and those who succeeded them.

The validity of narratives passed down on the authority of the Prophet has been the subject of significant disagreement among Muslim scholars, who have held widely divergent views on the method by which one needs to verify that a given hadith was actually passed down on the Prophet's authority. According to some scholars, no method can guarantee with even a reasonable degree of certainty that a given account about the Prophet's sayings or actions is accurate and reliable. Consequently, they deny the validity of acting on anything that has been passed down on the Prophet's authority. Such scholars essentially reject all reports about the Prophet's words and deeds, not because they actually believe that the Prophet did not do or say these things, nor because such reports have no use as evidence in argumentation, but, rather, because the accuracy and reliability of such reports cannot be proven. Our purpose here is not to detail these debates or to argue in favor of one view or another. However, we have alluded to them briefly in the hope of clarifying to readers that these disagreements have not revolved around the authoritativeness of the Sunnah itself.

Leading Jurists and Their Approaches to the Sunnah

The following presents a brief look at the approaches taken to the

Sunnah by six Muslim scholars: Imam Abū Ḥanīfah, Imam Mālik, Imam al-Shāfiʿī, and Imam Aḥmad ibn Ḥanbal from the Sunni schools, and from among the Shiites, Imam Zayd ibn ʿAlī, and Imam Jaʿfar al-Ṣādiq.

1. *Imam Abū Ḥanīfah (d. 150 AH/767 CE)*

Abū Ḥanīfah was accused of violating the Sunnah, although he denied the charge. When Abbasid Caliph Abū Jaʿfar al-Manṣūr wrote to him saying, "Word has it that you place higher priority on analogical reasoning (*qiyās*) than you do on the hadiths!" Abū Ḥanīfah replied:

> It is not as you have heard, O Commander of the Faithful. Rather, I work first on the basis of the Book of God. I then turn to the Sunnah of the Prophet and, after this, to the legal rulings issued by Abū Bakr, ʿUmar, ʿUthmān, and ʿAlī. Lastly, I look at the legal rulings issued by the other Companions of the Prophet. Only if there is disagreement among these do I resort to analogical reasoning. And God remains exalted above His creatures.

In the Hanafites' view, a hadiths that has not gained wide circulation (and has thus not been classified as *mashhūr* or *mustafīḍ*) is of only tentative value. As such, it neither specifies what is stated generally in the Qur'an, nor qualifies what the Qur'an has stated in absolute terms.

Abū Ḥanīfah would reject a solitary hadith (*āḥād*) if: (1) its content was in conflict with the overall message or apparent meaning of the Qur'an; (2) it contradicted other, widely circulating hadiths; (3) the narrator of the hadith was not a jurist or scholar of Islamic jurisprudence; (4) the narrator, after passing on the hadith, acted in a manner contrary to the hadith's content; (5) it dealt with punishments or means of atoning for serious offenses, since such measures lose their validity if they are subject to the slightest doubt, and the narrator may have lied or been mistaken in what he said; (6) some of the pious early Muslims had challenged its reliability; and (7) it had ceased to be employed in argumentation due to disagreement over it among the Companions. (The last condition was sufficient basis for rejection of a solitary hadith by some early Hanifite scholars, and most later ones).

2. *Imam Mālik (d. 179 AH/795 CE)*

Based on a reading of Imam Mālik's works, scholars of the Malikite school concluded that he had given the apparent meaning of the Qur'an priority over the Sunnah. In this respect Mālik was in agreement with Abū Ḥanīfah except in cases where the hadith in question was supported by something else. If such support was available, the hadith could be understood to provide specification for something stated generally in the Qur'an, or qualification for something stated by the Qur'an in absolute terms. For example, if a hadith was supported by the recognized practice of the Muslim community in Madinah (as in the case of the hadith prohibiting the consumption of fanged predators), it was to be deemed valid and acted upon. In his book, *al-Muwāfaqāt*, al-Shāṭibī listed a set of questions in relation to which Imam Mālik had given recognized human interests (*al-maṣlaḥah*) or other general principles priority over other considerations. On this basis he dropped solitary hadiths, since he viewed the principles he had adopted as being of indubitable certainty, whereas the hadith he had rejected, he viewed as providing tentative certainty only.

At the same time, Mālik accepted hadiths classified as *mursal* as well as so-called *balāghāt*, and even cited them as the basis for legal rulings, even though it was he who had been so exacting in his criteria for deciding which narratives to accept as valid. Mālik would approve hadiths with broken chains of transmission if he had heard them from someone whom he trusted and whom he had chosen precisely because he qualified as a reliable source based on Mālik's stringent list of criteria for trustworthiness. The demanding process by which Mālik vetted the men from whom he would accept hadiths in the first place gave him confidence in the accounts they related to him. His decision to approve hadiths with broken chains of transmission was thus based on personal considerations, and not only on methodological ones.

Mālik stipulated that a solitary hadith could only be rejected based on evidence of definitive certainty; he also stipulated that the hadith in question not be supported by any other evidence (in the form of a well-authenticated text or principle). If these two conditions were not met, a solitary hadith could not be rejected simply because it only had one narrator. Moreover, definitive evidence can only be rejected if it is opposed by some other piece of evidence which is equally, or more, definitive than the evidence in question. It bears noting here that Mālik understood the Sunnah to consist of practices of the Prophet's Companions. He observed, for example, that when ʿUmar ibn ʿAbd al-ʿAzīz wanted to spread knowledge of the Sunnah, he ordered the collection of the legal rulings that had been issued by the Prophet's Companions.

The Qualitative Classification of Mālik's Statements in Al-Muwaṭṭa'

Imam Mālik sometimes used the term *sunnah* in *Al-Muwaṭṭa'* in a sense close to that given for it in Arabic lexicons, that is, in the sense of a plan or a method. However, when he used it to refer to actions and statements attributed to the Apostle, he would accompany it with expressions that had become more or less obsolete in juristic circles. In particular, he tended to marshal a plethora of superlatives, describing the practices he was citing in clarification of this or that Qur'anic verse as "the best thing I have ever heard.," "...the most remarkable ruling ever made..." and the like. Hence, it is apparent from the rather flowery expressions Mālik introduced into his usage of the term that he was not employing the word *sunnah* in a formal or technical sense, since such language was more or less unheard of in juristic writings.

As for the matter of consensus (*al-ijmāʿ*), Imam Mālik makes reference to it both indirectly, as when he speaks of "that which is agreed upon" (*al-amr al-mujtamaʿ ʿalayhi*), or "things about which there is no dispute" (*alladhī lā khilāfa fīhi*) and directly, as when he states his belief that his book reflects "the consensus of the Muslim community in Madinah" (*ijmāʿ ahl al-madīnah*). As used by Mālik, then, the term *ijmāʿ* refers not to some general consensus of the Muslim community everywhere but, rather, specifically to that of the community in Madinah. As for the phrases "that which is agreed upon" (*al-amr al-mujtamaʿ ʿalayhi*) and "things about which there is no dispute" (*alladhī lā khilāfa fīhi*), Imam Mālik uses them when reasoning from the Qur'an. Therefore, Mālik's understanding of the term *ijmāʿ* cannot easily be equated with the understanding of it which developed subsequently among *uṣūl* scholars. He defines *ijmāʿ* specifically as the consensus of the Muslim community in Madinah, since it was they who had inherited the Sunnah of the Prophet and passed it down in their turn to others. The Madinan community was more knowledgeable than anyone else of the rulings that best reflected the Prophet's legacy and the sources from which these had been derived. Consequently, Mālik set out to collect the hadiths that had been passed down by the Madinans and the fatwas that had been issued by the Companions who were residents of Madinah and who had lived during the period when the Qur'an was revealed. He then recorded these in *Al-Muwaṭṭa'*.

3. *Imām al-Shāfiʿī (d. 204 AH/819-820 CE)*

As discussed in Chapter Three, al-Shāfiʿī devoted an entire section of his book *Al-Risālah* to the five levels of the process of *bayān*, or elucidation of the Qur'an.

In addition, al-Shafiʿī stipulated rigorous conditions that had to be met in order for a solitary hadith to be deemed acceptable. These conditions were as follows: (1) The narrator must be trustworthy, known for his piety and honesty. (2) He must understand the events that occurred well enough that he can either word them in more than one way, or pass on the account verbatim, exactly as he heard it. (3) He must have memorized the narrative in the written form in which he possesses it. (4) He must actually have heard the account from the person he claims to have heard it from. (5) The hadith must not contradict some other hadith on the same topic which has been passed down by trustworthy people of knowledge. (6) The previous conditions must be met at every level of the *isnād* reaching all the way back to the Prophet, or to a Companion or one of his Successors.

It should be remembered that the debates raging in al-Shāfiʿī's time between the People of Opinion and the People of the Hadith had produced a good deal of confusion in relation to the way in which the concept of *sunnah* was understood and employed. As we observed earlier in the writings of Imam Mālik, the People of Opinion would only accept a hadith if it was (a) classified as *mashhūr*, (b) the subject of unanimous agreement among scholars (*mujmaʿ ʿalayhi*), and (c) consistent with the practice of the Muslim community in Madinah. The

People of Opinion would reject any solitary hadith which failed to meet these criteria or which conflicted with the apparent meaning of the Qur'an. In defense of the People of the Hadith, al-Shāfiʿī marshaled evidence to demonstrate that the Sunnah could serve as a valid basis for Islamic legal rulings even if it was in the form of solitary hadiths, provided that the individual who had passed the hadith down could be shown to be trustworthy. The evidence cited by al-Shāfiʿī was compiled in *Al-Risālah*, while his debates with his opponents are recorded in *Al-Umm*.

The intellectual skirmish that took place between al-Shāfiʿī and his challengers marked the beginning of the shift in which the Sunnah ceased to be understood in its original sense and came to be defined as the hadiths and reports narrated by hadith transmitters in keeping with specific criteria. Al-Shāfiʿī emerged so victorious from this battle that he was dubbed "defender of the Sunnah."

4. *Imam Aḥmad ibn Ḥanbal (d. 241 AH/855-56 CE)*

According to Ibn al-Qayyim, Imam Aḥmad viewed the Sunnah as the second half of the primary source of Islamic teaching, that is, the Qur'an. The wisdom in this position is easily discernible, since the Sunnah is what elucidates and completes the Qur'an. Therefore, there should be no contradiction between them, and if there appears to be some conflict, it will be subject to resolution. Moreover, Imam Aḥmad more than once expressed the view that Muslims should seek enlightenment about their religion through the Sunnah.

As a hadith transmitter Imam Aḥmad was keen to write his *Musnad* to be a guide to people. He wrote nothing in the field of jurisprudence, nor did he dictate anything on this topic to his students. In fact, he was unwilling for anything to be passed down on his authority in this area. However, his students persuaded him to let them pass on his thoughts in the area of jurisprudence, and he may well have spent his younger years approving what was passed down and verifying the correctness of its attribution to him.

The majority view among Muslim scholars has been that solitary hadiths are acceptable as the basis for practice, but not as the basis for belief or doctrine. However, Imam Aḥmad accepted solitary hadiths as the basis for belief as well. Nor did he require the narrators from whom he received accounts, whether orally or in writing, to fulfill the stringent conditions that had been set by Abū Ḥanīfah and Mālik. At the same time, he established a rule according to which he was sometimes lenient in relation to the *isnād* and sometimes strict. In this connection he wrote, "If the hadith in question has to do with virtuous actions and the reward they bring, I am lenient with its *isnād*; if, however, it has to do with religious duties, prescribed punishments and means of atonement, I am strict."

Imam Aḥmad only included in his *Musnad* accounts narrated by individuals whom he deemed trustworthy, upright, God-fearing and truthful. He would only reject a hadith due to criticism of its content if it was in conflict with some other hadith judged to be authentic; however, he did not require that a hadith be compared to the Book of God. Rather, he viewed the Sunnah as explanatory of the Qur'an and its meaning. In a letter to Musaddid ibn Musarhid al-Baṣrī, he wrote:

> We define the Sunnah as the accounts that have been passed down on the authority of the Messenger of God. The Sunnah explains the Qur'an by clarifying its meanings. The Sunnah is not to be approached through the use of analogical reasoning, nor is it to be understood, whether via reason or on the basis of whim or fancy. Rather, one is simply to follow it, leaving personal desire and caprice behind.

In Imam Aḥmad's day, hadiths were classed as either well-authenticated (*ṣaḥīḥ*) or weak (*ḍaʿīf*). A third category included hadiths classed as good (*ḥasan*), as well as weak hadiths which, if they had been passed down via multiple lines of narrators, had been raised to the status of 'good.' According to Ibn Taymiyyah, the first person ever known to have divided hadiths into the three classes of well-authenticated, good and weak was al-Tirmidhī. Explaining what he meant by these terms, al-Tirmidhī defined 'good,' or *ḥasan*, as a hadith with multiple lines of narrators, none of whom had ever been accused of lying, and which was not inconsistent with any other hadith which had already been approved as trustworthy. By weak, or *ḍaʿīf*, he referred to a hadith whose transmitter had been accused of lying and was not good at memorizing. If a hadith had been narrated by an unknown individual, it was feared that he might be untruthful or weak at memorization. However, if the narrator was in agreement with some other narrator from whom he had not transmitted his account, it could be concluded that if he had transmitted an untruth, it was not done deliberately.

Imam Aḥmad's *Musnad* contains weak hadiths because, in keeping with the practice of his contemporaries, he wanted to include in his compilation everything that had been narrated on the authority of those of his generation. He thus compiled everything he received from the narrators of that period, and only rejected an account if he had proof that there was another, already approved, hadith that conflicted with it. In other words, as we are told by his son ʿAbd Allāh, Imam Aḥmad would not reject anything he had received unless there was a related hadith that refuted it.

Imam Aḥmad was known never to give analogical reasoning priority over a hadith, even if it was a weak report, as long as he had no evidence of its being forged. On this point he was in agreement with his teacher, al-Shāfiʿī, who had held that in dealing with hadiths there is no room for personal opinion. However, Imam Aḥmad went even further than al-Shāfiʿī, who had not been willing to recognize any weak hadiths whatsoever. So, while [al-Shāfiʿī] gave [sound hadiths] priority over opinion, [Aḥmad] gave them priority over analogical reasoning as well]. In clear contrast to Aḥmad's and al-Shāfiʿī's approaches – and particularly that of Aḥmad – Abū Ḥanīfah and Mālik are known to have given priority to analogical reasoning over solitary reports.

As an example of how these scholars decided what hadiths to accept or reject, let us take the hadiths classified as *mursal* by way of illustration. Hadiths classed as *mursal* were among the types of hadiths that had been used in legal argumentation. Such hadiths were defined in two different ways. Hadith transmitters used the term *mursal* to describe a hadith whose chain of transmission is unbroken as far as one of the Companions' Successors, who then attributes the hadith directly to the Messenger of God without mentioning the name of the Companion through whom he received the hadith in question. Jurists of that era, by contrast, used the term *mursal* to describe any hadith whose chain of transmission was not continuous all the way back to the Messenger of God, whether the break was at the point of a Companion or anywhere else in the transmission process.

The authoritativeness of hadiths classed as *mursal* as the basis for legal rulings has long been a subject of disagreement among Muslim scholars. The majority view among the jurists who established the four Sunni schools of jurisprudence (Abū Ḥanīfah, Mālik, al-Shāfiʿī and Aḥmad ibn Ḥanbal) was that such hadiths were admissible as evidence in favor of legal rulings. Some of them admitted such hadiths without exception; others even placed them on a par with well-founded hadiths (*musnad*). Still others gave them a lower status than well-founded hadiths, and still others, while placing them on a level lower than that of well-founded hadiths, laid down conditions for their acceptance. It is in this last category that we find al-Shāfiʿī.

5. *Imam Zayd Ibn ʿAlī (d. 122 AH/740 CE)*

The Zaydite school vis-à-vis the Sunnah: Solitary hadiths

According to the Zaydite school, solitary hadiths provide only tentative certainty. Consequently, they can be relied on as a basis for practical rulings, but not for doctrine. When reasoning from evidence, the Zaydites view solitary reports as lower in status than both the Qur'an and hadiths classed as *mutawātirah*. As for all other hadiths, they can lend specificity to general statements in the Qur'an. The reason for this is that specifying or restricting the meaning of a text is not the same as abrogating it but, rather, is a form of application. On this point, the Zaydites hold a position similar to that held by al-Shāfiʿī, who views specification simply as a form of elucidation. We read in *Al-Kāshif* that:

> solitary reports cannot be relied upon in relation to the fundamentals of the religion, definitive principles of jurisprudence, or principles of Islamic Law, because these things require full certainty, whereas solitary reports yield only partial certainty.

Zaydite conditions for narrators of solitary reports

In order for a report to be deemed trustworthy by the Zaydites, the following conditions must be met by its narrator: (1) The narrator must be reputable and trustworthy, though it is not necessary that he be a Zaydite or a descendent of the Prophet. (2) The report must not relate to an obligation that is required of all morally accountable individuals, since obligations of this nature must be announced and passed on publicly and, therefore, must be transmitted via a report that is *mutawātir*, not solitary (*āḥād*). (3) Although the Zaydites do not stipulate that priority be given to accounts narrated by a Zaydite, an account narrated by ʿAlī ibn Abī Ṭālib would nevertheless be accorded higher status than an account attributed to any of the other Companions. (4) The Zaydites accept hadiths classified as *mursal* as long as the Successor in its chain of narration is trustworthy. If he was a mujtahid, his account will be given more weight than if he was not. This is the view of Abū Ḥanīfah and Mālik. As for al-Shāfiʿī, he would accept a hadith that was *mursal* on two conditions, while Aḥmad would have deemed it weak. (5) A narrator who was a *faqīh*, or scholar of Islamic jurisprudence, would be accorded greater reliability than one who was not.

6. Imam al-Ṣādiq (d. 148 AH/765 CE)

Overall, the Twelver Shiites seem to agree to a significant extent with the Shafiites' approach to the principles of jurisprudence. Imam al-Ṣādiq stated, "In the Qur'an, God sent down clarification of all things. He left out nothing that His servants might need. Hence, no one can say, 'If only such-and-such had been revealed in the Qur'an....'" In *al-Kāfī*, al-Killīnī (d. 319 AH/941 CE) wrote:

> Abū ʿAbd Allāh al-Ṣādiq said, "If you find that a hadith is supported by the Book of God or by something said by the Messenger of God, accept it. Otherwise, what you have already been given is more worthy of trust."

The Twelver Shiites also accept as valid the statement attributed to the Prophet:

> If you are told that I said a certain thing, compare the account to the Book of God. If it is consistent with the Book of God, then I said it, and if is not consistent with the Book of God, I did not say it. How could I go against the Book of God through which God Himself has guided me?

This hadith in paraphrase form is found in *al-Kāfī*. Imam al-Ṣādiq taught his students to identify the Qur'anic basis for whatever hadith they encountered saying, "If I narrate a hadith to you, ask me where it is supported in the Qur'an." It is clear, then, that Imam al-Ṣādiq viewed the Qur'an as the foundation for everything, and the Sunnah as that which clarifies the Qur'an.

The Twelver Shiites are divided into two camps on the matter of whether to accept solitary reports. Earlier Twelver Shiite scholars rejected such reports unless they were accompanied by unassailable evidence that the report could be attributed to the Messenger of God or to the infallible Imam. However, the majority of Twelver Shiite scholars recognize solitary reports, with some of them stipulating that the report must have been passed down by two or more narrators. On this point these scholars have adopted the view of Imam ʿAlīṢ, who insisted that in order for him to accept an account, it had to have been passed down by two or more narrators on the Prophet's authority.

The Twelver Shiites' acceptance of solitary reports also requires that: (1) the narrator be a Twelver Shiite, and (2) the person on whose authority the account was passed down also be a Twelver Shiite. Hence, if a Twelver Shiite transmits a solitary report on the authority of individuals who are not themselves Twelver Shiites, it will not be accepted as valid. The Twelver Shiites thus accept only those accounts that have come down through the descendants of the Prophet.

[SECOND]
The Hadith Sciences: 'Narrative' and 'Knowledge'

The study of hadiths is comprised of two branches – narration-based hadith science (*ʿIlm al-hadith riwāyatan*) and understanding-based hadith science (*ʿilm al-hadith dirāyatan*) – under which all knowledge of hadiths can be classed.

1. *What is Meant by the Word 'Science' (ʿIlm)?*

The concept of *ʿilm* rests on four principles: (1) strict adherence to method, (2) objectivity, or academic integrity, (3) the ability of the discipline's principles and premises to accommodate new developments, and (4) its capacity for self-renewal. Every discipline must be willing to monitor and revise its own discourse by critiquing it, discussing it, and adjusting it in light of facts and events. If the results it is yielding are inconclusive, this indicates a flaw in its method. The scientific spirit is embodied in an ongoing effort to pursue truth, and science can only advance through critique and revision, since it does not always rest on solid ground. As for the dictionary definition of the word *ʿilm*, generally translated as 'science,' it is synonymous with knowledge (*maʿrifah*) and understanding (*fahm*). If knowledge is marked by certainty, it is referred to as *ʿilm*.

Philosophers have used the word *ʿilm* to refer to the formation of an image of something in the mind; as such, it is a level of perception, other levels being, in descending order, surmise (*ẓann*), suspicion (*shakk*), and illusion (*wahm*). The opposite of *ʿilm* is ignorance (*jahl*), whether compound (in which the ignorant person thinks himself to be knowledgeable) or simple (in which the ignorant person knows himself to be ignorant).

This plethora of definitions and differences aside, *ʿilm* may be identified as perception or understanding, the realities perceived or understood, or the abilities and skills acquired by the individual engaged in the act of perceiving or understanding.

a) The First Sunni Scholars to Compile ʿIlm of Various Types

- Al-Ḥasan ibn ʿAbd al-Raḥmān al-Rāmihramzī (d. 360 AH/971 CE) in his book entitled, *Al-Baḥth al-Fāṣil bayn al-Rāwī wa al-Wāʿī*, which was preceded by a number of works on the same theme.
- Al-Ḥākim al-Nīsābūrī (d. 405 AH/1014-1015 CE), who wrote a book entitled, *Maʿrifat ʿUlūm al-Ḥadīth* in which he listed fifty types of *ʿilm*. However, the book was never edited into final form.
- Abū Naʿīm Aḥmad ibn ʿAbd Allāh al-Iṣfahānī (d. 430 AH/1038-1039 CE), who added to al-Ḥākim's book but did not do full justice to the topic.
- Al-Khaṭīb al-Baghdādī (d. 463 AH/1071 CE), who compiled rules of narration in his book *Al-Kifāyah*, and the protocols associated with narration in *Al-Jāmiʿ li Ādāb al-Rāwī wa al-Sāmiʿ*. Al-Khaṭīb al-Baghdādī devoted a written work to virtually every one of the hadith sciences, and all those who came after him were indebted to his works in this area. His successors include al-Qāḍī ʿIyāḍ, who

wrote *Al-Ilmāʿ ilā Maʿrifat Uṣūl al-Riwāyah wa Taqyīd al-Samāʿ*, and Al-Miyānjī, author of *Mā Lā Yasaʿu al-Muḥaddith Jahlahu.*

- Abū ʿAmr ʿUthmān ibn al-Ṣalāḥ al-Shahrazūrī (d. 643 AH/ 1245-1246 CE), who brought together the works of his predecessors in his book, *ʿUlūm al-Ḥadīth*. Better known as *Muqaddimat ibn al-Ṣalāḥ*, this work became the object of intense study. Commentaries on it were written and abridged versions of it were composed, with some opposing it and others defending it. Al-Shahrazūrī's work became the mainstay of hadith study for those who came after him, including al-Zarkashī (d. 794 AH/1392 CE), al-Zayn al-ʿIrāqī (d. 806 AH/1403-1404 CE), and Ibn Ḥajar (d. 852 AH/1448 CE). Ibn al-Ṣalāh's work was abridged by al-Nawawī (d. 676 AH/ 1271-1272 CE) in his books *Al-Irshād* and *Al-Taqrīb*. It was summarized by Ibn Jamāʿah (d. 734 AH/1333-1334 CE) in *Al-Manhal al-Rawī*, by Ibn Kathīr (d. 774 AH/1373 CE) in *Al-Bāʿith al-Ḥathīth*, and by al-Bulqīnī (d. 805 AH/1402-1403 CE) in *Maḥāsin al-Iṣṭilāḥ*.
- Al-Zarkashī wrote a book known as *Istidrākāt ʿĀ'ishah ʿalā al-Ṣaḥābah*, which is a significant contribution to the discipline of text criticism.
- Other abridged works dealing with the terminology employed by Sunni scholars include *Al-Iqtirāḥ* by Taqī al-Dīn ibn Daqīq al-ʿĪd (d. 702 AH/1302-1303 CE) and *Nukhbat al-Fikr* by Ibn Ḥajar al-ʿAsqalānī, who also wrote a detailed commentary on this work known as *Nuzhat al-Naẓar*.

b) ʿIlm as Understood by the Twelver Shiites

The first to compile knowledge from the Twelver Shiite perspective was al-Rāmihramzī, followed by Abū ʿAbd Allāh al-Ḥākim al-Nīsābūrī and Aḥmad ibn Ṭāwus (d. 673 AH/1274 CE), who established new Twelver Shiite terminology as it related to the division of hadiths into the three categories of *ṣaḥīḥ*, *muwaththaq*, and *ḍaʿīf*.

In the area of understanding-based hadith study we have ʿAlī ibn ʿAbd al-Ḥamīd al-Ḥusnī, who wrote *Sharḥ Uṣūl Dirāyat al-Ḥadīth*, also known as *al-Dāyah fī ʿIlm al-Dirāyah*. Another scholar who worked in this area was Abū Manṣūr Bahā' al-Dīn al-ʿĀmilī, who wrote *Al-Wajīz fī ʿIlm Dirāyat al-Ḥadīth*. Commentaries were written on this work by Hasan al-Sadr (*Nihāyat al-Dirāyah*) and Muḥammad Bāqir al-Dāmād (*al-Rawāshiḥ*). However, most of the Twelver Shiites' writings in the area of understanding-based hadith study took the form of chapters in books on the fundamentals of jurisprudence, or introductions to books on Islamic jurisprudence.

c) The Zaydites

Apart from minor differences, most Zaydite terminology was based on that of Sunni scholars. Among Zaydite hadith scholars we have Ibn al-Wazīr al-Zaydī (d. 840 AH/1437 CE), whose work entitled *Tanqīḥ al-Anẓār fī ʿUlūm al-Āthār* was explained by Muḥammad ibn Ismāʿīl, known as al-Amīr al-Ṣanʿānī, in his *Tawḍīḥ al-Afkār*. Al-Ṣanʿānī is also known for his *Subul al-Salām* and *Thamarāt al-Naẓar*, where he discussed the criterion of uprightness and good repute (*ʿadālah*) which hadith transmitters require a narrator to meet in order for his accounts to be deemed acceptable.

Ibn al-Wazīr penned another book entitled, *Al-ʿAwāṣim wa al-Qawāṣim fī al-Dhabb ʿan Sunnat Abī al-Qāsim*, and he summarized the former work in *Al-Rawḍ al-Bāsim*, which contains wide-ranging studies on hadiths and hadith-related terminology from the Zaydite point of view. Another relevant work by Ibn al-Wazīr is his *Qaṣab al-Sukkar Naẓmu Buḥūth Nukhbat al-Fikr li ibn Ḥajar*.

2. *Narrator-Based Hadith Study (ʿIlm al-Ḥadīth Riwāyatan)*

Early scholars defined the field to which we refer here as 'narrator-based hadith science' as "a discipline which concerns itself with the way in which hadiths are traced back to the Messenger of God, with an emphasis on their narrators' precision and moral character and a description of their chains of transmission (as *muttaṣil*, 'continuous,' *munqaṭiʿ*, 'broken' and the like). This discipline might also be referred as 'the fundamentals of hadith' (*uṣūl al-ḥadīth*) on the pattern of 'the fundamentals of jurisprudence' (*uṣūl al-fiqh*). As for later scholars – those who came after al-Khaṭīb al-Baghdādī (d. 463 AH/1071 CE) – they defined it as "a discipline that treats the transmission of sayings, actions, and attributes attributed to the Prophet, including sayings and actions of others to whom he lent his approval. Such actions include even gestures and times of stillness while waking or sleeping." Later Shiite scholars also replaced the phrase "the Prophet" with "the infallible one" (*al-ma*ʿ*ṣūm*).

The difference between these two definitions inheres in the fact that the earlier one takes as its subject the characters of hadith narrators without regard for the content of the accounts they narrated. The only exceptions to this rule were situations in which the content of the hadith might shed some light on the narrator's character. As for the later definition, it focuses on the content of the accounts transmitted about the Prophet. In sum, then, earlier scholars' focus of study was the characters of hadith narrators, while the focus of later scholars was the character of the Prophet. The scholar credited with establishing narrator-based hadith science was Ibn al-Shihāb al-Zuhrī (d. 124 AH/742 CE), who drew on everything that might help him to ascertain the strength or weakness of narrators' characters so as to determine whether their accounts should be accepted or not.

As for whether one was required to learn this science, the ruling was that given the existence of a good number of individuals with the capacity to acquire this skill, it would be deemed a collective duty, whereas it would be deemed an individual duty for those persons gifted with ability in this area, since the aims and benefits of such a discipline are evident.

3. *Understanding-Based Hadith Study (*ʿ*Ilm Ḥadīth Dirāyatan)*

Earlier scholars defined the field to which we are referring as understanding-based hadith study as "the discipline which concerns itself with the meaning being conveyed by the words of hadith narratives based on the rules of the Arabic language, the principles of Islamic Law, and the character of the Prophet." Its topic of study was the hadith narratives themselves; the sources on which it drew were Arabic morphology, grammar and the like, as well as the principles of jurisprudence. The discipline had been established by the Companions of the Prophet, who had studied his life, witnessed his words, actions and character traits and had then communicated these things to others as a means of elucidating the Qur'an and showing how to apply its teachings and emulate the Prophet. The Companions verified the accuracy of what they transmitted through a process of mutual correction which laid the groundwork for the method of text criticism that was developed by those who came after them. This discipline made it possible to determine, with reasonable or complete certainty, that the account in question was acceptable without qualification, acceptable given certain conditions, or unacceptable; in other words, whether it was fully authenticated (*ṣaḥīḥ*), weakly authenticated (*ḍaʿīf*), or inauthentic, that is, forged (*mawḍūʿ*).

Later scholars defined *ʿilm al-ḥadīth dirāyatan* as "a discipline by means of which one ascertains the character of both the narrator and that which is narrated so as to determine whether the account should be accepted or rejected." Based on the foregoing, one will see that the definition offered by earlier scholars allows for the study, critique and analysis of the text of a hadith so as to determine whether it is inconsistent with the Qur'an, the well-authenticated Sunnah, sensory experience, or any other known constant. All these matters are included, for earlier scholars, in the definition of 'understanding,' or *dirāyah*. As defined by later scholars, the discipline involves melding the study of the narrator with that which is narrated. Consequently, "narrator" and "understanding" are almost treated as one and the same thing. It may be for this reason that these scholars devoted most of their efforts to the study of chains of transmission and narrators' characters, and lent only secondary attention to text criticism. If the chain of transmission was judged to be sound, rarely was any effort expended on critiquing the hadith's content. Hence, a hadith's acceptance or rejection hinged primarily on its *isnād*.

However, critiquing the text of a hadith is just as important as, if not more important than, critiquing its chain of transmission, especially given the fact that many hadiths have been narrated in terms of their overall meaning rather than word for word. In fact, both earlier and later scholars laid down criteria for text criticism which can be induced from their writings and employed as the foundation for a methodology in which the two approaches – *isnād* criticism and *matn* criticism – complement and reinforce each other. If there is a flaw in the text (*matn*) of a hadith, this is more likely than not related to a flaw in one or more links of the chain of transmission (*isnād*) unless the same account was passed down through an additional, fully sound, line of narrators. Therefore, if a flaw appears in the *matn*, the hadith scholar will need to undertake a thorough, painstaking review of all the narrators who transmitted the account. As for the actual process of text criticism, we shall have more to say on this below.

At this point one might ask: Is it possible to view narrator-based and understanding-based hadith study as a single discipline? As we have seen, earlier scholars tended to view them as two separate fields of inquiry, each of which makes a distinct contribution to the researcher's final conclusions and the decision whether to accept or reject a hadith. Among later scholars, by contrast, we observe a tendency to combine the two lines of inquiry. This merger produces a kind of overlap which, in these scholars' view, is necessary given the interrelated nature of the conclusions one reaches. Nevertheless, I personally prefer the approach adopted by the earlier hadith scholars, who maintained a separation between narrator-based critiques and understanding-based critiques. My reason for this preference is that by maintaining this separation or distinction, we make it easier to employ the two approaches in a balanced and sound manner. As the saying goes, "Too many cooks spoil the broth." For as we have seen, the merger of these two approaches has often resulted in two much weight being given to *isnād* criticism at the expense of *matn* criticism.

4. *Division of Hadiths into the Twin Categories of Mutawātir and Āḥād*

For later Sunni hadith scholars, the Arabic terms *ḥadīth*, *athar*, *khabar*, and *sunnah* are synonymous, all of them referring to a report of something the Prophet or one of his Companions or their Successors said, did, or approved. This being the case, these four terms include not only hadiths attributed specifically to the Prophet (*marfū*ᶜ), but, in addition, those classified as *mawqūf* (attributed to a Companion) and *maqṭū*ᶜ (attributed to a Successor). Some scholars defined hadiths strictly as accounts that pertained to things said or done by the Prophet himself; hence, their definition excluded accounts that could be described as *mawqūf* or *maqṭū*ᶜ. Others, by contrast, held that an account referred to as an *athar* was, by definition, *mawqūf*. Some defined a hadith as something that relates specifically to something the Prophet said or did, and a sunnah as one that relates his words, actions, approval of others' words and actions, and character traits.

As for the Twelver Shiites, they defined all four terms above as referring to "an account that relates something which the Infallible One said or approved," where the title "the Infallible One" (*al-maʿṣūm*) could refer either to the Prophet or to one of the twelve imams. The term 'the Infallible One' might also be applied to someone who had been a companion to an Imam, or to a companion to one of his companions. As for the word *qawl*, it referred to "an action or approval on the part of the Prophet," and "an action on the part of an Imam." For most scholars, the term *qawl* is synonymous with the words *khabar* and *athar*, although the words *athar* and *khabar* might be used to refer to "that which was said or done by the Infallible One or by someone else." For these scholars, the term *ḥadīth* might refer to something someone had said, and the term *sunnah* to an action or the approval granted to something someone had done or said. The term *khabar* might be used to refer only to accounts describing the actions or words of someone not considered to be infallible, and the term *athar* to refer to a narrative passed down on the authority of an Imam or a companion.

a) Hadiths Classified as Mutawātir

Hadith scholars have differed over the definition of the term *mutawātir*. Some hold that whether a hadith is *mutawātir* depends on the number of narrators. Imam Ibn Ḥajar wrote:

> A hadith may be classed as *mutawātir* if it meets the following four conditions: (1) The number of individuals who narrated the account is so large that it would be virtually impossible for them to have colluded in deceit. (2) All individuals in the chain of narration are of equally unquestionable integrity. (3) The last individual in the chain of transmission physically witnessed the action or heard the statement in question. (4) The account in question conveys genuine knowledge to those who hear it.

Al-Khaṭīb al-Baghdādī defined the term *mutawātir* as referring to reports "which have been transmitted by a sufficiently large number of people that, upon seeing them, one would know that it would have been impossible for them to have agreed amongst themselves to lie."

The question, then, is: How can we expect to acquire meaningful knowledge from a report simply because it was passed down by a certain unspecified number of people? And on what basis can we determine how large this group of people has to be in order for it to be impossible for them to collude in deception? One cannot help but note, moreover, that all the proposed definitions of *mutawātir* revolve around the notion of lying and deliberate deception, whereas none of them makes any mention of the possibility of error, illusion, forgetfulness and the like, to which even the most trustworthy narrator could fall prey.

Scholars have never settled amongst themselves on the number of narrators required for a report to be classified as *mutawātir*, with some specifying three as the minimum, and others specifying as many as 1,500! Each number proposed is based on the conclusions these scholars have drawn from relevant texts or situations. With reference to scholars' speculations on the number of narrators required for a hadith to be *mutawātir*, Indian scholar Abdul Hayy Lucknawi (d. 1304 AH/1887 CE) wrote:

> All such statements and their like are invalid. The more correct view, put forward by numerous hadith scholars, is that the classification of *mutawātir* does not require a hadith to have been transmitted by a particular number of narrators. Rather, what matters is that it convey certain knowledge.

In the view of thinkers such as Lucknawi, the classification of a hadith as *mutawātir* has to do with one's reason, emotions and sense of trust or confidence in what an account is saying. After reviewing the various points of view on the number of narrators required for a hadith to be termed *mutawātir*, Fakhr al-Dīn al-Rāzī (d. 605 AH/1209 CE) stated:

> None of these restrictions and qualifications has anything to do with the question at hand. You might say: "If you define knowledge based on the fulfillment of a certain, undefined quota of narrators, you will not be able

> to argue from this against an opponent." And to this I reply, "We do not argue in favor of certain knowledge on the basis of reports classed as *mutawātir*, that is, based on a requisite number of narratives that is not even specified. Rather, as we have explained, the matter of whether one may gain certain knowledge has to do with one's perceptions."

Is it Possible for a Report to be Truly Mutawātir?

Hadith scholars have disagreed as to the possibility of a report's being *mutawātir*. Ibn al-Ṣalāḥ, for example, held that only rarely would one find a report that qualifies as *mutawātir*. In his *Muqaddimah*, he wrote, "If someone were asked to produce an example of a hadith that is *mutawātir*, he would be hard pressed to find one." However, as hadith scholar al-Bulqīnī (d. 805 AH/1403 CE) noted, "An account might qualify as *mutawātir* in relation to matters of undisputable certainty even if it would be difficult or impossible to produce a chain of transmission." In *Nuzhat al-Naẓar*, al-Ḥāfiẓ ibn Ḥajar quotes the aforementioned statement by Ibn al-Ṣalāḥ, after which he comments:

> His [Ibn al-Ṣalāh's] claim that it is difficult to produce hadiths that are truly *mutawātir* is incorrect, as is the claim made by others that such hadiths do not exist. Such claims grew out of a lack of familiarity with the many paths of narration, narrators' lives and circumstances, and the character traits which necessitate that we rule out the possibility that they would have colluded in deceit.

Ibn Ḥajar preceded his earlier statement in *Nuzhat al-Naẓar* with the words:

> The conditions a hadith must meet in order to be classed as *mutawātir* are obscure in the source (that is, in *Nukhbat al-Fikr*), because they are not among the themes investigated by the science of *isnād*. For the science of *isnād* deals with a hadith's authenticity or inauthenticity so as to determine whether it is a valid basis for action given its narrators' characters and the formulations used in passing on accounts (such as, "So-and-so informed us," "So-and-so related to us," "We learned on the authority of so-and-so," and the like). In the case of a hadith classed as *mutawātir*, by contrast, no investigation is made into its narrators' characters; rather, it is to be acted upon without such an investigation.

The Claim that no Hadith Qualifies as Mutawātir

In the introduction to his *Ṣaḥīḥ*, Ibn Ḥibbān wrote saying:

> All hadiths [concerning things said and done by the Prophet] must be classified as *āḥād*, or solitary reports; that is to say, none of them is *mutawātir*. For no report has been passed down by two narrators of good repute, each of whom heard the account from two other narrators of good repute, each of whom, in turn, heard it from two other narrators of good repute and so on all the way back to the Prophet. Given the impossibility of such a scenario, it must be concluded that all hadiths are solitary reports, that is, not *mutawātir*.

b) Āḥad, or Solitary Reports

Based on a specified set of criteria, Sunni scholars divide *āḥād* reports into two categories: acceptable (*maqbūl*) and unacceptable (*mardūd*). Those that are deemed *maqbūl* can be used as the basis for Islamic juristic rulings that Muslims are obliged to act on, and they are viewed as yielding speculative certainty. Moreover, Muslims' obligation to act on them stands regardless of whether or not there is external evidence demonstrating their validity.

Both well-established later Twelver Shiite scholars and the Zaydites agree with Sunni scholars that *āḥād* reports are a valid basis for binding Islamic legal rulings even if they lack external evidence in their support. In fact, most beliefs that are viewed as being essential tenets of Islam are based on reports that yield only speculative certainty, and we have no statements by any of their imams to the effect that reports yielding only speculative certainty are not to be acted upon. Indeed, both hadith transmitters and *uṣūl* scholars have acted on such reports themselves, and a good many imams indicate that they should be acted upon, as we find, for example, in the hadith compilation of al-Kulaynī (d. 329 AH/941 CE) and al-Ṭūsī's *Al-Istibṣār*.

As for later scholars, the majority of them held that *āḥād* reports should be rejected and not acted upon if they lack external support. In fact, al-Murtaḍā tells us that later scholars were unanimously in favor of not relying on such reports as a basis for Islamic legal rulings. The most well-established scholars among them saw this as a weakly supported position. However, those who did rely on such reports as evidence for legal argumentation stipulated that in order for them to be the basis for action, they had to be listed in what they deemed authoritative Shiite works. Such works would have to include other, more strongly attested reports that were not in conflict with them. A hadith included in an authoritative Shiite work could be relied on even if its narrator was not well-reputed and even if the hadith was *ḍaʿīf*, *mursal*, *mawqūf*, *munqatiʿ*, *muʿallal*, or *muḍṭarib*, since it was deemed sufficient that scholars had accepted it based on its having a continuous chain of transmission, and its being free of inconsistencies with hadiths of established authenticity or other flaws. Earlier scholars applied the term *ṣaḥīḥ* (authentic) to every report that was supported by evidence recognized as authoritative, including fulfillment of these conditions.

Solitary Hadiths Yield Only Speculative Certainty

Al-Khaṭīb al-Baghdādī devotes a passage in *Al-Kifāyah* to a refutation of "the dubious claim that a solitary hadith communicates certain knowledge." He then goes on to say, "Solitary hadiths are not acceptable in relation to aspects of the religion which morally accountable individuals are required to know and act upon... However, they are acceptable for use in relation to matters that do not require certainty." Al-Manāwī states in this connection, "Contrary to the majority opinion according to which solitary accounts afford no knowledge of any kind, Imams al-Ghazālī, al-Āmidī, Ibn al-Ḥājib and al-Bayḍāwī hold that a solitary hadith can provide certain knowledge if it is accompanied by external evidence."

Uṣūl scholar al-Shanqīṭī (d. 1393 AH/1973 CE) states, "A solitary hadith provides no knowledge under any circumstances even if the narrator is of good repute, and whether or not it is supported by external evidence. This is the view of the majority of discerning thinkers, although there are some who hold the opposite opinion." As for al-Shāṭibī, he stated, "It is clear that a solitary hadith yields no definitive certainty."

According to Fakhr al-Dīn al-Rāzī, "If a solitary hadith deals with matters relating to the fundamentals of the religion, it holds no validity, since matters such as these require definitive certainty, whereas a solitary hadith provides only tentative certainty." Al-Bāqillānī (d. 403

AH/1013 CE) wrote, "Jurists and scholastic theologians have agreed to term every report that fails to provide certain knowledge as a solitary report, and this regardless of whether it was narrated by a single individual or a group." Al-Dhahabī (d. 749 AH/1348 CE) wrote in *Tadhkirat al-Ḥuffāẓ*, "This gives us all the more reason to provide numerous lines of narrators for hadiths in order for them to be elevated to the status of reports that afford genuine knowledge, since a single narrator might be affected by forgetfulness or a flight of fancy." As for al-Nawawī (d. 676 AH/1277 CE), he states in *Al-Taqrīb*:

> If a hadith is said to be authentic, this does not necessarily mean that it is indisputably certain... According to Shaykh Ibn al-Ṣalāḥ, any hadith included in the *Ṣaḥīḥ* of either al-Bukhārī or Muslim is most definitely authentic, and yields definitive knowledge. However, this point of view is disputed by the majority of well-established scholars, who hold that any hadith which is not *mutawātir* affords only tentative knowledge.

After quoting Ibn al-Ṣalāh in the introduction to *al-Minhāj*, his commentary on *Ṣaḥīḥ Muslim*, al-Nawawī states:

> What the Shaykh states here is in contrast to the view held by the majority of well-established scholars, who hold that the hadiths found in the compilations of Muslim and al-Bukhārī which are not *mutawātirah* yield only tentative certainty, since they are solitary reports... Despite the Muslim community's unanimous agreement on the necessity of putting the contents of these two hadith collections into practice, they do not necessarily agree unanimously that these hadiths are traceable with definitive certainty back to the Messenger of God. Ibn Burhān al-Imam, for example, disagreed vehemently with those who adopted Shaykh [Ibn al-Ṣalāḥ's] perspective.

In a similar vein, al-Bazdawī (d. 480 AH/1087 CE) stated, "As for the claim that we can acquire certain knowledge through solitary hadiths, it is without foundation, being refuted by logic and common sense. The reason for this is that a solitary report inevitably entails probability, and that which entails probability cannot be fully certain. Whoever denies this to be the case exposes his own foolishness and ignorance." Al-Ghazālī voiced a similar position, saying, "A solitary report does not provide certain knowledge. This is necessarily the case, since we do not believe everything we hear. If we believed everything we heard and we happened to hear two conflicting stories, how could we reconcile the two opposites?"

The quotations above are a mere sample of the numerous statements that have been made by well-established scholars in affirmation of the intuitively obvious fact that solitary reports yield only tentative knowledge.

5. *Methodological Differences Between Earlier and Later Hadith Scholars*

One can observe a clear difference on the levels of both method and terminology between early hadith scholars – generally identified as those who preceded and were contemporaries of al-Khaṭīb al-Baghdādī – and later hadith scholars, that is, those who came between al-Khaṭīb al-Baghdādī (d. 463 AH/1071 CE) and al-Ḥāfiz ibn Ḥajar (d. 852 AH/1449 CE). What this tells us is that the hadith sciences were engaged in by two major groups, each of which was marked by its own distinctive methods, concepts and academic protocols. The first of these groups was marked by a practical bent, while the second adopted a theoretical approach.

Earlier scholars, who approached the hadith sciences from a practical point of view, were the major hadith critics. It is this group that bequeathed us most of our modern sources of information on hadith scholarship during that era, whose foremost works were *Ṣaḥīḥ Muslim* and *Ṣaḥīḥ al-Bukhārī*. The distinctive feature of this era, which spanned approximately the first five centuries AH, is that its scholars only received and circulated hadiths via direct oral transmission.

As for the later group of scholars, their approach to the hadith sciences was to extract and define terminology found in existing writings. These later scholars also formulated rules of hadith criticism based on the practices of their predecessors. Unlike that of their forebears, the later scholars' work was marked by a reliance on written materials for the transmission of hadiths rather than direct individual narration. This later period also witnessed the development of logical principles derived from Greek philosophy, which exerted a deepening influence on the Islamic legal sciences as a whole, and, in particular, on definitions and distinctions.

The various differences between earlier and later hadith scholars touched upon both understanding-based and narrator-based hadith study. These differences impacted the definition of the phrase 'hadith science' itself as a technical term, as well as all hadith-related terminology and the legal rulings to which it gave rise. The changes that had been witnessed in the field of hadith study resulted in a fair degree of confusion in the methods its scholars were employing. Such confusion went deep, in fact, affecting nearly all of the principles and foundations on which later scholars based their endeavors.

The early hadith critics had a perspective on narratives and narrators that set them apart from everyone who came after them. For one thing, the accounts they worked with were derived from actual eyewitnesses. Hence, their work was based on direct contact with hadith narrators, as a result of which they could familiarize themselves with these narrators' characters and circumstances. Consequently, they possessed a thorough understanding that was not available to later generations. In addition, when arriving at judgments about this or that narrator, they refrained from adhering to unbending rules. Rather, and unlike those of their successors, their assessments were founded upon a consideration for specific circumstances and conditions. They did not have a single rule which they applied to situations in which there was a contradiction between a hadith with a continuous chain of transmission and another with an incomplete one, or between a hadith that was traceable all the way back to the Prophet and another attributable only to one of the Companions, or when there were additions to, or omissions from, a given hadith, and this regardless of whether it was done by one narrator or more than one. Rather, all judgments were subject to surrounding contexts. They might reject an addition made to a hadith account by a trustworthy narrator even though it was not in conflict with the account narrated by someone else. Conversely, in a case involving a choice between a hadith with a continuous *isnād* and another with an incomplete *isnād*, they might rule in favor of the hadith with the continuous *isnād*; however, they might rule in favor of a hadith with a discontinuous *isnād*, or an account someone had traced to a weak narrator if the surrounding evidence indicated that what he had done was right.

Consequently, their method tended to be quite selective, a fact which is made clear by al-Ḥāfiẓ ibn Rajab al-Ḥanbalī (d. 795 AH/1393 CE) in his work entitled *Sharḥ ʿIlal al-Tirmidhī.* One also notes that earlier scholars' assessments of narrators tended to be relative rather than absolute. Thus, for example, even if the hadith master Shuʿbah ibn al-Ḥajjāj (d. 160 AH/777 CE) or someone else said that a given narrator was trustworthy or weak, this was not a once-for-all verdict that required one to accept, or reject, everything he had narrated. Rather, the judgment would be applicable to a specific case, circumstance, or hadith. Scholars might declare a hadith weak due to an error the narrator had committed even though, generally speaking, they saw this narrator as trustworthy. Or, conversely, they might deem a hadith to be authentic in some respects, despite its overall weakness, while at the same time remaining skeptical of other hadiths related by the same narrator.

The prevalence of this phenomenon may help to explain the inconsistencies one observes in the narrator assessments offered by a single imam such as, for example, Yaḥyā ibn Maʿīn, whose book *Al-Tārīkh* is full of illustrative examples. However, the appearance of inconsistency actually results from our own ignorance of the circumstances on the basis of which the narrator in question was being assessed. Similarly, by the end of the fourth century AH, it had become difficult, if not impossible, for hadith scholars to familiarize themselves with narrators' life circumstances now that hadith study took place only through books.

The aforementioned facts raise questions about the objectivity and reliability of the rules, criteria, terms and definitions that were laid down by later hadith scholars. Those who articulated these principles had to engage in a good deal of interpretative work in their attempt to make sense of the numerous statements they had inherited from their predecessors on narrators and narratives. They lacked knowledge of the specific circumstances that had surrounded the formulation of such statements; hence, they disagreed over how to interpret them, and derive principles and rules from them. For, as we have seen, most of the statements by earlier hadith scholars were relative in nature and, as such, incomprehensible apart from the circumstances and situations to which they were a response. Nevertheless, later hadith scholars formulated rigid rules, criteria and definitions. They then proceeded to assess the rightness or wrongness of their predecessors' words against these standards, and classified the hadiths they had passed down as authentic or inauthentic based on their own criteria and in light of their own circumstances rather than those of the scholars whose work they were evaluating.

[THIRD]
The *Uṣūl* Method's Influence on Later Hadith Scholars

Imam al-Shāfiʿī was the first scholar to write on the subject of the fundamentals of Islamic jurisprudence in his book *Al-Risālah*, a work that testifies to his mastery of the Sunnah and its related disciplines. Yet, although al-Shāfiʿī was highly critical of scholastic theology and theologians, the method adopted by his followers who wrote on the fundamentals of jurisprudence was heavily influenced by scholastic theology. In fact, his students' approach to the classification of Islamic jurisprudence came to be known as "the scholastic theological method" which came to be associated specifically with the Shafiite school of juristic thought. This method was also employed by the Malikite and Hanbalite schools; however, it was the Shafiites who first initiated its use in writings on the fundamentals of jurisprudence.

It should be remembered in this connection that the scholastic theological method relies on Greek logic in resolving issues relating to the principles of jurisprudence and standardizing juristic rules, and that *uṣūl* scholars view the Sunnah of the Prophet as the second source of Islamic legislation. Moreover, the scholastic theologians' practice of studying the Sunnah based on concepts and terminology borrowed from Greek philosophers and logicians opened up a chasm between theory and practice in the hadith sciences, much like the wedge that *uṣūl* scholars had driven between jurisprudence and its principles.

Hence, beginning with the field of jurisprudence (*fiqh*) and its principles (*uṣūl al-fiqh*), the Islamic sciences overall – including, of course, the hadith sciences – came to be weighed down with the accretions of Aristotelian logic and philosophy.

Examples Illustrating the Disparity Between the Approaches Adopted by Earlier and Later Hadith Scholars

According to Burhān al-Dīn al-Buqāʿī (d. 855 AH/1451 CE), "Ibn al-Ṣalāḥ combined the methods of *uṣūl* scholars and hadith scholars who, unlike scholastic theologians and *uṣūl* scholars, had no fixed rules for establishing the trustworthiness of a narrator or narrative."

In a discussion of types of flaws that might come to light in a hadith, contemporary hadith scholar Ḥamzah al-Malībārī quotes Imam al-Ḥākim al-Nīsābūrī (d. 405 AH/1014 CE) as saying: "The proof for us lies solely in [a narrator's] knowledge, understanding, and ability to memorize." Al-Malībārī goes on to say:

> The phenomenon of eclecticism – that is, the practice of mingling the methods of jurists, *uṣūl* scholars, and hadith scholars – complicated matters in a significant way. The first book to adopt this dual method was *Al-Kifāyah fī ʿUlūm al-Riwāyah* by al-Khaṭīb al-Baghdādī. This method then became standard practice among later scholars, who filled their books with citations of the opinions of scholastic theologians and *uṣūl* scholars, along with the arguments given by each group, to the point where these thinkers' opinions drowned out the voices of hadith critics themselves.

As for Ibn Rajab al-Ḥanbalī, he tells us that:

> Al-Ḥāfiẓ Abū Bakr al-Khaṭīb (i.e., al-Khaṭīb al-Baghdādī) wrote an excellent book entitled, *Tamyīz al-Mazīd fī Muttaṣil al-Asānīd* (On Distinguishing Among Additions Made to Hadiths with Continuous Chains of Transmission) which is divided into two parts. In the first part, he rules that it is valid either to mention additions that have been made to a hadith's chain of transmission, or not to mention them. In the second, he rules that such additions should be rejected... al-Khaṭīb is inconsistent here. On one hand, he mentions in *al-Kifāyah* that people disagree concerning differences among narrators with respect to whether or not they trace their accounts back to the Messenger of God. However, none of their points of

> view comes from early scholars who knew the Qur'an well. Instead, they come from the books of scholastic theologians. In addition, he favors the view that an addition made [to a hadith's text or chain of transmission] by a trustworthy narrator is to be accepted unconditionally. This view, in which he is supported by scholastic theologians and numerous jurists, contrasts with the position he took in his book, *Tamyīz al-Mazīd fī Muttaṣil al-Asānīd*, for which he was criticized by some jurists and hadith scholars who had agreed with the position he took in *Al-Kifāyah*.

Commenting further on the writings of Ibn al-Ṣalāḥ, al-Ḥāfiẓ al-ʿAlā'ī (d. 761 AH/1359 CE) wrote saying:

> Shaykh Taqī al-Dīn ibn al-Ṣalāḥ, who steered a middle course between hadith scholars and *uṣūl* scholars, divided additions to hadiths into three types. However, in relation to such additions, appeal should be made to hadith critics alone. Indeed, this matter lies at the heart of their specialization, and only their approach can be relied upon in determining which additions to hadiths are acceptable and which are not. The authority of these critics is derived from their broad memorization of hadiths, their understanding of their content, and their knowledge of the circumstances surrounding their narration... It has been made clear by those knowledgeable in the field of hadith study that there are innumerable ways in which to argue for a hadith's authenticity, and that there is no set criterion on the basis of which all hadiths can be judged. Rather, each hadith has to be argued for individually. This argumentation is to be engaged in by experienced, discerning researchers with knowledge of a hadith's many lines of narrators and forms of narration. This is why early hadith scholars did not make blanket judgments. Rather, their view differed depending on what they found in any given hadith. And God knows best.

According to al-Malībārī, "According to a group of leading scholars of jurisprudence and its fundamentals, an addition made by a trustworthy narrator to a hadith or its chain of transmission should be accepted unconditionally." This is the position that was taken by Shaykh Muḥyī al-Dīn al-Nawawī (d. 675 AH/1277 CE) in his writings. However, it is a questionable view. Take, for example, a hadith which is traced back to a single source, or original narrator, but which is narrated in one way by a group of trustworthy hadith memorizers, and in another way by a solitary narrator known to be less precise and skilled at memorization than the aforementioned group. This solitary narrator has included additions that conflict with what was narrated by the group. How, then, are we to accept such an addition? This question becomes especially pointed if these narrators' shaykh is one who, like al-Zuhrī and others of his ilk, collected and preserved his hadith narratives. For in such cases it might be said: If the shaykh had narrated the hadith, it would have been heard by students of his who had memorized vast numbers of hadiths. And if they had heard it, they would have passed it on themselves, and would not have allowed it to be forgotten or neglected. In this and similar situations, it would seem most likely that the narrator who included the addition is in the wrong.

This line of reasoning is adopted by al-Shāfiʿī in *Al-Umm*, where he discusses the addition included by Mālik and others to a hadith concerning the freeing of a slave.[1] According to al-Shāfiʿī:

> the narrator [who introduced the addition] is in error, unlike those who have memorized more and better than he has. He may also have erred by including something which is shared in common with the other narrators' account, but which he did not memorize on their authority. It should be borne in mind here that the group in question represents a larger number of people than this one individual. Hence, an addition which goes against an account narrated by others, who have memorized more and who outnumber the person who narrated said addition, should be rejected.

Hence, it can be concluded from Ibn al-Ṣalāḥ's writings as they relate to the weakness in a hadith that the decision whether to accept an addition to a hadith as valid depends on the contextual evidence. Al-Malībārī states in this connection:

> The contextual evidence will differ from one hadith to the next. There is no one criterion against which all hadiths can be measured. Nor is it simply a matter of whether a single trustworthy narrator has contradicted a group of trustworthy narrators, or a narrator deemed to be more trustworthy. The only people who are qualified to evaluate the quality of the evidence, what it means, and its scientific dimensions, are hadith critics. Ibn al-Ṣalāḥ refers to this point when he speaks of "additional evidence which alerts the knower (*al-ʿārif*) in this regard," where the term *ʿārif*, or 'knower,' refers specifically to the hadith critic.

Two other types of hadiths that relate to additions made by reliable narrators are referred to as *shādhdh* ('irregular') and *munkar* ('unacknowledged'). Ibn al-Ṣalāḥ divides the category of *shādhdh* into two types. The first type is an individual hadith that conflicts with another hadith related by a trustworthy narrator, while the second type is a hadith which, although related by a weak narrator, does not conflict with the account of some other narrator. The first type includes hadiths related by a trustworthy narrator and whose content conflicts with the account of someone viewed as a more qualified memorizer. This conflict may take numerous forms, one of which is an addition to, or deletion from, the hadith's chain of transmission, its main text, or both. If a narrator adds to the hadith something that was left out by someone who would have been in a better position to memorize the account in question, the hadith belongs to the first type of *shādhdh* mentioned above. If, on the other hand, the narrator who includes the addition is in a better position to have memorized the account than the narrator who left it out, then the hadith is classed as authentic, or *ṣaḥīḥ*. This indicates clearly that before validating an addition to a hadith account made by a trustworthy narrator, we must consider the factors and circumstances that qualify the narrator in question to have memorized the hadith accurately.

Consequently, al-Ḥāfiz ibn Ḥajar draws a close connection between the matter of whether a hadith is classified as irregular, or *shādhdh*, and additions made by a trustworthy narrator. He states:

> Hadith critics stipulate that in order to be authentic, or *ṣaḥīḥ*, a hadith must not be classed as *shādhdh* (irregular), where the term *shādhdh* describes an account which, although it was related by a trustworthy narrator, is contradicted by the account related by someone known to be more accurate at memorization, by a group, or by someone more scholarly. The question is then: Should such a hadith be deemed authentic (*ṣaḥīḥ*), or irregular (*shādhdh*)? In such a case we have no choice but to recognize the contradiction between unconditional acceptance of an addition made to hadith by a trustworthy narrator and stipulating that no authentic hadith can be classed as irregular, or resolve the difference between the two forms of the hadith.

It will be seen from the foregoing that hadiths over which there is disagreement due to additions made by a trustworthy narrator, whether to the chain of transmission or to the main text, are included in the category of 'irregular,' or *shādhdh*, if the additions resulted from error or misperception. Hence, not every addition made by a trustworthy narrator can be accepted as valid. Commenting on this matter, al-Ḥāfiẓ ibn Ḥajar notes that whereas hadith scholars stipulate that in order to be judged authentic, a hadith cannot also be deemed irregular, *uṣūl* scholars accept additions which might be viewed as irregular by hadith scholars. In explanation of this difference in approach, al-Ḥāfiẓ ibn Ḥajar suggests that in his discussion of weaknesses in hadiths, Ibn al-Ṣalāḥ relied on concepts derived from hadith scholars rather than stating his own point of view, whereas in his discussion of irregular hadiths, he may have lent greater weight to the views of jurists and *uṣūl* scholars. And God knows best.

[FOURTH]
Narrator Evaluation: Objectivity and Subjectivity

The Definition and Scope of This Science

The discipline which in Arabic is termed *ʿilm al-rijāl* (literally, "the science of men") concerns itself with the circumstances and characters of hadith narrators with a view to deciding whether to accept or reject their accounts. Given the many factors which have a bearing on whether an account should be accepted or rejected, this science branched into numerous subdisciplines. These subdisciplines dealt with topics such as: the history of births and deaths; names, agnomens and titles; genealogies; countries and travelogues; shaykhs and their pupils; narrator assessment; ways of differentiating between narrators when, for example, names are the same but refer to different people, names are written without voweling and are thus liable to be misread or confused with each other, and so on; identification of weak vs. trustworthy narrators, and others.

The topic with which this science concerns itself is whether a given narrator's accounts are to be accepted or rejected. The term "narrator" (*al-rāwī*), although masculine in form, includes both men and women;

hence, the term *ʿilm al-rijāl* is non gender exclusive. This discipline is by no means self-contained or autonomous; rather, it is a branch of historiography which examines the history of a particular class of people. We read in *Miftāḥ al-Saʿādah* by Ṭāsh Kubrā Zādah that: "this discipline is, in one respect, a branch of history and, in another respect, a branch of the hadith sciences." The discipline of history concerns itself with human beings and time in general, whereas *ʿilm al-rijāl* concerns itself with narrators in particular: with their characters, the times in which they lived, their travels, and their lifespans.

Who Were the Prophet's Companions?

Early researchers into the characters of narrators exempted from examination those whom they termed 'Companions' of the Prophet, since they deemed everyone belonging to this category as individuals of such integrity that there was no need to inquire into their moral rectitude.

Hadith scholars defined the Companion of the Prophet as "anyone who met the Prophet, believed in him, and died a Muslim." According to these scholars, the act of meeting the Prophet referred to in the definition above includes any meeting whatsoever, if even for a single moment. The definition of Companion thus does not require the person to have spent a year or more with the Prophet, or to have taken part in warfare under his leadership. By contrast, hadith scholar ʿĀṣim al-Aḥwal (d. 140 AH/757 CE) stipulated that the person must have been a Companion of the Prophet in the more commonly accepted sense of the term; this condition is likewise stipulated by *uṣūl* scholars. There are, in addition, numerous other definitions of the term, a discussion of which space does not permit.

Uṣūl scholars themselves differed over what the term 'Companion' meant. Some defined it as referring to anyone who had seen the Prophet, without having been with him for a significant period of time, and without having narrated accounts on his authority. Others stipulated that in order to be referred to as a Companion, the individual had to have seen the Prophet and been with him for a long time, even if he narrated no accounts on his authority. Still others defined the term

Companion exclusively as someone who had spent a significant period of time with the Prophet and received knowledge on his authority.

In order for someone to qualify as a Companion of the Prophet, he or she had to have died a Muslim; hence, the term does not apply to someone who saw the Prophet and believed in him, but died a non-Muslim. Some scholars, such as al-Nawawī and al-ʿIrāqī, included among the Prophet's Companions those who, during his Prophetic calling, were youths who had reached an age of sufficient discernment that they could understand and engage in intelligent discussion; included in this group were individuals such as the Prophet's grandsons al-Ḥasan and al-Ḥusayn, Maḥmūd ibn al-Rabīʿ, and others. As for youths who had not yet reached the age of discernment, their accounts were not recognized as authoritative, but were classified as *mursal* even though they were honored with the title of Companion. Al-Bukhārī defined the Companions as "all Muslims who saw the Prophet." This definition is rejected by many jurists based on the two verses from *Sūrah al-Munāfiqūn* which read:

> When the hypocrites come unto you, they say, "We bear witness that you art indeed God's Apostle!" But God knows that you art truly His Apostle; and He bears witness that the hypocrites are indeed false [in their declaration of faith]. They have made their oaths a cover [for their falseness], and thus they turn others away from the Path of God. Evil indeed is all that they are wont to do. (63:1-2)

The hypocrites referred to here were residents of Madinah who claimed to be Muslims and who had seen the Prophet. However, they secretly waged war on the Islamic message and conspired against the Muslim community. The Qur'an thus warned them and threatened them with banishment from the presence of the Messenger of God, saying:

> Thus it is: if the hypocrites, and they in whose hearts is disease, and they who, by spreading false rumors, would cause disturbances in the City [of the Prophet] desist not [from their hostile doings]. We shall indeed give you mastery over them, [O Muhammad] – and then they will not remain your neighbors in this [city] for more than a little while. (*Sūrah al-Aḥzāb* 33:60)

How is a Given Individual Shown to Have Been a Companion of the Prophet?

Someone can be said to have been a Companion of the Prophet if one or more of the following conditions are fulfilled: (1) There is an account deemed *mutawātir* that bears witness to such companionship – such as the account relating the Prophet's declaration to ten of his Companions, who are mentioned by name, that they would be among the inhabitants of Paradise. (2) There is a widely circulating account bearing witness to this companionship. (3) There is a statement confirming the fact by someone else who was known to be a Companion of the Prophet. (4) There is a statement by a Successor judged to be trustworthy based on someone else's endorsement. (5) A claim to such companionship was made by someone who lived during the Prophet's lifetime and who, being known for his upright character, would not have lied.

The Uprightness of the Companions

Sunni scholars, as well as some Zaydite scholars and some of the Muʿtazilah, held that all of the Prophet's Companions, including those who took part in the uprisings that took place during and after the assassination of ʿUthmān ibn ʿAffān in 35 AH/656 CE, were upright. According to this view, such individuals could be classed among the Prophet's Companions even if they had committed serious sins. On the other hand, some scholars held that the characters of the Prophet's Companions needed to be investigated just as those of other hadith narrators did. According to another view, all of the Companions were upright until the time when divisions arose among them; if, however, the account in question was narrated after this point in history, a Companion's character would be subject to investigation just as any other narrator's character would be. In the view of still others, any account narrated by a Companion following these events should be rejected, since one of the two sides had to have been in the wrong; however, which of them was wrong is not known for certain. And lastly, there are those who hold that we should accept hadiths narrated by a Companion following these events if it is individual in nature, since our basic knowledge of the Companions is that they were upright; hence, we have no proven basis for suspecting them of immorality, and such a suspicion cannot be confirmed given evidence to the contrary simply because we know that one, as yet unidentified, side of the conflict was in the wrong.

The Study of the Companions

Not all of the Companions were equally knowledgeable about the things the Prophet had said and done. In this connection, Masrūq wrote, "I have sat with Muhammad's Companions, and I found them to be like depressions in the ground where rainwater collects. Some of these are so small that their water would suffice only one man. Others, somewhat larger, would suffice two men. Others, being medium-sized pools, would suffice one hundred men. And still others, the size of ponds or lakes, would suffice the population of an entire land." Ibn Khuzaymah (d. 311 AH/923 CE) acknowledged the possibility that the Companions could forget some hadiths, saying:

> The Companions of the Prophet may have shortened some of the stories from the Prophet's life when they narrated them, while in other cases they may have related events with perfect accuracy. Some of those who heard the reports may have memorized some of the events, but not all of them, and they may have forgotten some of the report after memorizing it.

So, if this could happen to the Companions themselves, what should we expect from others?

In the course of discussing how to assess the knowledge possessed by one of the Companions, Ibn Ḥazm stated:

> His [a Companion's] knowledge can be ascertained through one of two means. The first is the number of accounts he narrates and the number of fatwas he issues. And the second is the degree to which the Prophet pressed him in to his service. For the Prophet would certainly not have employed someone with no knowledge. Hence, these are the principle witnesses to the breadth of someone's learning.

[FIFTH]
The Terminology Employed in *ʿIlm al-Rijāl*

Is there a systematic method for assessing narrators' characters that was shared by earlier and later scholars? If so, what technical terms were used in this process, and how were they used by earlier and later scholars? And lastly, what indicators will help us to arrive at the correct assessments?

1. *Systematic Rule Formulation vs. Subjective Interpretation in Narrator Assessment*

Early hadith critics frequently differed in their assessments of a single narrator. In fact, the same narrator might be given varying assessments by one and the same critic. In response, later scholars often read their own interpretations into earlier scholars' statements and terminology in a misguided attempt to reconcile what they saw as inconsistencies. This occurred despite the fact that an experienced, knowledgeable, trustworthy critic was sure to have had reasons for reaching different conclusions about the same narrator in different situations. For example, the critic's judgment concerning a narrator might be influenced by something else he had heard from the same narrator. Commenting on this sort of situation, al-Muallimi (d. 1966 CE) wrote in *Al-Tankīl*:

> A hadith collector might ask about a given narrator, and then judge him based on what he knows about him overall. He might then hear another hadith transmitted by the same narrator and arrive at a judgment in which he is prone to take another position. As a result, there appears to be some contradiction among his various statements. And as a matter of fact, this is what happened with Dāraquṭnī, whose *sunan* and other works contain numerous examples of this phenomenon. He might even convey two or three different verdicts of his own, imagining each of them to be absolute.

Elsewhere in *Al-Tankīl*, al-Muʿallimī wrote:

> What a hadith collector says about a narrative grows out of two processes. The first involves making inquiries about the narrator and reflecting on both his personal character and the hadiths he has narrated; from this the

> researcher derives an overall picture of the narrator and his work. The second involves absorbing this overall picture and employing it as a broader framework in the context of which he draws conclusions about this or that particular hadith related by the narrator in question.

The first process leads to a judgment that might be termed 'absolute' in the sense that it will not be challenged by some other judgment unless the scholar's interpretation of things has changed. As for the second process, it may involve a shift in the scholar's perspective with regard to his assessment of a particular hadith. Suppose, for example, that the scholar's general observation about the narrator is that he is "truthful, but with a tendency to imagine things." If the scholar then discusses the narrator in the course of examining two different hadiths of his, we might well observe differences in the scholar's assessments from one hadith to another. Illustrating this phenomenon with particular examples, al-Muʿallimī cites a situation in which the assessment of a given narrator is not entirely clear. A hadith critic presents his personal assessment of the narrator; however, the things he says about the narrator differ from one situation to the next or one time to the next.

After mentioning a number of scholars in the field of hadith study and narrator assessment before the time of Yaḥyā ibn Maʿīn (d. 233 AH/848 CE), al-Dhahabī wrote:

> Another leading scholar in the field of narrator assessment was Yaḥyā ibn Maʿīn, who was once asked about various hadith narrators by ʿAbbās al-Dūrī, ʿUthmān al-Darāmī, Abū Ḥātim and a number of others. He answered each of these men based on his personal interpretation. As he spoke, his opinions and his ways of expressing himself about certain narrators differed, just as the interpretations and opinions of jurists and other mujtahids had differed. For in fact, the critics who express the most widely varying opinions on a given narrator are the ones who engage in the most ijtihad in this connection; they are also the ones who have written the most about hadith narrators, and the ones who are asked the most questions about them. And it was to this group of scholars that both Ibn Maʿīn and Dāraquṭnī belonged.

In fact, one even finds situations in which a critic expresses two different opinions on the same hadith. One of these opinions will be influenced by the circumstances of the hadith's narrator, while the other will be influenced by the manner or tone of the person who asked him for the opinion, or the setting in which the question was asked. The questioner might have a stern demeanor and thus appear to want the critic to be strict in his assessment, which will in turn color the assessment he receives. Ibn Rajab's commentary on al-Tirmidhī's *al-ʿIlal al-Kabīr* includes an account related by ʿAlī ibn al-Madīnī, who said:

> I once asked Yaḥyā ibn Saʿīd about Muhammad ibn ʿAmr ibn ʿAlqamah. He replied, "Do you want me to be lenient, or stern?" "I want you to be stern," I told him. Then he said, "He is not the man you want. He used to say, 'Our shaykhs are Abū Salamah and Yaḥyā ibn ʿAbd al-Raḥmān ibn Ḥāṭib.'"

Al-Khaṭīb al-Baghdādī wrote in *al-Kifāyah*:

> Critics' views on narrators are puzzling and convoluted. A critic, having heard something uncomplimentary about a given narrator, may stop citing his hadiths even though what he heard may not justify rejecting this narrator's accounts or doubting his integrity. If the narrator is alive, then the hearer may view what he has done to be preferable in hope that the narrator will exercise self-restraint and refrain from actions that would reflect a weakness of character. If the narrator is no longer living, the person who related the hadith on this narrator's authority should be placed in the same class as the narrator himself. Others hold that it is more apt to take precautions for the religion's sake by investigating to see whether other, similarly suspicious reports, have been circulated. After all, it is human nature to reveal one's virtues and conceal one's vices. However, if someone should act in an unseemly manner, one should beware that he might act in a similar manner in some other situation. This is why ʿUmar ibn al-Khaṭṭāb said, "If someone acts well toward us, we place our confidence in him, and his inward intentions are of no concern to us. But if someone acts badly toward us, we will not trust him or believe what he says even if he protests that his intentions were good."

In his book entitled *Al-Taʿdīl wa al-Jurḥ*, al-Bājī (d. 474 AH/1096 CE) stated:

> The critic who has deemed a narrator to be upright may say, "So-and-so is trustworthy," yet without meaning by this that the hadiths related by the

> narrator in question can be used in legal argumentation. Or he might say, "So-and-so is acceptable," by which he means that the hadiths related by the narrator in question can be used in legal argumentation. A critic might be asked about a virtuous, pious man who is more or less reliable in his accounts and who is being compared to weak narrators. Someone asks, "What is your opinion of so-and-so and so-and-so?" To which the reply comes, "He is trustworthy," by which he means that he is more trustworthy than the individuals to whom he is being compared.

After providing numerous examples of the phenomena he has described and citing evidence for his statements, al-Bājī explains: "What this shows is that the statements such critics make reflect the questions they have been asked and differ accordingly, and will be based on the comparisons among those being asked about." Similarly, a narrator might be deemed to have a faulty character because of something which, had it been done or said by someone else, would not be a basis for such an assessment due to the person's overall reputation for virtue and knowledge. Al-Bājī concludes his discussion with the words:

> Therefore, the words used by critics in their negative or positive assessments of narrators need to be interpreted by those who have a good understanding of their intentions and aims. The only persons who have such an understanding are those with specialized knowledge about this sphere of inquiry. As for those who lack such expertise, they are in no position to understand critics' words however they see fit.

Commenting on this field of study, contemporary scholar Shaykh Hassan Abd al-Mannan states:

> It first needs to be understood that the decision as to whether a hadith is well-attested or weak is a matter of interpretation. As such, it tends to depend on how one conceptualizes things. Specifically, it depends on an investigation of lines of narration and of the other hadiths related by the same narrator. A given narrator might, in the view of Aḥmad and Abū Ḥātim, for example, be viewed as unreliable, whereas al-Bukhārī, Yaḥyā ibn Maʿīn and others might disagree with this assessment. All of these scholars may have investigated the hadiths in question, but on the basis of differing criteria. Similarly they may have adhered to inconsistent methods. In fact, the hadith scholar concerned might judge a hadith to be well-attested

or weak without revealing the proof on the basis of which he made this judgment, a phenomenon of which there are numerous examples.

2. *Observations on the Science of Narrator Assessment (ʿIlm al-Rijāl)*

We tend to assume that the circumstances of narrators were well known to hadith critics from the time when narrations began to be passed down. However, the establishment of the science of narrator assessment was delayed by more than 160 years. In his *Ṣaḥīḥ*, Muslim quoted Ibn Sīrīn (d. 115 AH/733 CE) as saying:

> They [hadith collectors] did not used to ask about an account's chain of transmission. When the great uprising took place, people said, "Name your narrators for us." Then, if the narrator was found to be orthodox, his hadiths were accepted, whereas if he was found to be an innovator, they were rejected.

Discussing the beginnings of the science of narrator assessment, Ṣāliḥ ibn Muḥammad al-Baghdādī (d. 293 AH/906 CE) tells us that

> the first person to pose the topic of narrators' characters was Shuʿbah ibn al-Ḥajjāj (d. 160 AH/777 CE). He was followed by Yaḥyā ibn Saʿīd al-Qaṭṭān (d. 198 AH/813 CE), who was succeeded by Aḥmad ibn Ḥanbal (d. 241 AH/855 CE) and Yaḥyā ibn Maʿīn (d. 233 AH/847 CE).

However, the method employed in investigating narrators differed from one critic to another. Yaʿqūb ibn Shaybah once asked Yaḥyā ibn Maʿīn, "Do you know of any Successor who picked and chose his narrators the way Ibn Sīrīn did?" "No," he replied, shaking his head.

[SIXTH]
Loopholes in Narrator Assessment Methodology

1. *Falsification (al-Tadlīs) and Falsifiers (al-Mudallisūn)*

The dictionary definition of the Arabic verb *dallasa* is to engage in deceit by concealing a flaw or fault. As a technical term in the field of hadith study, the verb refers to a narrator's act of concealing a fault or flaw in an account in order to mislead the hearer. As such, it is an act of cunning and duplicity which has been widely condemned by hadith scholars.

Despite the fact that the practice of hadith falsification was alarmingly widespread among narrators in general, and among those of Iraq in particular, books written on narrator assessment contained descriptions of no more than one hundred such hadith falsifiers. An examination of writings on hadith falsifiers reveals that they number approximately one hundred thirty. If we subtract those who were only probably falsifiers, the number comes to around one hundred twenty. If we then subtract those narrators who were judged to be weak for some reason other than hadith falsification, there remain no more than seventy-five. These seventy-five were the only narrators whose hadiths were accepted by early hadith scholars only on condition they stated explicitly that they had heard a hadith from a specific person by saying, "My shaykh related to me....," "So-and-so related to me," etc. So, does this number include all narrators who engaged in hadith falsification? Most certainly not.

Ibn ʿAbd al-Barr (d. 423 AH/1071 CE) stated in *al-Tamhīd*: "There is a great deal of hadith falsification among the narrators in Kufah." Similarly, Shuʿbah ibn al-Ḥajjāj wrote, "The only narrators I have encountered who do not engage in hadith falsification are ʿAmr ibn Murrah and Ibn ʿAwn." For this reason, Imam Mālik dubbed Iraq "the hadith mint," since hadiths were produced there for public circulation the way money is produced in a mint! Not only this, but hadith falsification was practiced by the imams themselves, and by those who narrated on their authority! Ibn al-Mubārak (d. 181 AH/797 CE) stated, "Baqiyyah ibn al-Walīd would be an excellent hadith transmitter were it not for the fact that, instead of using the name by which a narrator is well-known, he uses this person's agnomen ("Father of so-and-so" – Abū Fulān) and, instead of using the agnomen by which the narrator is best known (Abū Fulān), he uses the person's regular name (So-and-so, son of So-and-so)." Ibn al-Mubārak went on to add that a certain narrator "had been relating hadiths to us for years on the authority of someone known as Saʿīd al-Waḥḥāẓī, only for us to discover much later that the person from whom he was passing on his accounts was ʿAbd al-Quddūs (whose hadiths were unanimously viewed as untrustworthy)." Other examples also make clear how difficult it was to detect hadith falsification even among individuals who were one another's contemporaries.

2. *Lying*

The number of false hadiths continued to proliferate as time went on. Shuʿbah ibn al-Ḥajjāj wrote, "No one has examined existing hadiths as rigorously as I have, and I have discovered three-fourths of them to be lies." If we trace this phenomenon back in time, we find (as have other hadith scholars) that it began in the days of the Prophet's Companions! ʿUthmān ibn ʿAffān commented, "People relate things about the Messenger of God that I have never heard of before!" In a similar vein, Muʿāwiyah ibn Abī Sufyān once wrote a letter saying:

> It has come to my knowledge that some men among you relate narratives that are not consistent with the Book of God, nor have they come down to us on the authority of the Messenger of God. Such men are ignorant!

As for al-Bukhārī, he wrote in his *Ṣaḥīḥ* with his own chain of transmission:

> Ḥamīd ibn ʿAbd al-Raḥmān told me that he had heard Muʿāwiyah, speaking of Kaʿb al-Aḥbār, say to a group of Qurayshites in Madinah, "He [Kaʿb] was one of the most truthful hadith narrators to relate accounts on the authority of People of the Book. Yet despite this fact, we cannot rule out the possibility that he may have passed on lies without intending to."

3. *Obscurity of the Narrator*

Hadith scholars deem a hadith weak if its chain of transmission contains the name of a narrator judged to be obscure.[2] However, the criteria on the basis of which it was decided whether a narrator was obscure or not differed from one period to another and from one place to another. Consequently, the same hadith might go from being judged authentic to being judged weak, and back again. In this connection, Aḥmad ibn Ḥanbal stated, "A narrator who has been deemed obscure will no longer be deemed thus if it is learned that an imam related hadiths on his authority. However, an imam might relate a hadith on the authority of someone who is not trustworthy." After quoting examples of such hadiths, Ibn Rajab commented:

> The fact that a trustworthy person relates a hadith does not mean that the person on whose authority he related it is himself trustworthy. For we know that many trustworthy narrators such as Sufyān al-Thawrī, Shuʿbah, and others, have related accounts they received from weak narrators.

4. *Provinciality*

Provinciality is a kind of prejudice or bigotry. If a critic is found to have been influenced by such prejudice or bigotry, his assessment of hadiths will be invalidated, and this regardless of whether he has deemed them to be authentic or inauthentic, and whether he has deemed a narrator to be strong or weak. Nevertheless, Wakīʿ ibn al-Jarrāḥ said, "There is no one from our region that we deem to be upright." As for Sufyān ibn ʿUyyaynah, he stated, "If one is looking for reliable hadiths and chains of transmission that will inspire confidence in people's hearts, let him take his accounts from the people of Madinah." Conversely, al-Zuhrī wrote, "Never have I seen a people more prone to sever the ties of Islam than the people of Makkah." When ʿAbd al-Raḥmān ibn Mahdī was asked about the hadiths related by narrators from the Levant, he replied with a dismissive gesture of the hand, while Abū Sulaymān al-Juzjānī (d. 823/1422 CE) denigrated the people of Kufah for being Shiites and for their habit of swindling others.

5. *Sentimentality*

Sentiment has nothing to do with knowledge. Unfortunately, however, it has colored many a critic's assessment of both narrators and hadiths. Imam Mālik, for example, grew very fond of Ayyūb al-Sakhtiyānī (d. 131 AH/749 CE) and declared him to be a trustworthy narrator, saying, "Whenever the Prophet is mentioned, he weeps most pitifully. Hence, seeing his immense reverence for the Prophet, I began writing down his accounts." Conversely, al-Nasāʾī (d. 303 AH/915 CE) refused to transmit accounts narrated by Imam Aḥmad ibn Ṣāliḥ due to the latter's refusal to relate accounts directly to him.[3] If space permitted, we could cite numerous other examples of situations in which sentimentalism has tainted the better judgment of otherwise outstanding religious scholars.

6. Imitation

A number of hadith critics who were unfamiliar with narrators' circumstances and characters simply parroted their associates' opinions and assessments of such narrators. Some of these critics then retracted opinions they had voiced earlier after having the opportunity actually to know the people they had been speaking about. The master of hadith critics, Yaḥyā ibn Saʿīd, used to imitate others in denouncing Rawḥ ibn ʿUbādah (d. 205 AH/821 CE) even though, without knowing his name, he had found Rawḥ ibn ʿUbādah to be a trustworthy narrator so that, in effect, he had made one person into two. Imagine…

7. Juristic and Scholastic Denominationalism

Differences among juristic schools or denominations have nothing to do with whether a given hadith account should be accepted or rejected, especially when the hadiths in question are not promoting one school or denomination over another. Alas, however, it was precisely this sort of difference of opinion that impacted scholars' assessment of particular hadith narrators. Abū Ḥanīfah stopped transmitting hadiths on the authority of ʿAṭā' ibn Rabāḥ (d. 114 AH/732 CE) because he had issued a legal ruling in favor of temporary marriage (*zawāj al-mutʿah*), and Aḥmad ibn Ḥanbal stopped transmitting hadiths on the authority of ʿAlī ibn al-Madīnī (d. 234 AH/849 CE) and everyone who had cooperated with the Mutazilah authorities in the theological inquisition carried out against those who, like Aḥmad, held the view that the Qur'an was created. And the list goes on. Given the extremes to which the People of Hadith went in the proliferation of hadith narratives, inter-denominational battles, and hadith falsification and forgery, some hadith experts began pining for "the old days" before the Islamic heritage had been glutted with hadith narratives of every shape and size. In this spirit we find Sufyān al-Thawrī saying, "Would that I had never involved myself in any of it [i.e., in the collection of hadiths], be they favorable toward me, or unfavorable!"

8. *Fraudulent Claims for and Against Hadith Narrators*

Hadith narrator assessment, whether negative or positive, should be governed by integrity and objectivity rather than by personal inclinations. However, the course of events in the field of hadith criticism has been otherwise. Al-Shāfiʿī related that Sufyān al-Thawrī once told Shuʿbah, "If you should criticize Jābir al-Juʿfī, who is a Rafidite, then I shall criticize you..."[4] Perhaps this is what led Shuʿbah to say once, "If I passed hadiths on to you from none but reliable narrators, I would only pass them on to you from a very small number." Similarly, al-Qaṭṭān stated, "If I passed on hadiths from none but those narrators I approve of, there are only five from whom I would pass them on," to which Yaḥyā ibn Saʿīd added, "If I put the narrators whose accounts I pass on to the test, I would pass them on only from a very few."

[SEVENTH]
Narrators' Memory

Hadith scholars divide memory (*ḍabṭ*) into two types. The first is *ḍabṭ al-ṣadr*, literally, "preservation of the chest," which refers to memorization – preservation – of things stored in one's mind or heart, and the second is *ḍabṭ al-kitāb*, literally, "preservation of the book," which refers to the ability to memorize and preserve accounts that have been recorded in writing. Now, we know that no matter how advanced a person is at memorization, his or her memory will still be subject to error. He or she could still forget, imagine things, have a lapse of attention, be confused, or undergo some change. Fearful that he would forget the revelation, the Prophet kept repeating it until God said to him, "Move not your tongue in haste, [repeating the words of the revelation:] for, behold, it is for Us to gather it [in your heart,] and to cause it to be read [as it ought to be read]" (*Sūrah al-Qiyāmah* 75:16-17).

1. *Ḍabṭ al-Ṣadr (Preservation of What is in the Mind, That is, Unwritten)*

Hadith collectors acknowledged that their accounts sometimes contained errors. Yaḥyā ibn Maʿīn once said, "Whoever claims not to have made any errors is a liar." As Sufyān al-Thawrī put it, "Hardly anyone can avoid making mistakes," and, "If we were determined never to relate an account to you unless it was exactly as we had heard it, we would not relate to you a single one." There are two types of hadith-related situations on which the act of forgetting has a bearing. The first category includes things one forgets without noticing that one has forgotten them, (this type accounts for most cases). The second category includes situations in which a narrator relates an account, and then forgets it until he is reminded of it by others who do remember it. If a narrator has had a lapse of memory, there is disagreement over whether or not to accept his account, with some accepting it and others, such as the Hanafites, rejecting it. One hadith that falls into this category states, "If a woman marries without her guardian's consent, the marriage will be null and void." Another is the hadith narrated by Abū Hurayrah concerning reaching a legal verdict based on a single witness and an oath.

In sum, errors are bound to occur in the transmission of at least some oral accounts, a fact which may lead to the appearance of contradictions in the contents of various hadiths. Some of these contradictions are easily detected, while others are not, which brings us to the topic of paraphrased accounts.

2. *Narratives Passed Down in Paraphrase*

Passing down a hadith in paraphrase form involves substituting some words of the narrative with synonymous terms. There have been differing views on this practice. Imam Mālik held that it was not permissible to paraphrase hadiths that were traced back to the Messenger of God for fear that those who did so would be liable for the punishment due to someone who lies about the Prophet. In the view of Abū Bakr ibn al-ʿArabī, it is a practice that was permissible only to the Companions of the Prophet. The majority view, however, holds that it is permissible to paraphrase accounts with unambiguous meanings by translating them into other languages, since it is good to explain the law of Islam to the peoples of the world in their native tongues. As for paraphrasing hadiths in Arabic, it is held to be permissible for those who have a solid grasp of the hadiths in question. However, it is not permitted in cases where the text contains homonyms, general concepts, and ambiguous and comprehensive terms.

Hadith scholars are in agreement that most accounts that have been passed down have been narrated in paraphrase. This is why ʿUmar ibn al-Khaṭṭāb was so insistent on the importance of a precise understanding of any account that was narrated, since the narrator might use terms which he believes to be synonymous with those in the original account, or which he thinks to be identical in meaning to what the Prophet said. Ibn Sīrīn said, "I might hear a given hadith from ten people, every one of whom narrates it in a way different from all the others, yet the meaning remains the same." He also said, "Anas ibn Mālik narrated few hadiths on the authority of the Messenger of God. But when he did relate a hadith from the Prophet, he would say: 'Or, as he said...'" Qatādah quoted Zirārah ibn Abī Awfā as saying, "I have met several of the Prophet's Companions, who spoke of him in different terms, yet conveyed the same message."

There is unanimous agreement among scholars that someone who is ignorant of the meaning of what he is transmitting should not be allowed to narrate the hadith in question in paraphrase form, and that those who did allow hadiths to be narrated in paraphrase only allowed it on certain conditions. In this connection, al-Māwardī wrote:

> If you have forgotten how the original hadith was worded, you may paraphrase it. Since you have taken responsibility for both the words and the meaning but find yourself unable to convey one of the two, you must therefore convey the other, since failure to do so might entail suppression of a legal ruling which you are obliged to communicate. If, on the other hand, you have not forgotten the original wording, you are not permitted to convey it in any but these words, because the Prophet's way of speaking was more eloquent than anyone else's.

Describing the qualities a narrator must have, al-Shāfiʿī wrote:

> A narrator of hadiths must be genuinely pious and known for his honesty. He must understand the account he narrates and be aware of which words would, if used, change the account's meaning. [Otherwise], he must relate it exactly as he heard it, and not in paraphrase form. Someone who paraphrases an account without knowing which words would change its

> meaning has no assurance that he will not portray the forbidden as permitted, whereas if he relates it word for word, there will be no danger of his changing its meaning.

As we have seen, then, al-Shāfiʿī held that one may only paraphrase a hadith if one understands it so thoroughly that there will be no danger of distorting its meaning.

3. *Preservation of Written Sources of Hadiths (Ḍabṭ al-Kitāb)*

We have thus far been discussing the preservation of oral accounts; we now turn to the preservation of written accounts, which were likewise subject to being corrupted through additions, deletions or other changes. Books were most frequently tampered with by their authors' relatives, close associates and students – without their knowledge, of course. Authors whose works are known to have been tampered with include the Iraqi hadith collector and scholar, ʿAlī ibn ʿĀṣim ibn Ṣuhayb, Kufan hadith scholar Sufyān ibn Wakīʿ al-Ḥāfiẓ ibn al-Ḥāfiẓ, Sufyān al-Thawrī, Abū Muqātil al-Samarqandī, Ibn Abī Maryam, ʿAbd Allāh ibn Ṣāliḥ, and Shuʿbah ibn al-Ḥajjāj. The errors that occurred were of the type that most people would be unable to detect, such as the omission or addition of a diacritical mark that would change the meaning of a word entirely, failure to include the letter hamzah, and so on.

[EIGHTH]
Isnād Criticism vs. *Matn* Criticism

Hadith scholars who engaged in *isnād* criticism – criticism of a hadith's chain of transmission – did so essentially in service of the *matn* – the body of the hadith. Ibn al-Qayyim (d. 751 AH/1350 CE) wrote in his book, *Al-Furūsiyah*:

> Let it be known that the authenticity of a hadith's *isnād* is a necessary, but not a sufficient, condition for the authenticity of the hadith itself. Rather, in order for a hadith to be deemed authentic, a number of other conditions must also be met. These are: (1) its *isnād* must be authentic, (2) it must be free of weaknesses, (3) it must not be either irregular (*shādhdh*) or

unacknowledged (*munkar*), and (4) its narrator must be known not to have contradicted other, trustworthy narrators or introduced variations into their accounts.

1. *Putting the Isnād to the Test of Academic Inquiry*

Given the foregoing facts, the question arises: How credible is the *isnād* in question, academically speaking, when judged in light of the various factors which impact such credibility, such as: the assessment of the narrator's character, knowledge of narrators' and scholars' dates of birth and death, the science of *ʿilal al-ḥadīth*, that is, the various weaknesses to which hadiths are subject, careful examination of the lines of narrators included in the *isnād*, and external textual evidence?

If we reflect for a moment on the idea of relying entirely on our examination of a hadith's chain of transmission, including the characters of its narrators, as a basis for determining the authenticity of a hadith attributed to the Messenger of God, we will see that we have placed ourselves in a dangerous situation, since we are no longer allowed to determine a hadith's authenticity based on its actual content by comparing it to that of the Qur'an – the only text that we know to be free of error. However, this kind of comparison is precisely what the Prophet's Companions engaged in.

The question that needs to be asked here is: What led hadith scholars onto this slippery slope – the method of hadith criticism that relies on the study of chains of transmission and narrators' characters – when the most we can derive from this method is tentative judgments on such narrators and their accounts? Is it not sufficient for us to appeal to the authority of the Qur'an itself – which God sent down as a confirmation of previous revelations and a measuring rod by which to assess them – when seeking to arrive at such conclusions? Did the original Muslims place their faith in the Qur'an and follow the guidance it had provided based on an inquiry into the character of the Prophet? Or was it, rather, the Qur'an itself which served as the proof of the Prophet's truthfulness and the validity of his claims? The hesitation to measure not only hadiths and other historical reports and narratives but, in addition, opinions, ideas, and various interpretations, against the Qur'an is simply a sign of the kind of mental paralysis that has afflicted Muslims, who have for centuries remained shackled to the evidence afforded by hadiths' chains of transmission. Such hesitation is also an admission that because of our lack of freedom to appeal to the Qur'an, we are no longer able to sift through and properly scrutinize this vast accumulation of narratives.

The leading Companions, such as Abū Bakr, and ʿUmar and the Prophet's wife ʿĀ'ishah, were well aware that assessment of narrators' characters was not the true criterion on the basis of which to accept or reject hadith accounts. They realized that such decisions had to be based on the Qur'an, and on the hadith accounts that they knew with certainty to be trustworthy and reliable. This decision-making process required that they examine the actual content of the hadiths, and not just their chains of transmission. Focusing on hadiths' contents and comparing them to the teachings of the Qur'an would provide a kind of natural protection against allowing falsehoods to infiltrate the Sunnah. Only this approach would be consistent with the Qur'an's edict found in *Sūrah al-Ḥujurāt*: "O you who have attained to faith! If any iniquitous person comes to you with a [slanderous] tale, use your discernment, lest you hurt people unwittingly and afterwards be filled with remorse for what you have done" (49:6). What believers were urged to verify was not a person's character but, rather, the report they had received, and the only way to verify the truth or falsehood of claims relating to the religion would be to check them against the Revelation they had at their disposal, the Revelation that had been preserved by God Himself, and against the Sunnah they had been given as a way of clarifying and applying this Revelation. This is not to say that we should reject the *isnād* as a means of hadith verification. However, examination of the *isnād* is meant to be merely a first step in the process of sifting through hadiths, the second step being to measure the conclusions reached through the first step against the yardstick of the Qur'an. If the contents of a hadith with an acceptable *isnād* are confirmed by the Qur'an, it will stand; otherwise, it should be eliminated. What happened, however, was that the first step was allowed to expand until it took up nearly all of hadith collectors' time and energy, and the Sunnah was taken captive by *ʿilm al-rijāl*, the science of narrator assessment.

By advocating this approach I am not, like some, issuing a call to abandon the hadith collections that have come down to us. Such a step would be unacceptable according to both the teachings of the Qur'an itself and the demands of academic inquiry. At the same time – bearing in mind the need for our approach to harmonize with both Qur'anic imperatives and the scientific method – we must not view the hadith collections we have been bequeathed by Islamic tradition in a hierarchical fashion, considering some to be "authentic" and others "more authentic." Rather, it should be remembered that every one of them contains both authentic and inauthentic hadiths.

In fact, the whole concept of "authenticity" (*aṣaḥḥiyyah*) has been clothed in such sanctity that it poses a danger to Muslims' intellectual soundness, since it prevents us from thinking for ourselves. The claim that there is a book, or set of books, that is "the most authentic" after the Book of God is symptomatic of the methodological crisis into which Muslim thinkers entered as they allowed their thinking to be taken captive to the inviolability of the *isnād* and the written tradition. After all, the Qur'an did not acquire its respected position because it had been transmitted via well-authenticated lines of narrators but, rather, because the One who had sent it down took it upon Himself to preserve and protect it, saying, "Behold, it is We Ourselves who have bestowed from on high, step by step, this reminder, and behold, it is We who shall truly guard it [from all corruption]" (*Sūrah al-Ḥijr*, 15:9).

If we consider any book comparable to the Qur'an, this indicates a flaw in our ability to distinguish between what it means for the Qur'an to be well-authenticated, and what it means for historical reports to be well-authenticated. The Qur'an receives its authentification from within itself, not from those who passed it down. The authentication of historical reports, by contrast, must take place based on whether they are confirmed by the Qur'an.

The scholars who recorded the Sunnah compilations which have come down to us made no claims to have critiqued the contents of the accounts they contained. Nor did the author of any of the Sunnah collections claim to have compared hadiths one by one to the contents of the Qur'an. Their task had been limited to the collection of hadiths via the science of narrator assessment. Moreover, although some of them referred to what they had collected as "well-authenticated" (*ṣaḥīḥ*), they were defining the term "well-authenticated" in terms of the criteria they themselves had adhered to in their processes of collection and selection. For if they had been striving for absolute reliability, how could the same report be deemed "well-authenticated" by one scholar, and "weakly authenticated" by another? This could occur because the hadiths contained in these "well authenticated" compilations had not been subjected to both *isnād* criticism and *matn* criticism. After all, these very compilations also contain reports that have been classed as "strange" (*gharīb*), that is, as hadith one tier of whose chains of transmission contained only one narrator. If we were to compare reports in this category with the Qur'an, we would be certain to find disparities and contradictions between them. Indeed, not a single *ṣaḥīḥ* hadith compilation is free of reports belonging to this category.

2. *Matn Criticism (Hadith Text Criticism)*

As we have stated, it is essential that we not simply critique a hadith's chain of transmission (*isnād*), but its text (*matn*) as well. This is the case whether the *isnād* in question is "high" (*ʿālin*) or "low" (*nāzil*),[5] *ḥasan* or less than *ḥasan*. There are three reasons for the urgency of hadith text criticism:

One: Al-Shāfiʿī stated in *al-Risālah* that:

> every practice for which the Messenger of God established a precedent was in agreement with the Book of God. If it was a practice that had been ordained explicitly in the Book of God, then it was in perfect conformity to what had been ordained. If it had been stated in general terms in the Book of God, the practice of the Prophet provided further clarity on God's authority… The Messenger of God was a native speaker of the Arabic tongue who lived among Arabs. As such, he might say something which he intended to be applied generally; he might also say something specific which he intended for only specific application…If something was prohibited in general but allowed in specific situations, these exceptions would not cancel out the general prohibition. Similarly, if something was allowed in general but prohibited in specific situations, these exceptions would not cancel out the general allowance.

Al-Shāfiʿī, who was dubbed the Champion of the Sunnah, points in the passage just quoted to types of hadith narratives whose meaning he could only determine by subjecting their texts to a thoroughgoing critique and analysis as to how they were narrated, and how transmitters received them and passed them on.

Two: Based on these and other statements made by al-Shāfiʿī, many hadiths had been passed down in paraphrase form. Additionally, many hadiths had, for one reason or another, passed undetected through the porous sieve of the highly subjective *isnād* methodology.

Three: Critiquing a hadith's *matn* helps to uncover hidden flaws in the *isnād*; it may also help to attenuate the effects of subjectivity on *isnād* assessments. By "subjectivity," I refer to the judgments issued by numerous hadith scholars deeming this or that hadith trustworthy or untrustworthy based on nothing but the scholar's personal opinion of the narrator and his attitude toward the narrative in question. This can be seen in the tendency of al-Shāfiʿī and others to use phrases such as, "I was told by the trustworthy...," "I was told by someone I would not accuse...," and the like, which makes it difficult to view the scholar's assessment of the hadith concerned as an impartial evaluation resting on precise, objective data. Moreover, as was noted by the late Ahmad Muhammad Shakir (d. 1958), among other researchers in the fields of narrative-based and understanding-based hadith study (*ʿilmay al-riwāyah wa al-dirāyah*), those who recorded biographical information about hadith narrators did not write down the dates of narrators from Makkah, and particularly not those of Madinah; hence, here was confusion in their transmissions. When it came to the dates of narrators from Iraq and the Levant, however, they did write them down.

In sum, only a combined critique of a hadith's text (*matn*) and its chain of transmission (*isnād*) will afford us a reasonable level of certainty in our assessment of the hadith's validity and reliability.

3. *Criteria for Hadith Text Criticism*

Although standards for hadith text criticism have received some consideration from hadith scholars, they have received the most attention from jurists and *uṣūl* scholars. In fact, it has been reported of virtually every leading *uṣūl* scholar, jurist, and mujtahid that he rejected some accounts that hadith scholars had deemed reliable. Similarly, we have hadiths that were approved and applied by some *mujtahids* but rejected by others, who then – on the basis of this rejection – reached contrary conclusions on relevant issues. Such scholars raised issues relating to the critique and interpretation of the hadiths in question, and of this we have countless examples.

An examination of the various standards these scholars left for us in the area of hadith text criticism yields a list of nineteen basic criteria which, if not fulfilled, require a hadith to be rejected. These criteria are as follows:

1. It must not conflict with the explicit, unambiguous import of the Qur'an, the well-authenticated Sunnah, or necessary tenets of the religion.
2. It must be consistent with sensory experience and what we know of the observed world.
3. It must not conflict with established scientific knowledge or natural laws.
4. It must not be counter-intuitive or conflict with indisputable evidence or established experience.
5. It must not be inconsistent with established scientific knowledge in the fields of medicine, astronomy, and the like.
6. It must not be marked by a weak linguistic style that falls short of the standards of eloquence established by the Prophet, who has been described as "the most eloquent speaker of the language of *ḍād* the world has ever known." It must also be devoid of terms that were not in circulation during the lifetime of the Prophet.
7. It must not promote immoral behavior inconsistent with Islamic law.
8. It must not contain superstition or nonsense.
9. It must not promote allegiance to a particular school of thought, sect or tribe.
10. It must not conflict with firmly established historical facts and events, or with archeological evidence acknowledged by experts in the field to verify such events and the time of their occurrence.
11. It must not recount significant events that have been witnessed publicly on the authority of just one or two individuals.

12. It must not conflict with fundamental Islamic doctrine on the divine attributes – those attributes which *must* be predicated of the Divine, those that *cannot* be predicated of the Divine. and those that *may* be predicated of the Divine; similarly, it must not conflict with fundamental Islamic doctrine with respect to what must, what must not, and what may be reasonably said about God's honorable messengers.
13. It must not promise a tremendous reward for some trivial act, or threaten a severe punishment for a minor offense.
14. The narrator must not have stood to gain personally from relating the account in question, nor have related it under some external influence.
15. It must not promote belief in doctrinal or philosophical teachings taken from bygone religions or civilizations.
16. There must be no irregularity or serious weakness in the hadith's text or chain of transmission.
17. It must not have been rejected by the leading Companions or have been a subject of dispute among them. If it was, this would indicate that it was not viewed as authentic by the Companions themselves. And if the account was not viewed as well-authenticated during the Companions' day, there would have been no reason to view it as such thereafter.
18. It must not have happened that, after the account had been attributed to a given narrator, this narrator denied having related it.
19. It must have been passed on in exactly the words in which the original was phrased, without omissions or additions.

As may be seen, some of these conditions have to do with the narrator; most, however, have to do with the narrative itself: its content and wording. Moreover, the list is open to further additions. One also notes that these conditions draw upon numerous approaches, including the historical, the juristic, the linguistic, the scientific, the analytical, and the sociological. This is not surprising given these hadiths' multidimensional nature. Moreover, by welcoming the contributions of these various fields of inquiry, we can help to purge the *Ṣaḥīḥ* collections of accounts that have not been borne out by a comprehensive critique methodology.

Hadith scholars should be in the forefront of those who adopt the use of this type of methodology. We have no reason to fear that the application of these approaches will do the Sunnah any harm. Rather, we should pursue this endeavor with confidence rather than leaving work on the Sunnah to those who imitate contemporary Western schools of criticism and counter-criticism that end up deconstructing everything. Muslims' thinking has been plagued by many an errant idea, and the invading hordes keep flooding in. Hence, we need to cling as never before to the Book of God and to the clarification provided in the Sunnah of the Prophet, for this alone may be our salvation.

I urge my colleagues and all students of the sciences of Islamic law and written tradition to learn and teach this methodology, to enrich and crystallize it, and, in so doing, to thwart the efforts of those who call for reliance on "the Qur'an alone" but who are the farthest possibly cry from being supporters of the Qur'an. Rather, they have fallen under the influence of modernist philosophies and tools of textual criticism. Such people suppose that the Muslim community knows nothing of this type of criticism when, in reality, Muslim scholars have engaged in numerous forms of this discipline over the centuries, with some of them (such as *isnād* criticism and the narrative-based and narrator-based methodologies) having been unique to Muslim academics.

In the face of modern deconstructionist thought, hadith scholars need to reexamine the mistaken notion that "the hadith sciences" are a world unto themselves rather than being part and parcel of the broader sphere of academic inquiry. Just as jurists have sometimes failed to carry out their functions properly because they have not been well-versed in the hadith sciences, we find that the *Ṣaḥīḥ* hadith collections were infiltrated by accounts which, had it not been for some hadith scholars' lack of expertise in the sciences of jurisprudence and practical life issues, would never have acquired the status they did.

Hence, the approach taken to the hadith sciences needs to be an integrated one that takes careful consideration of the *isnād* and the *matn* of each narrative within the broader context of juristic issues and the ongoing social, economic, intellectual and spiritual challenges presented by the world in which Muslims live their daily lives.

Glossary of Terms

Āḥād: Linguistically, the term *āḥād* ('solitary') describes a hadith transmitted by only one narrator. Practically speaking, however, the term applies to any hadith which is not *mutawātir*.

Ahl al-Ra'y: Rendered here as "the People of Opinion," this term refers to the followers of Imam Abū Ḥanīfah, who derived Islamic legal rulings through the use of his reason and discernment, and who only accepted the hadiths that came his way if they passed a set of exacting criteria.

Balāghāt: Hadiths whose chains of transmission contain the phrase *balaghanī min fulān*, meaning, "It came to my hearing through so-and-so."

Ḍaʿīf: Meaning "weak," the term *ḍaʿīf* describes a hadith whose chain of transmission is marked by discontinuity, and one or more of whose narrators has some weakness in his character. There are numerous subcategories of weak hadiths.

Gharīb: Literally, "strange," the term *gharīb* is used to describe a hadith one tier of whose chain of transmission includes only one narrator.

Ḥasan: Meaning simply "good," *ḥasan* is an adjective used to describe a hadith whose authenticity is not as well-established as those classified as *ṣaḥīḥ*, but which is sufficient for use as religious evidence.

Ijtihād: The effort exerted by a suitably qualified scholar of jurisprudence to derive legal rulings from Islamic sources (the Qur'an, the Hadith, analogical deduction and consensus).

Isnād: The chain of transmission for a hadith narrative.

Kharijites: The Kharijites (Arabic, *al-khawārij*) were a sect that revolted against the authority of Caliph ʿAli ibn Abī Ṭālib after he agreed to arbitration with his rival Muʿāwiyah ibn Abī Sufyān to decide the succession to the Caliphate following the Battle of Siffin in the year 36 AH/657 CE. They held that "judgment belongs to God alone," and that God would decide succession by determining the victor in battle, whereas arbitration would be decided by human beings. The Kharijites developed extreme doctrines that set them apart from both mainstream Sunni and Shiite Muslims.

Maqṭūʿ: Meaning "severed," *maqṭūʿ* is an adjective which describes a narration attributed to a Successor of one of the Prophet's Companions.

Marfūʿ: An adjective describing a narration attributed specifically to the Prophet.

Mashhūr: Meaning famous or well-known, the term *mashhūr* describes an account that was reported by more than two narrators. According to some scholars every narrative which comes to be known widely is called *mashhūr*. A hadith might be reported by only one or two narrators in the beginning, but become widely known, that is, *mashhūr*, at a later time.

Mawqūf: An adjective describing a hadith attributed to one of the Prophet's Companions.

Muʿallal: A 'defective' hadith.

Mujtahid: Someone qualified to engage in *ijtihād*.

Munkar: Meaning "unacknowledged," the adjective *munkar* describes a hadith which conflicts with another, authentic hadith, and which is related by a weak narrator.

Munqaṭiʿ: Meaning "broken," the adjective *munqaṭiʿ* describes a hadith whose chain of transmission is disconnected at any point. If any narrator in the chain of transmission is known never to have heard accounts from the next narrator in the chain, even though they were contemporaries, the hadith concerned is deemed *munqaṭiʿ*.

Murji'ites: A sect which, as opposed to the Kharijites, held that human beings should always defer judgments on others' beliefs, since only God can judge what is in a person's heart. The name of the sect is derived from the verb *arja'a*, which means to postpone or defer. Also in contrast to the Kharijites, the Murji'ites held that a Muslim who commits a grave sin will remain Muslim provided that he or she repents and retains his or her faith.

Mursal: An adjective used to describe a hadith whose chain of transmission goes back only as far as a *tābiʿī* (one of the Successors to the Prophet's Companions).

Musnad: Used as an adjective, the word *musnad* describes a hadith which is "well supported" in the sense that it has a chain of transmission which goes back without interruption to a well-known Companion, and from him to the Messenger of God.

Mutawātir: An adjective used to describe a report narrated by a group of individuals sufficiently large and disparate that it would be impossible for them to have colluded in falsification.

Muttaṣil: Meaning "connected," the adjective *muttaṣil* describes a hadith whose chain of transmission is free of any breaks.

Muwaththaq: Meaning "authenticated, documented, certified," the term *muwaththaq* describes a hadith whose chain of transmission goes back to the Prophet via a narrator who has been judged by the Companions of the Prophet and the Imams to be trustworthy, but whose doctrine is 'corrupt' in that he belongs to a sect other than the Twelver Shiites.

Qadarites: Adherents of the doctrine of free will.

Rafidites: Derived from the Arabic *rāfiḍah*, meaning "rejector," the term Rafidite is used to refer to someone who, in the view of the speaker, refuses to recognize legitimate Islamic authority.

Sunan: Plural of the word *sunnah*, the word *sunan* also refers to a collection of hadiths compiled by a Muslim scholar. Some of the best known collections of this genre are *Sunan Abū Dāwūd* and *Sunan Ibn Mājah*.

Sunnah: When upper case and un-italicized (Sunnah), this word refers to the entire corpus of hadiths relating the words and actions of the Prophet viewed as the model that Muslims are to emulate in their practical lives. When lower case and un-italicized (sunnah), the word refers to a particular example set by the Prophet in a particular situation. For example, the act of eating with one's right hand rather than one's left might be referred to as 'a sunnah.' Lastly, when lower case and italicized (*sunnah*), the word is being used in reference to the Arabic word as such, or to the concept underlying the word.

Uṣūl scholar: A scholar who devotes himself to the study of the principles of Islamic jurisprudence (*uṣūl al-fiqh*).

Notes

INTRODUCTION

1. The term "later" refers generally to scholars of the third century AH and beyond, that is, who came after the generations of the Companions, the Successors, and the Successor's Successors.

CHAPTER TWO: SUNNAH AS CONCEPT AND AS TECHNICAL TERM

1. The differences between a concept (*mafhūm*) and a technical term (*muṣṭalaḥ*) are subtle, but significant. A concept is associated with a definition that can be expressed in a number of different ways, or what is sometimes known as a procedural definition. A technical term, by contrast, is generally associated with a more rigid definition consisting of a distinct set of related words. As a result of this difference, the individual word referred to as a "concept" might be associated with numerous other words, each of which communicates the same meaning from a different angle or perspective. This is not so for the individual word referred to as a technical term, which is viewed as conveying the intended meaning uniquely, and which defies being treated as synonymous with other words. This singularity or uniqueness is a trait special to what I mean by a "technical term." Hence, on the practical level, the notion of "concept" has gone beyond the logical meaning of the word *mafhūm* associated with a broad conceptualization or understanding viewed within an inclusive, comprehensive semantic and linguistic framework, and has come to be linked to a particular word denoting a particular meaning. In this connection, see *Binā' al-Mafāhīm: Dirāsah Maʿrifiyyah wa Namādhij Taṭbīqiyyah* (Concept Building: An Epistemological Study and Applied Models), Ibrahim Bayyumi Ghanim et. al., Foreword by Taha Jabir Alalwani, (Cairo: IIIT, 1998).
2. The word *sunnah* has been defined by Arab linguists as "observed manner, custom, and law," by scholars of the fundamentals of jurisprudence as "the second source of Islamic legislation," by jurists as "actions whose commission merits reward but whose omission merits no punishment," and by hadith transmitters as "sayings, actions, or approval attributed to the Prophet."

3. The homonym, or *mushakkik*, is a universal which may not be predicated equally of all its individual instances, as, for example, the way existence can be predicated more fittingly, and more eternally, of that which exists of necessity – such as God – than it can of something that exists only contingently – as in the case of created beings.
4. The pronoun "her" apparently refers to another woman, also a grandmother, who had approached the Prophet in an analogous situation.
5. See al-Shāfiʿī, *al-Risālah*, paragraphs 300, 303, 308, 314, 419, 440, 465, and 479.

CHAPTER THREE: THE QUR'AN AS CREATIVE SOURCE AND THE SUNNAH AS PRACTICAL CLARIFICATION

1. In his outstanding work entitled *Mufradāt Gharīb al-Qur'an* (Unusual Terms in the Qur'an), al-Iṣfahānī sets out to clarify the Qur'anic concept of *waḥy* through a painstaking study of the word's uses throughout the Qur'an. He begins by tracing the linguistic meaning of the word *waḥy*, which forms the foundation and starting point for constructing a sound network of Qur'anic terms and concepts. Al-Iṣfahānī's study represents one of the best and most important contributions to the study of the concept of *waḥy* and its multiplicity of meanings. Of course, *waḥy* in the sense of divine revelation is a supernatural phenomenon. God chooses whom He wills of His servants to receive His revelation. He also chooses an angel to receive the revelation and to deliver it to His messengers and prophets, who in turn are charged with delivering it to their communities. Such an angel may approach the human messenger in his angelic form, or in some other form. Believers hold that the angel comes to God's prophet or messenger as a genuine human being, not merely as an apparition; he also comes when the prophet or messenger is awake, not only when he is asleep.
2. A reference to Jesus' disciples.
3. The hadith in question relates that when the Messenger of God was about to dispatch Muʿādh to Yemen, he asked him, "How will you issue legal rulings if you are presented with a case that requires adjudication?" Muʿādh replied, "I will rule based on the Book of God." "So," the Prophet asked him, "what if you find nothing in the Book of God that addresses the situation?" "I will base my ruling on the Sunnah of the Prophet," Muʿādh replied. The Prophet then asked, "What if you find nothing that addresses the situation in either the Book of God or the Sunnah of the Prophet?" "In that case," said Muʿādh, "I will do

my best to form an opinion on my own." Upon hearing Muʿādh's reply, the Prophet struck his chest and exclaimed, "Praise be to God for leading the Prophet's envoy to that which is pleasing to the Prophet!" Ibn Ḥajar al-ʿAsqalānī tells us in *Talkhīṣ al-Ḥabīr* that this hadith "was cited by Aḥmad, Abū Dāwūd, al-Tirmidhī, Ibn ʿUdayy, al-Ṭabarānī, and al-Bayhaqī from the hadith of al-Ḥārith ibn ʿAmr on the authority of some of Muʿādh's companions, on the authority of Muʿādh." Al-Tirmidhī wrote, "We know it from no other source, and its chain of narrators is not continuous." In *al-Tārīkh al-Kabīr*, al-Bukhārī tells us that the hadith was narrated by "al-Ḥārith ibn ʿAmr on the authority of companions of Muʿādh and on the authority of Abū ʿAwn. It is not authentic nor is it known through any other source." As for Ibn Ḥazm he stated, "It is not authentic, because al-Ḥārith is not recognized as a narrator, and his shaykhs are unknown." Ibn Ḥazm went on to say, "Some claim that this hadith is *mutawātir*, but this is untrue. In fact, it is a far cry from being *mutawātir*, since it was narrated by no one but Abū ʿAwn on the authority of al-Ḥārith." In *al-ʿIlal al-Mutanāhiyah*, Ibn al-Jawzī wrote, "It is not authentic. However, all the jurists cite it in their books and rely on it for their arguments. Besides, its meaning is correct..." See Ibn Ḥajar al-ʿAsqalānī, *Talkhīṣ al-Ḥabīr fī Aḥādīth al-Rāfiʿī al-Kabīr*, ed. Abd Allah Hashim al-Yamani al-Madani, (Madinah: no publisher, 1964), vol. 4, p. 206.

CHAPTER FIVE: THE CHRONICLING OF THE SUNNAH AND ITS HISTORICAL CONTEXT

1. I did not find the account with this particular wording in the places where I would have expected it to be. However, I did find an account similar to it narrated by Muslim ibn al-Ḥajjāj on the authority of Bishr ibn Saʿīd, who said, "Fear God, and be wary of the hadiths you hear. For I tell you truly: When we sat once with Abū Hurayrah, he narrated hadiths on the authority of the Messenger of God and on the authority of Kaʿb al-Aḥbār. When speaking to some of those who were with us, he related things on the authority of the Messenger of God as though they were on the authority of Kaʿb, and other things on the authority of Kaʿb as though they were on the authority of the Messenger of God." According to another version of the account, Bishr said that Abū Hurayrah "quoted things said by the Messenger of God as though they had been said by Kaʿb, and other things said by Kaʿb as though they had been said by the Messenger of God." Bishr then added, "So fear God, and be wary of the hadiths you hear." This account was listed by one scholar under the

heading, "His [Abū Hurayrah's] deceit by concealment" (*tadlīsuhu*), quoting from *Al-Bidāyah wa al-Nihāyah* by Ibn Kathīr (109/8). See Mahmud Abu Riyyah, *Aḍwā' ʿAlā al-Sunnah al-Muḥammadiyyah* (Cairo: Dār al-Maʿārif, 1994), Sixth Printing, p. 176 and its footnote.

In Muslim ibn al-Ḥajjāj's Introduction to his *Ṣaḥīḥ* collection, he discusses the weak points of certain narrators, and mentions the prohibition against relating hadiths passed down on the authority of narrators who are known to be weak. Assuming the aforementioned account to be validly attributable to him, this is the place where I would have expected to find it. However, I found no sign of it. See Muslim ibn al-Ḥajjāj al-Qushayrī, *Ṣaḥīḥ Muslim*, ed. Muhammad Fuad ʿAbd al-Baqi, (Cairo: Dār Iḥyā' al-Kutub al-ʿArabiyyah, 1955), Part 1, p. 43-144.

The aforementioned account is likewise cited by al-Muʿallimī, who writes, "Yazīd ibn Hārūn said, I heard Shuʿbah say: Abū Hurayrah used to engage in deceit by concealment (*tadlīs*). In other words, he used to relate what he had heard from Kaʿb and what he had heard from the Messenger of God without being careful to distinguish one from the other. This has been mentioned by Ibn ʿAsākir." See this narrative and the one prior to it both in this source and in *Al-Bidāyah wa al-Nihāyah*, cited above. See also al-Muʿallimī's comment on this matter in ʿAbd al-Raḥmān ibn Yaḥyā al-Muʿallimī, *Al-Anwār al-Kāshifah li mā fī Kitābi Aḍwā' ʿalā al-Sunnah min al-Ẓalāl wa al-Taḍlīl wa al-Mujāzafah* (Beirut: ʿĀlam al-Kutub, 1402 AH/1983 CE), Part 1, p. 171.

2. These jurists were: Ibn al-Musayyab, ʿUrwah ibn al-Zubayr, al-Qāsim ibn Muḥammad, Khārijah ibn Zayd, Abū Bakr ibn ʿAbd al-Raḥmān ibn Ḥārith ibn Hishām, Sulaymān ibn Yasār, and ʿUbayd Allāh ibn ʿAbd Allāh ibn ʿUtbah ibn Masʿūd.

CHAPTER SIX: THE AUTHORITATIVENESS OF THE REPORTING OF THE SUNNAH

1. The hadith in question consists of a saying of the Prophet concerning a situation in which a slave is owned jointly by more than one person. If one of the owners pays his share of the price of the slave in order to free him but has enough money to pay the other owner's share as well, he should do so. To this content, some versions of the hadith add a phrase to the effect that if the owner who wants to free the slave does not have enough money to pay the entire price of the slave, then "what has been freed, has been freed" (*faqad ʿatiqa mā ʿatiqa*).

2. Hadith scholars divide obscure narrators into two categories. The first is termed *majhūl al-ʿayn*, that is, someone on whose authority only one other narrator has related accounts, and who was not deemed trustworthy by said narrator. The second category is referred to as *majhūl al-ḥāl*, or someone on whose authority one or more other narrators have passed on accounts, yet whose circumstances indicate that they had only superficial or general knowledge about him. However, if there is evidence that the other narrators knew him to be of good, upright character, then he is no longer deemed obscure.
3. Al-Nasā'ī spoke of Aḥmad ibn Ṣāliḥ as being "neither trustworthy nor reliable," adding that Yahyā ibn Maʿīn had described him as "a lying pedant." According to Ibn Ḥajar, "Al-Nasā'ī declared him [Aḥmad] weak because of something he had related on the authority of Yaḥyā ibn Maʿīn..." Ibn Ḥajar then went on to mention that the reason for al-Nasā'ī's increasingly vocal prejudice against Aḥmad was that the latter had refused to relate hadiths to al-Nasā'ī because he (al-Nasā'ī) had kept company with certain hadith scholars whom Aḥmad did not think well of.
4. What Sufyān was supposed to have said to Shuʿbah was, "If you criticize Jābir al-Juʿfī, then I shall defend him." Jābir ibn Yazīd al-Juʿfī's hadiths were transmitted by Abū Dāwūd, al-Tirmidhī and Ibn Mājah. However, a number of scholars stopped transmitting his accounts when they learned of his dishonesty and the impertinence with which he spoke against the religion of God. See al-Mizzī, *Tahdhīb al-Kamāl fī Asmā' al-Rijāl*, Part 4, p. 467. Yaḥyā ibn Maʿīn once stated, "I once saw Abū Shaybah's two sons come to him (that is, to Yūnus ibn Bukayr), but he sent them away. They asked him for something written, but he would not give it to them. So they went off and spoke badly about him." See al-Mizzī, *Tahdhīb al-Kamāl*, Part 32, p. 496.
5. A "high" *isnād* is one in whose first tier there are few, or fewer, narrators between the last person to relate the hadith and the shaykh from whom this person received it, while a "low" *isnād* is one in which there is a larger number of narrators between the last person to relate the hadith and the shaykh from whom he received it. For example, al-Tirmidhī had a shaykh by the name of Qutaybah ibn Saʿīd from whom he received many hadiths. If the *isnād* for one such hadith began, "I was told by Abū Mūsā ibn al-Muthannā, who was told by Ibn Saʿīd al-Dārimī, who was told by Qutaybah...," while the *isnād* for another began, "I was told by Abū Mūsā ibn al-Muthannā, who was told by Qutaybah...," the first *isnād* would be "lower" than the second, which has fewer narrators between al-Tirmidhī and his shaykh.